For God's Sake:

Work by the Book!

Management Explained from Within

For God's Sake:

Work!
by the
Book!

Management Explained
from Within

Sarah Zohn
Manager and Leader LLC, US

WS Professional

NEW JERSEY · LONDON · SINGAPORE · BEIJING · SHANGHAI · HONG KONG · TAIPEI · CHENNAI · TOKYO

Published by

WS Professional, an imprint of
World Scientific Publishing Co. Pte. Ltd.
5 Toh Tuck Link, Singapore 596224
USA office: 27 Warren Street, Suite 401-402, Hackensack, NJ 07601
UK office: 57 Shelton Street, Covent Garden, London WC2H 9H

British Library Cataloguing-in-Publication Data
A catalogue record for this book is available from the British Library.

FOR GOD'S SAKE! WORK BY THE BOOK
Management Explained from Within

ISBN 978-981-3222-48-9

For any available supplementary material, please visit
http://www.worldscientific.com/worldscibooks/10.1142/10502#t=suppl

Desk Editor: Sandhya Venkatesh

Typeset by Stallion Press
Email: enquiries@stallionpress.com

Printed in Singapore

The only source of knowledge is experience.

— Albert Einstein

Praises for the Book

Mike Ruettgers

Former CEO and Chairman, EMC Corporation

"The high growth years at EMC taught us a lot. One of the hidden problems with high growth companies is the lack of experienced middle line managers. Sarah captures the needed lessons perfectly in this book. My favorite motto... "You have to plan for success" ...is right there, fully explored."

Israel Makov

Chairman of Sun Pharma Board

Former CEO and President of Teva Pharmaceutical Industries

"I find interesting and useful how she distills her experience from industries that are so different into management practices that apply everywhere. It's simple — translates the philosophies into clear actions. The stories make it real and interesting."

Orna Berry, Ph.D

Former Chief Scientist of the State of Israel

Entrepreneur and industry executive

VP, Dell EMC, Israel Center of Excellence, Brazil & Skolkovo R&D Centers

"A solid bridge between theory and practice — from how to write an email to a full strategy. Lots of gems, pleasure to read."

Philip Tamer

VP, 3PAR Engineering and Storage Networking at Hewlett-Packard Enterprise

Former GM & VP, Symmetrix Business Unit at EMC Corporation

"A feat of great engineering... Condensing such a broad range of management topics into one book that's usable, easy and makes so much practical sense. Mandatory read for anyone who wants to advance and lead from the front. Bravo !"

Benjamin Soffer

CEO, T3 Technion Technology Transfer

"As a Technion graduate loyal to her training Sarah brings it all together — engineering approach to management. Her vast experience and the many sources she uses are truly impressive. Here are the practical approaches and tools for most of today's management situations, in business and in operations - you'd feel as if she wrote it for you. Read it once and keep it close..."

Gil Zimmermann

Founder and CEO of Cloudlock – A Cisco Company

"Growing a company from an idea and a core team to a large acquisition by Cisco, we've been learning and improving through all stages, just as she describes the corrective processes of management. I was inspired to continuously inspect, correct and advance how we do things in our company. Page by page, I was curious to see what else she reminds me to do."

Tom Heiser

CEO ClickSoftware

Former President, RSA, The Security Division of EMC

"The way she goes from large to small, and makes it relevant to all... even with my years of experience I see that she extracted the common language that unites us all, managers and leaders of businesses in high technology."

Prof. Shlomo Maital

Technion, Israel Institute of Technology

"Mid-level managers are a forgotten, neglected nation, even though they do the real work. Sarah Zohn has written her book for them. It is a treasure chest of valuable to-do tools, gleaned from her long experience. And she offers ongoing help, Ask Sarah, at the very end. For those managers who want to excel, this is one of a very few must-read books."

Dedicated to the memory of my father

— My first mentor

Contents

Foreword

In the hope of avoiding a lot of politically correct repetitions, I took the liberty to use just the male gender in this book. In some languages, nouns, verbs, and pronouns are always masculine when used for a mixed audience of males and females, even if there's only one male and many females in audience. Women have been living peacefully with this discriminating bias; these languages did not create the combinations of *he or she* and *him or her* as in English. As a woman, I hope I am forgiven for the male bias, which is only in my writing — I promise.

This book is intended for men and women alike; the subject of gender bias is not covered here at all. I hope that many women read the book and become better managers and leaders. If I contribute to increasing the percentage of women in managerial ranks to 50%, all the way to the top levels, my reward will be in watching these numbers rise.

And I am thanking my friends Ira Schild, Chuck Urmson, and Cheryl LaMontagne for reading the manuscript and making valuable contributions.

A Manager's Cookbook

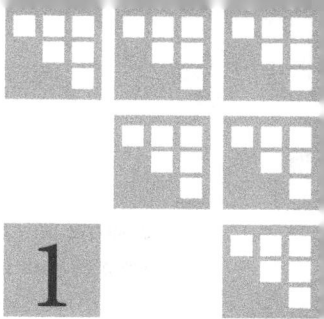

PART I

The Cook

1

All my friends are aware that I love to cook; so much so that it has become one of my distinguishing features. During cocktail hour of a conference I once attended with hundreds of business people, an executive — a colleague — introduced me to his acquaintances. As you'd expect, they were standing in a circle holding their wine glasses, engaged in small talk. With some apprehension — as I'm not so great at these events — I slowly walked over, expecting to be presented to these people with my short bio — highlights, title, and a cute anecdote to garnish our new acquaintance. What he chose to do, however, was utterly different. *I want you to meet my colleague and friend*, he addressed them, *you must know, she is such a great cook!* I knew then and there that indulging my friends with great dinners is far more impressive than any of my career accomplishments.

My annual dinner is a social event for my close friends, and for me it is an adventure in creativity — cooking the meal and putting on the event. These dinners are 6-hours of food samplings and togetherness. A couple of months in advance I set the date and start thinking of the theme for the dinner. I like to tell a story through my choice of theme — usually the experience of a recent trip. I choose around 20 dishes from the typical cuisines of the latest parts of the world where I traveled, such as Tlayuda from a Tianguis in Oaxaca, Tapado soup from a riverside home in Livingston Guatemala accompanied by coconut challah bread from the same kitchen, and Secreto cutlets served with rich Mojo Picante from a plancha in the Canaries — yes, they are all served in their refined gourmet versions.

I need to be very careful in selecting the menu for such a long eating event; especially since every dish is accompanied by its matching wine — it has to be light, well balanced, and small, always leaving a taste for more.

I always was very serious about cooking. The French kitchen was my first love. The old French food was exotic, refined, and beyond the grasp of our diaspora-influenced tastes; the dishes left my guests delighted. My first French cookbook, however, was a challenge. In the beginning, whenever a photo seduced me, the recipe had so many steps and unfamiliar terms that I had to shelve it for some time. I didn't fail to produce; rather, I did not make it as a goal to accomplish. Since then, I have mastered the secrets of the French kitchen, but now I have this yearning toward Japanese, which is so delightful and tantalizing on the table, and still unapproachable in the kitchen. At least for me!

In a continuous quest to improve my techniques and delight my friends with surprises, just like Siddhartha's journey toward nirvana, I met my master and mentor somewhere along the way — the *Donna Hay* magazine. Australia's gift to its western cousins is unjustifiably hardly known outside Down Under. This magazine is so meaningful to me that I prefer to humanize it — we have a relationship. And I continue to be in awe of how much more I can learn from her, like from any good old master. Bite by bite, she augments my vocabulary, enriches the palette of flavors, and with her masterful wisdom she teaches me all the possible shortcuts.

Finally, I found a concise and clear source of variety with global reach, and oh so doable! Now, I can wait much more peacefully for my endless dinners of *shock and awe*.

In all those years of cooking, I've learned one important lesson for life: great cooking is a craft that grows with experience — not an art.

The Manager

M anagement and leadership are also forms forms of craft — with tools, methods, ingredients, and techniques that have to be mastered until they are second nature, just as in cooking.

Let's review a wonderful example from *The Checklist Manifesto* by Atul Gawande, a prominent surgeon and professor at Harvard Medical School. In his book, he offers expertise on how to reduce errors, improve safety, and increase efficiency in surgery — certainly a noble cause — and a story that has direct application to many organizations and fields. The story is simple. During his tenure as Massachusetts General Surgeon, research showed that about 6% of patients in surgery wards of hospitals developed infections and that the general conditions of these hospitals did not have any effect on this unbecoming statistic. In fact, hospitals in affluent Boston ranked in this research similar to those in India. According to Gawande, the main causal chain was as follows: the surgical environment engenders so much pressure on the medical staff that they make errors in following protective procedures, which in turn leaves the door open for microbes to enter and infect. Clearly, this problem occurred due to the failure of the entire system and not just a failed task.

His approach to solving this systemic problem appears to be very simple; yet, after studying other fields, he proved that using it in his own field is highly effective. A simple checklist, if enforced continually, can reduce human error and reverse the hospital infections trend. In his quest to create proper checklists, he found that designing the right checklist was not, however, a simple task; it required special skills and experience — the craft of creating checklists.

Gawande writes that despite these checklists providing an obvious and easy-to-prove positive effect, his major challenge was to overcome the resistance to checklists coming from surgeons. They, the most prominent and confident professionals in a hospital's hierarchy, had a hard time submitting to simple checklists despite the overwhelming evidence of their effectiveness. Conversely, members of the support staff, such as nurses, were far more open to this idea.

Similarly, in my practice, I usually find that managers and leaders are confident that their current toolbox and experience is sufficient for most tasks in their area of responsibility. After all, the fact that they hold the important positions in a group, a unit, a department, or a business is already enough reason for self-assurance. However, after being in quite a few management and executive positions, I know that underneath this confidence lies a great deal of insecurity — the higher the position, the more lonely and insecure one feels. On the one hand, there's nothing wrong with a small dose of paranoia to keep things in balance — I'm certainly not the first to advocate this. On the other hand, I believe that it is important to test this pervasive level of ostensible confidence.

In interviews with managers, I find that they feel confident about being able to execute at least 80% of their responsibilities in effective and efficient ways. It appears that they have a tolerance for up to 20% of their work being less defined or in need of revamp. Most managers who have been in their position for some time feel that they have already achieved this 80/20 state — 80% under control and 20% less so.

Here is where I like to challenge this view. I find that businesses and work environments are changing at a quick pace. Andy Grove, the legendary chairman of Intel Corporation, said, "leaders have to act more quickly today. The pressure comes much faster." He said this years ago, but it's even

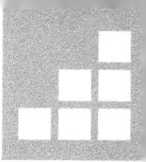

more relevant today. We see continuous shifts in competitive landscapes and in investors' demands and expectations. Shortages in skilled labor are prevalent. Many companies don't even have fully settled product portfolios or boundaries — product definitions and addressable markets are not constant, not to mention new technologies that make not-so-old ones obsolete at an ever-increasing pace. Managers, especially at middle and lower ranks, are very good at executing tasks, but in these constantly shifting conditions, company structures and management roles are so unstable that they don't achieve their units' best possible contributions to the business. The portion that seems to be under control — 80% of the manager's responsibilities — is in dire need of reevaluation in many cases that I have reviewed. All aspects of a manager's responsibilities — workload, priorities, human resources, and internal and cross-functional processes — should be assessed and corrected at all levels, periodically and not just once.

Why is it, then, that despite hiring educated, experienced, and success-driven people for management positions, we don't see optimal management in the organization? This problem is pervasive and well recognized — executives often report on the shortcomings and sub-par performance of their lower management ranks, while conveniently refraining from much self-assessment.

Most of the resumes I review clearly show that people change positions faster than before, whether within their companies or by moving to other companies. Managers who excel in one aspect of their role that's critical to another area of the business are likely to be promoted on a whim without consideration for the entire set of requirements of the new role. A single successful project is often followed by a premature promotion of the "hero" of the project to a higher management position. Looking from top-down, these decisions are hasty; and from bottom-up, the expectations of good performers are also too aggressive — they want to be promoted quickly, and not *waste their time.*

After such short tenures, it's impossible to attain the level of proficiency that is needed for higher management positions, which is that of a skilled craftsman who is ready to handle complexities, challenges, and changes, while driving the unit to meet its full potential for the benefit of the business. We see so much sub-optimal performance, and, yet, managers move from position to position as if they are already masters of their previous roles. They move fast and skip the training opportunities that a job used to provide. The business "chefs" are missing the basic skills of cutting, chopping, mixing, caramelizing, and emulsifying, and yet, they are expected to produce soufflés in an Iron Chef competition.

When I ask managers to define their roles — a straightforward and simple question — many have difficulties answering this and resort to generalities. I've yet to meet a manager who, at first attempt, is able to account for all the functions of his role. I help them with a simple exercise — make a list of all your constituencies and describe in detail the nature of your relationships with them. Typically, with this exercise, the manager develops deeper insight into the breadth and complexity of his responsibilities, and has his original excessive confidence rattled a little.

The comfortable balance of 80/20 — between the larger part of the manager's job that is ostensibly well executed, and the smaller part that requires refinement — does not exist in reality. In most cases, the 80% needs refactoring before it can be declared stable and ready for regular cycles of improvement. Only when it's well defined and established can the manager focus on the rest, where creativity, art, and inspiration may be applicable.

*

As a manager, you should never feel totally comfortable; on the contrary, you should periodically assess *important high-level questions about your unit and function*:

- Do we contribute the most to the business?
- Is morale at a good level?
- Is everybody working together to attain the best results?
- Do we have the right focus?
- Do other units give us what we need?
- Is it in the format that is best for us?

- Do we give other units what they need?
- Do we deliver it in the best way for them?
- How connected are we to customers?
- Do we understand the evolution of customer needs?
- Do we know our customers' future demands?
- How much wasteful repeated work occurs?
- Do we balance current needs with future needs?
- Do we provide the correct service levels?

Above all, you need to keep the improvement engine working at all times so that, in the words of Rabindranath Tagore, "the clear stream of reason has not lost its way into the dreary deserts of dead habit."

The essence of the manager's role is anchored in these questions. If you still feel relatively comfortable — *I think we are about 80% OK* — use these questions with your constituencies (customers, employees, partners and suppliers) and validate the consistency of the emerging picture. For example, if you are the head of marketing, check that your department's production of sales collateral material (product positioning, website content, presentations) is what the sales representatives need and use. Obviously, your department created the material according to directions from executives in the company, but do field personnel — sales and account managers — use it unmodified and as intended? Or is it only partially useful and off-target for their specific customers? Unfortunately, I see many situations where field personnel spend hours adapting their company's material to their needs while they should be spending these hours converting prospective customers. While both marketing and sales may behave correctly, they follow instructions and make the investment, the result for the company is waste, because of misalignment. This example relates to just one of the questions from the list above — more can be unearthed from digging into them all.

In this book, I've assembled my collection of recipes, checklists, and approaches to management situations and problems. Use them and you will be more comfortable and confident in the 80%. I've been adapting the skills and methods to today's ever-shifting requirements, the techniques to the latest management tools, and to the needs of contemporary generations of workers. I've been refining, using, and teaching them over the last 30 years in many types of businesses, industries, and organizations. These are not groundbreaking theories; rather, you'll find elegant recipes that work, and you will understand why they work!

We will work together — you and I — on techniques to deal with large and small tasks. We will follow a process to create a strategy and keep it updated; we will learn what to consider for organizational structure and how and when to reorganize. We will also look at smaller work items, such as creating and driving a program, setting goals, interviewing, assigning tasks, and even how to efficiently write an effective email.

These recipes are simple and linear, with as few steps as possible. Obviously, you have to adjust them to your situation; the effort will contribute toward making an organization more effective and more efficient, which is an organization that produces the intended results and increases productivity by eliminating clutter and waste.

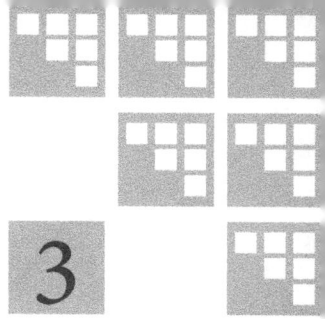

The Cookbook

The key to organizational success in a chaotic world is to ensure that we are not adding to the chaos, but rather, are finding ways to reduce it. Well-meaning managers often create and execute appropriate actions; however, I often see decisions that are not followed thoroughly and consistently. Adherence to a new cross-functional process, for example, quite often remains in a state of flux or disappears altogether once it hits its first difficulty. Before starting a process, procedure, or initiating any kind of reorganization, spend time discussing it with all involved in the activity and elicit their commitment to adopt it religiously — something which they cannot ignore or neglect. Address every difficulty with a commitment to improve the process until it's stable. Change always comes with a productivity price — friction and unexpected obstacles are natural. Without commitment to bring the change to a conclusive, stable state, the original problems persist *and* the organization continues to pay the price.

We, in business, cannot allow the high level of waste that exists in institutions such as in government. Cabinet Secretaries or Ministers make decisions, but a very small percentage of them are followed as intended. In good cases, results come after delays or with budget overruns. I know of one government controller who claimed that there was only a consistent 20% rate of follow-through on ministerial decisions. He didn't claim any bad intentions; it's just that these decisions were made without

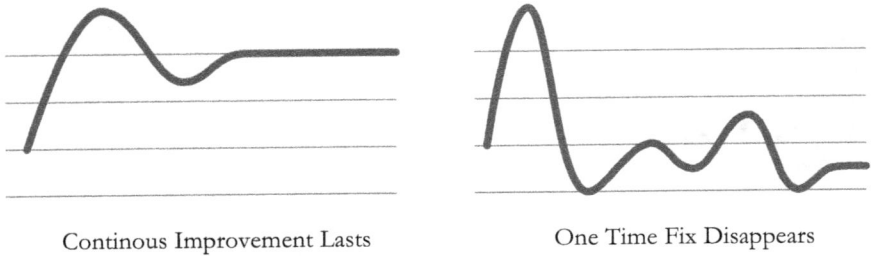

Continous Improvement Lasts   One Time Fix Disappears

Figure 1

checking feasibility, and the high turnover in political positions did not allow enough time for developing the experience to execute decisions properly. With such low performance, we would see our businesses die — while these ministers can stick around until the next election.

The manager's job is never easy, and it's not meant to feel natural. The approaches, techniques, and tools that I cover in this managers' cookbook will help you make good and thorough decisions, and stick to them (Figure 1). By mastering these techniques, you will improve the 80/20 to 80/20/20 — 80% of your responsibilities executed with 20/20 vision. It's within a manager's reach if he takes his job seriously.

The Manager's Job

PART II

So Much Change

Change is a topic that never goes away — whether it's change on the horizon or change that's already here. With entire industries transforming, moving, or relocating to cyberspace, change is a reality in every organization, large or small.

Entire industries are transforming. In the late 1990s, competition in the telecom industry centered on the question of who owned more physical conduits — CATV cables or phone wires. Telecom leaders and opportunistic investment companies were acquiring fiber infrastructure as if building muscle for a big ring fight. The push to wireless, however, quickly became the stronger technological wave for the future, with entire industries being restructured in its wake. Every business and operational model in telecom has been challenged, revised, or tossed out as irrelevant. Verizon has now purchased AOL and Yahoo — content companies. As I write, in 2016, big advertising budgets are still going to TV, even though the audience spends more time on mobile devices. Telecom companies are trying to figure out how to get their share of the advertising money that flows through their systems.

Another industry, content production and distribution — the media — is undergoing a complete reshaping as its consumers on the Internet demand free content with on-the-go access. Parts of the industry dissolve while others grow. The very definition of content is changing, and the behind-the-scenes money has begun to flow in new directions to technology that optimizes profits from advertising, and content that attracts new viewers. TV, newspapers, print, advertising, music, video, and movie producers are all changing the way that they function; as one business owner told me, "we used to be a video production company; now, with our nice Madison Avenue property, we are a real estate company."

These tectonic shifts, propelled by new technology, globalization, the Internet, and mobile adoption — all interwoven into one big fabric — dictate that every organization needs to adjust continuously. The new reality is change, which is roughly understood, at best.

Inside the organizations, the carriers of change are managers and leaders. Therefore, it is crucial for them to understand their jobs well, in their broadest definitions, because they have to stage it and perform in a moving reality. You have to keep running and win the race while changing your shoes — it's no longer a situational joke.

In the next few chapters of Part II, we drill deeper and go wider into the manager's role and build an understanding of what it entails. These are step-by-step guidelines — best done as a team — to build the first version of a detailed job definition for each manager. As a matter of good practice, we learn from the past, understand the present, and prepare for the future. In Part III, we see how to take this definition and adapt it continually to change, all the while staying in complete control and reducing the fallout from change.

Defining The Job — Five Pillars

W here do we start? The title of a job should reflect its actual functions i.e., area sales, marketing, engineering lead, product management, department manager, operations. These examples are very clear. However, if you are a CTO — *but I spend most of my time helping sales* — or a customer service manager — *but we actually do product testing* — your title is causing confusion, missed expectations, and hampered communication, both inbound and outbound. It is alright to have a mixed position with highly different components such as *Head of BI and Product Owner*; or *Field Operations* that includes customer service, implementation, professional services, order fulfillment; or *Head of Products and Offerings* that includes everything related to products and offerings, e.g., R&D, CTO, quality, manufacturing, and product management. A job title is not a decorative pin; therefore, try to find a sensible title that helps the organization be more effective and efficient.

Once the title is decided, we define in detail all the functions that constitute a job. I find many managers that see their role from a narrow point of view as a collection of tasks that they are responsible for. This is a completely outdated view which belongs to pure hierarchical organizations when cross-functional teamwork among managers was less crucial. In those organizations, you had a job and you coordinated with other managers, but you did not have to think how the other managers will succeed with your help. Nowadays, irrespective of your managerial role, you have to understand the roles of others and stay current with the latest version of the company's strategy. Top management should invest time and effort in developing this deep and broad understanding at least in mid-level managers.

This deep and broad understanding of management roles can be derived from five clusters of requirements that I call *The Five Pillars* (Table 1). These are summarized here and discussed further in the next chapters.

1. **Manager and leader**: You are both the manager of work and the leader of people, as in most management jobs you cannot choose to be one or the other. We will further discuss how to develop the correct balance in your job and become effective and efficient in both functions. Periodic staff meetings to manage work and departmental meetings to forge leadership are certainly neither enough nor executed properly in many places.

2. **Eco-system constituencies**: Your job is to satisfy the requirements of internal and external customers. We will review all the mutual needs with your constituencies as a collection of activities — taking inputs, processing them to add value, and producing outputs. These 360° examinations of the relationships with upper management, peer groups, employees, external customers, and partners aren't always straightforward. They require an understanding of the other side.

3. **Strategy** has two main components, namely business and operational. As a manager, the operational strategy is your framework, and the business strategy supplies the reasons for it. You need to understand these strategies thoroughly to create the right programs and tasks and to execute them correctly. Creating strategy often becomes more complicated than necessary. We will see step-by-step practical methods to build and maintain these strategies, first for the operational and then for the business.

4. **Workload and people management**: You manage work by prioritizing it, assigning the tasks, checking quality, delivering, and

communicating. In addition, you are responsible for the improvement of work methods. As a people manager, your employees expect you to act like a parent, i.e., help them succeed with their work, develop their professional skills, and nurture their mental state with a lot of appreciation; this is how the knowledge economy works. We will review potent *parenting* tools that are light and easy to use with no psychological pretentions. These tools are useful for all managers.

5. **Managerial relationships**. Can a regular manager do all that's detailed in the first 4 pillars? Are we being unreasonable in expecting all managers to be broad, thorough, and excellent with people? Obviously, a manager shares his responsibility with the team and both the manager and the team always grow together. As a manager, you develop relationships with your team members that mature with time, so that together the team can carry more load. You should always keep nurturing these relationships, and never take them for granted. Also, you cannot delegate the nurturing to others — HR cannot do it for you. We will discuss a model to help you bring these relationships out of the fuzzy zone into clear and practical actions.

Table 1   The Five Pillars of the Manager's Job

Manager and Leader	Ecosystem and Constituencies	Operational and Business Strategy	Work and People	Managerial Relationships
Manager's Job Definition				

Manager and Leader

6

What do you need to be more for your organization? Manager or leader? The common definitions are confusing and certainly not helpful to the manager who wants to improve. In workshops for client companies, I did a simple test with a few managers and leaders to check their perceptions of themselves as well as of others. The participants needed to be in the middle, between a manager and a leader, but usually that's not how it developed in the workshops. First, I asked the group to randomly suggest a few words or attributes that they associate with the concepts of *manager* and *leader*. I got the list of words for the respective terms as follows (Table 1).

I picked a few of these attributes and challenged the participants: would you like to have a leader who is *not responsible* or the one who *lacks knowledge*? Who should be the *planner*? Manager or leader? Would you like a manager who is *not supportive* and believes solely in *direction* and *execution*?

The exercise showed that when asked on a short notice to reflect, participants came out with a list of perceptions from their recent experiences. The list represented their concerns for improvements around them, perhaps about their managers, and less analytic thinking. It was also obvious that most good traits were not mutually exclusive — our preference is to have them both in managers and in leaders. When we prune the lists to real differentiating traits that can help us understand the two functions

Table 1   Attributes Casually Associated with Manager and Leader

Manager	Leader
Responsible	Vision
Effective	Targets
Efficient	Support
Influence	Lead
Goals	Quality
Passionate	Warm
Mission	Charisma
Knowledge	Relevant
Guide	Planning
Directive	Influence
Manage	Functional
Planning	Followers
Execution	Informative
Involved	Motivation
Results	

Table 2   Differentiating Attributes of Manager and Leader

Manager Distinct Attributes	Leader Distinct Attributes
1. Planning, workload management	1. Charisma
2. Quality	2. Influence
3. Execution, detailed knowledge	3. Ecosystem understanding

separately, we remain with three main traits that are somewhat unique for each of them (Table 2).

Clearly, a manager's role is to first understand the work, then split it into manageable parts, and finally assign them to available resources (people, skills, and systems). The manager has authority over *what to do* and *how to do*. The work plan, i.e., the sequence of tasks, is also the manager's job. Even in the democratic Agile method, although the team assigns the work, the manager still bears all the responsibility. The leaders benefit from understanding the workload, but it's the managers who own it.

In addition, one of the manager's most important functions is to ensure the quality of the work. It starts with setting quality goals, designing programs to achieve them, and driving these programs. The leader sets the tone, the quality religion of the organization, but it's the manager who gets the budget and delivers it. Managers should always dedicate time and resources to define and maintain the quality in their respective fields.

Above all a manager's role is about execution, i.e., delivering the results of a group of people effectively and efficiently through direct reporting or matrix relationships. Managers are like doctors, i.e., they have to continuously develop detailed knowledge on their work, and general knowledge about their customers and suppliers.

The managers own the work, its execution and quality, but as we have seen in the brief examination of the five pillars (Chapter 5), they also own a lot more.

Let's now look at the differentiating features of leaders.

It helps the leaders tremendously when they are naturally charismatic, though they could still be effective leaders even if they are not. If you look at the dictionary definition for charisma — *a personal magic of leadership arousing popular loyalty or enthusiasm for a public figure* — I'm not sure you'd want to be charismatic. Isn't that like a charlatan who uses magic to create irrational beliefs? Certainly, you shouldn't attempt to be charismatic if you aren't. Consider those politicians that try hard to present a warm side, even though everyone knows for sure that they are cold and calculative. Or, imagine this situation from my time in a company that had *true Puritanical New-England character,* when a new leader in the organization appeared on stage in a large corporate event wearing shorts and a Hawaiian shirt. He looked ridiculous, and no one forgot it for a long time. Charisma is a natural trait — you know if you have it, but don't try to fake it.

True leaders, with or without charisma, have followers and they accomplish their goals by influence. In my workshops, the name of

Steve Jobs is the first to spring to mind when I ask the participants for an example of a true leader. Watching him on a bare stage pointing to a small device in his hand is an unforgettable sight, especially when you know that hordes of people across the world were standing in queues in front of Apple stores, eager to spend $800 on a personal appliance. Few knew then how it would add to their lives, and many, including me, continue to carry this extra load with them. This is pure leadership and pure influence. Behind the scenes, many people worked on building the anticipation and the staging of this event, and collectively they accomplished a momentous feat. As opposed to charisma that has to be natural, influencing techniques can be learned.

Steve Jobs told us in his speech how we would behave in the future, and he was right; so whenever his team came up with new ideas, we were even more inclined to believe. He built a new user ecosystem which we had not been aware of and he described it to us. You can also use this technique and influence your team by providing information that's beyond their normal reach. In general, a team expects a leader to be more knowledgeable than they are and when you share technique and information with them you become a stronger leader. You spend more time than your team in visiting and understanding the wider ecosystem. Then inform them how their ecosystem looks, what other teams are doing, chart the road ahead, and explain the destination. Managers who share information only on *a need-to-know basis* lose the opportunity to lead. In the current information age, followers trust in your leadership with more information divulged. Always remember that a leader without followers cannot be a leader; therefore, assess your leadership through the eyes of the followers.

A true leader behaves and acts differently from a pure manager. The hunter and the gatherer both bring home food, but their goals and methods are completely different.

But whom do we *need* more? The manager or the leader?

In my workshops, at this point of the discussion, we already had a better understanding of the differences between leader and manager. So I asked the participants to assess their behaviors in their own jobs and environments.

I drew a line on the board with "Manager" written on one end and "Leader" on the other (see Fig. 1), and waited for the first participant to come forward with his self-assessment and put an "X" on the line.

Participants who see themselves more as managers were grouped on the left. Typically, one-third of the group was self-proclaimed managers, with a slight deflection toward leadership and only a small variation among them. And those who see themselves as leaders spread over the entire right half of the scale.

Once all participants had marked their X on the scale, I asked the group to do peer reviews — do you agree with the self-placements? First, they had to overcome their hesitation to tell what they think of each other, and then they came forward. I recorded their observations with arrows. In a typical group, at least half of the names moved significantly — some, from one side of the scale entirely to the other side.

Nonscientific as it is, this simple group exercise taught the workshop participants a few important lessons. Self-perception is very different from peer-perception even when peers work with you every day and know you well. We also see that more people typically position themselves on the Leader side, and that raised a question: do we think that managers are less valuable to the organization? Do we think the position of a manager is lower than a leader position? Once this realization sets in, the immediate question that bothers participants is what this means to them.

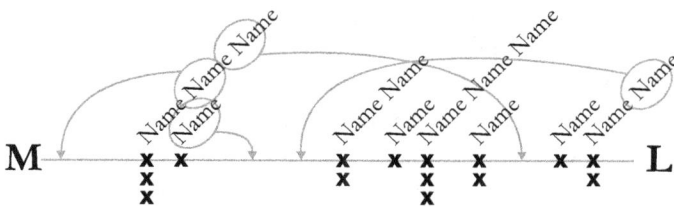

Manager vs. Leader
Self assessment - Group assessment

Figure 1

From here I steered the group toward the main point of the manager vs. leader conversation. Can a modern organization afford *pure* leadership positions, i.e., roles dedicated solely to vision and influence? Will a leader who is solely *high up* build enough credibility and gain trust to produce followers? Even the legendary leaders of hi-tech always maintain a foot on the ground and they like to be famous for it.

NO FOOT ON THE GROUND

I particularly like to tell this anecdote to illustrate my *foot on the ground* point. I was scheduled to meet the global head of sales in the giant company where I worked, to discuss an issue of mutual interest to his organization and my department. He was an Executive VP, a direct report to the CEO, and I, a mere VP in the product organization, two levels down in the hierarchy. The meeting had been postponed a couple of times, but finally, I was there. It was the last day of the quarter — the *hottest* in the life of American corporations. The door to his office was closed — I was in the waiting area. After about 15 minutes the secretary explained that he was aware that I was there and that he was on the phone. 15 minutes later, he was still on the phone and I was still waiting. 15 more minutes went by and I started to wonder. I offered to reschedule; after all, it was the end of the quarter and he must be busy. *Oh! there's no need to postpone,* she said in total calm, *he's got other people to worry about end-of-quarter business.* In a later conversation with my EVP boss — his peer — I said that I didn't believe he would survive in the company. My boss smiled — I could only surmise what it meant. Indeed, the head of sales did not survive much longer after this minor incident. The spectacular results of his organization didn't help him either; he had no supporters, no followers; his most important constituency — his employees — voted him out because he wasn't involved where it mattered to them.

On the other end of the scale, managers cannot afford to just be managers — focusing only on execution and leaving the rest to others. You have to pay attention to the needs of the team for information, attention, guidance, and professional development, as well as to drive and ensure teamwork. The quality of work and your team's productivity and motivation depend on these leadership activities, by influence and not by dictate. It's not optional and no manager is exempt.

By now the conclusion of the discussion is evident — if you are strong as a manager and want to improve, add leadership to your curriculum of self improvement. If you are more of a leader, get involved with the work and the people. Your peers will help you see the real you.

Make sure the push to the center of the scale is consistent; otherwise it will be perceived as fake. I once coached a leader who was known by his organization as removed and cold. His employees saw him mostly when he was unsatisfied with the results that he monitored from his desktop. When I suggested scheduling random one-on-one meetings with employees (Andy Grove style), he agreed to do it. Later, however, when I asked how it was going, he told me that he changed the action to: *I'll occasionally walk around the office with a smile on my face.* I would have preferred he did nothing — no action is better than fake action.

The right mix for today's work environment is to be both a hunter and a gatherer, i.e., a manager and a leader. For your own self improvement, pick a few attributes from the two columns, for example, being informative, improving team motivation, and increasing quality. Use your team to translate the intent into actions. Tables 3 includes examples for ideas in such an improvement plan.

Be both a Manager and a Leader is the short conclusion of the first pillar of your management responsibility (Table 4).

Table 3 Effective Manager and Leader: Example of Self-improvement Plan

Attribute	Intent	Action
Informative	Improve leadership by becoming a source of external information for the team	1. Simple presentation about industry trends + competitive landscape and comparison to our roadmap and position 2. Update and review with the group quarterly
Motivation	Improve motivation of individuals and team	1. Quarterly mini performance reviews focused on personal development 2. Monthly team meetings: 1–2 topics chosen and presented by employees
Quality	Improve quality of team output and service	1. Set quality benchmark and metrics. Develop improvement goals and plans. Continuous follow-ups 2. Educate team on service orientation and analyze current situation regularly

Table 4 Five Pillars of the Manager's Job

Manager and Leader	Ecosystem and Constituencies	Operational and Business Strategy	Work and People	Managerial Relationships
✓				
Manager's Job Definition				

Ecosystem and Constituencies

7

L et us consider the spatial ecosystem of an organization, small or large, with its manager at the center and surrounding him on all sides are the constituencies, i.e., groups or entities with whom he has relationships of *mutual expectations, needs*, and *give-and-take interactions*. These constituencies can be compared to those with voting power, as if they could vote the manager *in* or *out*, and the success of the manager and his organization depends on them.

In this chapter, we develop the understanding of the manager's relationships with the constituencies and translate them into essential parts of the managerial job. To complete the ecosystem, the conceptual worlds, i.e., industry, economy, and company vision, are located in the front and back of the manager's virtual space. Part IV, Global Company Strategy, describes how these conceptual worlds influence his routine functions as the manager.

I regularly meet managers who are busy beyond belief — streams of tasks flow and inundate their work lives. These managers struggle to control their movements in the deluge and their personal lives are often affected. The need to rationalize, manage, and control the requirements of all the constituencies is not just important — it is urgent.

From a manager's vantage point, we identify three types of work relationships: expectations, give-and-take interactions, and needs.

Starting at the top of the ecosystem, upper managers and executives have *expectations* from the manager. These are not always communicated clearly, regardless, the manager has to recognize them and live by them. Every manager should visualize a *personal board of directors* (P-BoD), real or imaginary. Even a sole owner of a business, with no one to report to, has his higher-ups such as investors, bankers, a mentor, or spiritual supporter. A smart manager makes a conscious effort to manage the *expectations* of the P-BoD to secure their continued support.

What are these formal or informal *expectations*? P-BoD members always think about the same two questions explicitly or implicitly: *is this manager the right person to be entrusted with the charge? Should we continue to support him?* Keep this in mind whenever you talk to your superiors; they are always thinking if you're the right person, no matter what else they talk about.

Therefore, you have to figure out those expectations, take them seriously, and manage them accordingly. These skies are full of dangers; some P-BoD members are like moons that appear nightly with their own sets of beliefs. Others might be comets with their own favorite people or supernova ideas — threatening, and you don't even know it. You work hard to build, and they can dissolve your fragile structures with close to no effort. It is not always logical. You have to manage these celestial bodies with art and finesse.

Moving on to the sides of the manager's space, i.e., peer constituencies, we find the external and internal suppliers and clients with whom he has mutual dependencies. We interact frequently with peers with an exchange of *give-and-take*.

Below the manager we find the team, direct and matrixed employees, with their *needs*. Your main role as a manager is to orchestrate, refine, and improve suppliers and clients, and to receive products and services from your team. The suppliers and clients provide the tasks, systems, tools,

processes, motivational drivers, and knowledge for your team. In reality, your job is to work *for* your employees' needs and not the vice versa.

How you manage these ecosystem relationships, i.e., P-BoD *expectations*, peers' *give-and-take*, and employees' *needs*, determines your professional career growth. If you want to avoid stagnation you have to go all the way out, be proactive, yet balanced. You cannot neglect activities that are less natural to you because they *are* as important. I have seen managers with new ideas working hard on detailed plans only to be blocked later by their P-BoDs, because they were not included in hatching those ideas. You have to straddle that fine line between being fully open with your ideas and disclosing too little. You already know what you can achieve within your comfort zone; to get more, you need to venture out.

Optimizing these ecosystem relationships starts with understanding the key functions, features, and challenges of the other side. For example, engineering manager and product manager depend on each other as peers. Stability of product specifications is a daily challenge for the engineering manager. The product manager, on the other hand, is sensitive to the market. He needs to deliver the right feature at the right time — when customers are willing to pay a premium, or to react to a competitive challenge. The needs of the two managers are inherently conflicting. Constant *give-and-take* between them, whenever effective, will produce the successful combination of minimal product that satisfies time-to-market needs. In Agile terminology, we call it MVP (minimal viable product). The regular revisions of the MVP balance the needs of the two sides continuously.

To understand your constituencies, a simple table can be made that captures the mutual needs and their related activities (Table 1). Do it in pairs, i.e., create two separate versions from either side of the relationship, then discuss and settle into one agreed version to review regularly (quarterly). Do not assume that you already have this agreement with the other groups. At the very least, the exercise will reinforce how deeply your team understands the needs of the other side — the devil is in the details. The development of mutual understanding is also the basis for teamwork; without it teamwork is only lip service and not true collaboration.

Table 1   Manager Ecosystem: Form for Mutual Needs

Internal and External Relationship	
Mutual Needs	**How**
I need from them: 1- 2- 3-	Activities 1- 2- 3-
They need from me: 1- 2- 3-	Activities 1- 2- 3-

To get the most out of this exercise, a constituency that's a large group can be split into coherent segments. For example, customers could be segmented into key customers, enterprise, and SMB's, and partners into revenue channel partners and technology solutions partners. Each segment has its unique set of needs. Examples of entries in the *Mutual Needs* column of the table are:

- A manager needs from his manager: executive level information
- Engineering manager needs: specific product decisions
- Customers need: offers, services, products, information
- Partners need: education on trends and company offerings

In the *How* column on the right, the activities to satisfy the needs are specified. The How activities are fairly simple to fill, if the Mutual Needs are specific enough. For example, for the needs mentioned above, the following activities may provide the right response.

- A regular managers' forum on corporate information
- Engineering product reviews
- Customer visits
- Quarterly partner visits for updates and webinars

CEO — Ecosystem and Constituencies

As a more complete example, let us examine the role of a CEO in a mid-size company. I chose a mid-size company because they have almost all the challenges of a large company, only with fewer means to address them. You can expand or reduce it according to your situation. The CEO is always challenged with the balancing act of assigning priorities and deciding what *not* to do. He can only make these decisions properly if he maintains a deep understanding of all of his constituencies, what's important to them, and what is less important.

This hypothetical multinational company, headquartered in an industrial park, has one thousand employees, and it sells products and services. It has two remote engineering units and several international and domestic offices for sales and services. They sell directly to large customers and also have major channel and service partners. Their investors and 70% of the sales activity are in the United States.

This CEO's ecosystem includes the following constituencies:

1. Board of directors
2. Executives in the company, e.g., VPs and GMs
3. All employees, segmented into headquarters and field
4. Key customers
5. Industry followers, e.g., reporters, analysts, sector investors
6. Surrounding community, e.g., city, universities
7. Investment firms
8. Major partners
9. Critical suppliers
10. Government entities, tax authorities, financial institutions.

The following sections capture *expectations, give-and-take,* and *needs* of the first five constituencies from the list. In small companies, majority of the activities fall on the CEO, while in large companies the responsibility is shared with the layers of upper management (Table 2 through Table 7).

Table 2 CEO Ecosystem — Board of Directors

Board of Directors	
Mutual Needs	**How**
I need from them:	**Activities**
1. Funds for investments	1. BoD meetings
2. Budget approvals	2. BoD meetings
3. Strategic decision making	3. Ad Hoc meetings
4. Industry presence of the company	4. Relationship building
They need from me:	**Activities**
1. Execution of approved plans	1 + 2. Policies, programs, plans, field and
2. Lead the company to success	organizational presence, BoD reports
3. Ideas for business expansion	3. M&A activity
4. Focus on shareholder value	4. Manage strictly top/bottom lines

Table 3 CEO Ecosystem — Executives in the Company, VPs and GMs

Executives: VPs and GMs	
Mutual Needs	**How**
I need from them:	**Activities**
1. Execution of plan	1. Monthly reviews/plan adjustments
2. Supervise productivity and quality	2. Quarterly Operational reviews
3. Collaborate with other departments on plans according to strategy	3. Cross-functional processes
4. Build and maintain excellent organization	4. Semiannual organizational reviews: talent, promotions, stability, skill coverage, training
They need from me:	**Activities**
1. Leadership and guardian of team spirit, vision, strategy	1. Periodical global communication events, departmental visits and programs to celebrate success
2. Professional coaching, focus, priorities	2. One-to-one meetings
3. Owner: top-level collaboration forums	3. Executive cross-functional status reviews and synchronization
4. Approval of department plans, budgets	4. Quarterly plan and budget reviews

Table 4   CEO Ecosystem — Headquarters Employees

Headquarters Employees	
Mutual Needs	How
I need from them:	Activities
1. Focus on quality delivery	1. Quality and excellence initiatives
2. Motivated, company ambassadors	2. Community involvement programs, university relations programs
3. Customer oriented	3. Field/HQ exchange programs, customer success stories, company internal periodicals
They need from me:	Activities
1. Involved manager and leader	1. Corporate culture programs, awards for quality and execution excellence Presence in departmental events
2. Quality leadership team	
3. Corporate and HR policies — hiring, promotions, compensation, etc.	2. 360° surveys on leaders, high potential programs for managers
4. Good working conditions	3. Semiannual reviews of policies, organization development
	4. Policies, reviews of working conditions

Table 5   CEO Ecosystem — Field Employees

Field Employees	
Mutual Needs	How
I need from them:	Activities
1. Be corporate citizens	1. Educational programs: service orientation, customer experience, how to represent the company
2. Focus on total customer value	
3. Expertise, professional excellence	2. Total customer value education
4. All items on headquarters' employees list	3. Training: technical, professionalism
	4. As for HQ employees
They need from me:	Activities
1. Educational programs, investment in field employees	1. Educational programs
2. Tight collaboration between field and headquarters	2. Field input to corporate functions, periodical satisfaction surveys, 3-way offering reviews quarterly: engineering–marketing–field
3. Service orientation focus in all HQ units	3. Education and service orientation Enforced metrics and CI programs

Table 6   CEO Ecosystem — Key Customers

Key Customers	
Mutual Needs	**How**
I need from them: 1. Repeat business 2. Openness to try new products 3. Be reference sites 4. Share needs and spend priorities 5. Information on competitive offerings	**Activities** 1. Consultative relationships, excellent service 2. Focus — customers competitive edge 3. Invest in the relationship 4. Executives' visits to customers, information exchange events 5. Invest in the relationship
They need from me: 1. High value products and services 2. Industry education 3. Consultative relationship at all levels 4. Interest in improving their revenue and cost structures	**Activities** 1. Customer-focused product and services roadmaps 2. Customer events, customer visits at HQ, executive visits at customer sites 3. Educational programs to field employees, solution orientation vs. product orientation 4. Executive exchange visits, win-win deals and attitudes

Table 7   CEO Ecosystem — Industry Followers

Industry Followers — reporters, analysts, sector investors	
Mutual Needs	**How**
I need from them: 1. Information on my company's industry perception and reputation 2. Exposure, PR 3. Competitive information 4. Information about industry trends and major players 5. General advice	**Activities** 1–5. Active relationships with company executives, meetings, conferences; occasional paid engagements Participation and contribution to analyst events
They need from me: 1. Good stories for publication 2. Exchange of information 3. Connections, networking 4. Participation, paid services engagements — analysis, articles, PR	**Activities** 1–4. Active relationships with company executives, meetings, conferences; occasional paid engagements Participation and contribution to analyst events

Completing these tables for all ten functions helps the CEO in educating, reinforcing, and driving improvements and stability in all areas. He can use them as checklists to do self-assessments with the leadership team and to reaffirm all the values of the company, such as quality, service orientation, and continuous improvement. In addition, these tables are the basis for structuring the company calendar. A regular schedule of the company's internal and external activities and processes is THE main source of stability and predictability and it's the best way to reduce chaos in an otherwise chaotic world.

How much of your time as a manager should you devote to your constituencies? A good balance is: two-third for them and one-third for your managerial tasks and unplanned activities and processes. If you struggle with time management, take a look at the tables above and decide what to delegate and what to defer or cancel. With this, we conclude the discussion on the second pillar (Table 8).

Table 8   Five Pillars of the Manager's Job

Manager and Leader	Ecosystem and Constituencies	Operational and Business Strategy	Work and People	Managerial Relationships
✓	✓			
Manager's Job Definition				

Heat

Miracles

GTM
Strategy

Light

Operational
Strategy

Romantic
Ideas

Partners

Industry
Waves

Galaxy
Storm

Quality

Ideas

Unexpected
Phenomena

Managers'
Skills

Managers'
Needs

Competitive
Landscape

Values

Customers

Employees

Clients

Suppliers

A lot to think about?

Operational Strategy →
Plan-Of-Record

8

We can look at strategy in two ways. First, strategy paints the picture of the desired future, charts the routes to get there, and pulls the organization forward; this is the operational strategy. The second is the global company strategy and it's the search for what to do. Global strategy examines industry trends, competitive landscape, buying patterns, and technology trends, and decides on customer segments, value proposition, technology, partnering strategy, etc. Strategy looks at the future. The time horizon depends on the industry, e.g., for the IT infrastructure industry — enterprise hardware and software — the visible future is still 5 years, but it's getting shorter; for the online media industry, 18 months is already beyond the horizon.

Every manager should have an operational strategy, or be part of a larger one that he understands thoroughly. A departmental operational strategy follows the global company strategy, though its scope is narrower. The manager is responsible for creating the operational strategy for his area, and revising it periodically with the team. You cannot make any decisions without a point of reference; the operational strategy is your reference — the plan-of-record.

You make daily decisions on work plans and programs. The operational strategy gives you and other managers a unifying point of reference in the future. All decisions have to make sense in the context of this future picture, i.e., whenever you need to choose between two options, you'd prefer the one that is more in line with the operational strategy. For example, you are choosing between two candidates, one is better for today's needs and the other for the future. For any function that is more than that of a small screw in a big machine, you choose the second candidate, just as the operational strategy guides you.

In this chapter, we build a generic *operational strategy in three main steps*. You can use this process as a guideline and build one for your organization, department, or business.

Step 1: Define value (revenue) streams
Step 2: Drill down of the value (revenue) streams
Step 3: Portfolio view

Operational Strategy — Value Streams

We start with an example in which the value streams are revenue streams. Let's assume we sell three products, A, B, and C, and we have several ways to reach customers such as online, resellers, and direct sales. We identify four revenue streams in Table 1: product A sold online (Rev stream 1), product B sold direct (Rev stream 2), and product C sold both online (Rev stream 3) and through resellers (Rev stream 4). Each of the four revenue streams is a way to earn money, and they differ from each other in decision making and allocating resources.

Table 1   Identifying Revenue Streams

Go-To-Market/Product	Product A	Product B	Product C
Online	Rev stream 1	—	Rev stream 3
Resellers	—	—	Rev stream 4
Direct	—	Rev stream 2	—

Another example is an order fulfillment company that receives products from the manufacturers and delivers them to customers. The company offers two types of service:

- Same-day delivery service to individual buyers
- Pallets with clustered products delivered to stores

These two types of service have different dynamics and operational metrics. The first would keep consumer customers happy by ensuring same-day service, and the second makes its customers (stores) happy by offering lower costs of logistics. Clearly, each of the two separate revenue/value streams has its set of decision criteria and they are very different.

Value streams are easy to understand when the value is revenue, but when it's not, we need to think of different work currencies. For example, a software engineering unit generates value in delivering products and solutions and in testing ideas. For an operational strategy of an engineering department, we divide their work into decision groups that we call value streams. Table 2 shows how to find these decision groups. First, we list all the projects, for example, a, b, c, etc. and then, we categorize them by purpose as product, feature, test software, debugging tool, integration, architectural change, and evaluations. We examine the combinations of projects and purposes, and look for groups with high dependency. These are the decision groups or value streams. We started with 19 software projects (from "a" to "s"), in 7 categories (from "product" to "evaluations") and reduced the number of combinations with high dependency to 10 value streams as shown in Table 2. Real environments have more dependencies among work items and therefore, for the operational strategy, it will result in a lower number of value streams to be analyzed .

The value streams are sometimes easy to identify but not always. The number of true value streams should be the lowest possible, so that further analysis is manageable and conclusive. With a client in the online media industry we used four categories for this divide-and-conquer analysis of their work and obtained 23 combinations. After examining the dependencies, we reduced

Table 2 Identifying Value Streams

Purpose/SW	a	b	c	d	e	f	g	h	i	j	k	l	m	n	o	p	q	r	s
Product	1	—	—	—	—	—	—	2	—	—	—	—	—	—	5	—	1	—	—
Features	—	3	—	—	—	—	—	—	—	—	4	—	4	—	—	—	—	—	—
Test	—	—	—	2	—	—	—	2	—	—	—	—	—	—	—	5	—	—	—
Debug	—	—	6	—	—	6	—	—	6	—	—	—	—	7	—	—	—	—	—
Integration	—	—	—	—	8	—	—	—	—	—	—	—	—	—	—	—	—	9	—
Architecture	—	—	—	—	—	—	7	—	—	—	—	—	—	—	—	—	—	—	—
Evaluations	—	—	—	—	—	—	—	—	—	—	—	—	—	—	—	—	—	9	10

the number to eight separate decision groups, i.e., eight revenue streams. After the completion of the rest of the operational strategy, as shown in the next steps, they decided to focus only on four of the revenue streams. The overall process created the focus that this company needed so badly.

Dividing the work into value steams helps in several ways, even before any further analysis:

- Value streams suggest the possible organizational structures. It makes a lot of sense to organize teams around work items with high interdependency.
- Wherever we assign revenue or profit to value streams, we can draw benefit pie charts and develop in the team the understanding of relative importance among value streams.
- If we know the costs of value streams — rough estimates are sufficient — we can compare the cost pie chart to the benefit pie, and create in the team a shared understanding of cost-benefit.

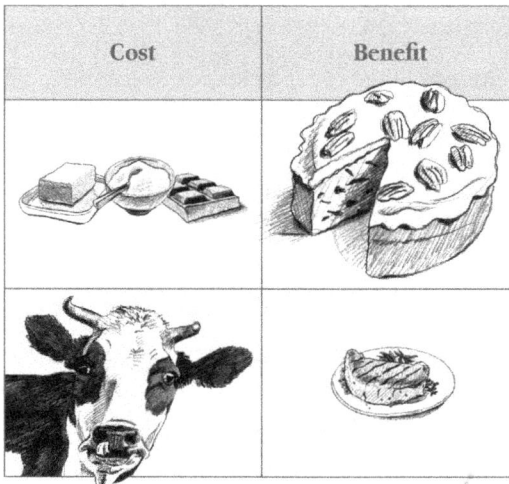

Operational Strategy — Drill Down of Value Streams

We analyze each of the identified value streams independently to get the potential value of each, as if it were a business on its own. Putting all constraints aside, i.e., budget, resources, or otherwise, we ask questions about the present, understand the past, and chart the future.

After completing this present–past–future drill-down, we have the potential, risk and value for all the value streams, individually. We compare them, and make decisions as we would in choosing investment options, i.e., we invest where the best returns are promised. The resulting decision set is as rational as it can be in a company environment. We will get to this comparison in the portfolio step, which comes next, but first we continue with our example in this drill-down step.

One of the revenue streams that we analyzed in this online media company is called performance campaigns. Its business model is success fees, i.e., only if their client is benefited from the advertising campaign, the company receives a fee. It is a high-risk model for the online advertising agency and no risk for the client, therefore, easy to close deals, but difficult to make money. Here the team created seven tables of present–past–future questions to capture the drill-down process.

Example: Performance Campaigns — The Present

We analyzed the present of the revenue stream by capturing all its vital signs, i.e., relevant metrics, trends, and dependencies. Then we added commentary in a SWOT format, in which the team captured market trends, competitive landscape, technology, organizational aspects, and other internal and external challenges. (Entries in Tables 3 and 4 are only for illustration.)

Example: Performance Campaigns — The Past

After drilling down and understanding the present, we wanted to learn the relevant lessons from history, when market and technology conditions were similar enough to what we expected them to be in the near future. The team chose to examine the actions from the past starting from revenue, contribution, and profit, and then to assess previous decisions and conditions to determine what worked and what didn't work, and how it affected the key performance indicators. Actions that failed in the past could still be relevant if the conditions were different. The relevant historical period was 1.5 years — three six-month periods including the current.

Table 3 Value-Stream Vital Signs

Performance Campaigns	Lead/Manager: Robert	Comments
	Date: May 2014	
Revenue	$800K/Mo	Spike in April
Gross profit %/$	25%/$200K	% Flat in recent months
Click through rate	1.5	Trending up
Conversion rate	2.1	Trending up
Earning per 1000 impressions	$0.5	Trending up
Number of clients	45	Stable
Clients generating 80% revenue	19	Stable
Trends — internal	Business metrics — up Team professionalism — up Stable team	Waiting for technology to improve results
Trends — external	Gaming demand — up Mobile restrictive regulations	—
Dependencies	Budget for media buying Exchange available supply More media sources	—
Reverse dependencies	Media	Mutual dependency

Table 4 Value-stream SWOT

Strengths	Weaknesses	Opportunities	Threats
Company-wide focus	Not enough investment in marketing	Email marketing, affiliates, others	Pressure on margins. Low growth opportunities
Sales knowledge	Dependency on a few experts	Affiliate networks as new revenue source	No commitment for investment period
Client service High retention	Usage data Availability of CDF	Optimization tools in Q3	Dependency on exchanges
Growth — healthy market demand	Automation tools	Implementation of CDF — beginning Q3	Dependency on other business units
Client retention	CF/LP — creation and quality	LATAM/ US — dedicated teams (sales + media)	Highly competitive environment
Centralized operation	Revenue concentration on 20 clients	Increase no. of clients lead generator	Dependency on RM
Strength in five market segments	—	CM team — dedicate to affiliate networks (6 CMs)	Market regulations and restrictions
Fast client onboarding	—	Creative Studio	Advertisers restricting media Deterioration of media effectiveness

The historical analysis showed us the evolution from a declining revenue stream to recovery and growth. We wondered why and concluded that focus, a dedicated team for each function, and specialization drove the recovery. The analysis and the picture that emerged from it reinvigorated the team — they could see that teamwork with one set of goals can be successful (Table 5).

Example: Performance Campaigns — The Future

Revenue and profit were the main metrics for this value stream; the team agreed to a realistic forecast for 1 year in quarterly increments. To realize this potential they also agreed on 10 action items (Tables 6 and 7).

To complete the drill-down of the independent revenue stream, i.e., performance campaigns, the team summarized its potential in cost–benefit terms in Tables 8 and 9: long-term potential, risk, cost, and dependence on technology. We also answered the question of importance of this revenue stream to the company's global strategy. With the cost breakdown that followed, this revenue stream was now ready to be compared with other revenue streams in the last step of building the operational strategy, i.e., portfolio view.

Operational Strategy — Portfolio View

After dissecting all value streams and analyzing each of them, we combine, compare and contrast, and then ask: where should we invest our time, effort, and money? I call this very difficult task *KIK — Keep–Invest–Kill.*

Due to vested interests or momentum, many projects tend to continue forward, always one more step, even when they aren't supposed to. It's human nature that we find it hard to say goodbye to failing ideas. Working as a team on the operational strategy helps overcome these difficulties. A team that's committed to focus, productivity, and quality will make the KIK decisions and remove the clutter. If we finish the portfolio view without dropping anything, we should repeat it to ensure that the projects that

Table 5 Value Stream — Relevant History

Historical Criteria	1 Year Ago	Half a Year Ago	Current Half
Avg. Rev/mo.	$640K	$620K	$800K
Gross profit $/mo.	$147K	$126K	$200K
Rolling avg. profit %	23%	21%	25%
Major observations and actions influencing business	Organizational split: Operations and Sales	Started DR concept under sales	Team moved from Sales to Operations
	No dedicated campaign managers for performance	Dedicated three CMs in Q3	Mixed AM + CM teams in two key markets
	10 clients — focused only on 3 clients	High turnover CMs — end of Q3	Centralized Sales and Client Management
	Rev decline monthly	Cutting long-tail clients — end of Q3	New methodologies
	—	—	LATAM decrease — loss of two major clients
	—	—	Major execution improvements

Table 6 Value Stream — Potential

	+1 Quarter	+ 2 Quarters	+ 3 Quarters	+ 4 Quarters
Revenue	30% increase	20% increase	15% increase	10% increase
Gross profit %	20% increase	20% increase	20% increase	20% increase
Required actions	Action List — Q3	Action List — Q4	Action List — Q1	Action List — Q2
Dependencies	Indirect: Agency performance Knowledge/expertise	Indirect: Linked Need more media	Same	Same

Table 7 Value Stream — Actions

Action #	1	2	3	....	10
Action	Media resources	Dedicated lead generator	6 mo. invest. Profit targets: RM — 20% EXTs — 30%	....	Data mining system, optimization tools
Key milestone	Early Q2	Early Q2	Q2, Q3	....	Q2
Resources	HR recruitment	Absorbed in daily ops	—	....	Development engineers
Ownership	Jim	Anna	Joe	....	Sheila

Table 8 Value Stream–Cost–Benefit

Long Term Potential	Risk	Cost	Portfolio Contribution	Dependency on New Technology
High Potential	Medium risk	High cost	Strategically debatable — not in line w/ company direction	High dependency
$2.5 M/month in 1 year 25%–30% profit	Technology	HR — media, external tools, dedicated sales	Contribution potential to revenues is clear	Optimization tools
Achievable	Profit margins	Technology development	—	Data mining interface

Table 9 Value Stream — Cost Items Breakdown

HR	Technology	Other
Media buy/account managers	Optimization tool development	LATAM — focus team
Lead generation	Data mining/reporting	6-month investment period: gross profit targets: 20% RM/30% EXTs
Graphic designers	Automation tools	—
External media buy	—	—
Outsourced team: affiliate	—	—

remain on the table compete well for the limited resources. Maintaining too many projects puts the entire portfolio under critical mass and it hurts the potential results.

The analysis of the portfolio view requires several iterations and much deliberation until you arrive at an operational strategy consensus and a plan-of-record. Killing projects is not a simple task. If customers are involved, you have to do it gradually in a sun-setting process. Even without customers, closing a project is a several step process — just like old items in the house that are kept neatly in the attic, never to look at them again. Separations are hard.

Use some of the following tools to do the iterations of portfolio-view analysis, and repeat periodically:

- Project list: You have to see the entire list of all value streams, and all other projects and new ideas, that receive attention from the organization. Sometimes you realize that something isn't quite right just by giving a quick look at the length of the list.
- Investment matrix: Add columns to the project list and review the investments in HR, technology, etc. From the resources point of view, you will see things you did not see before.
- Risk–benefit matrix: Divide projects into four groups based on potential and cost, or any other way you look at risk and benefit (Table 10).
- Betting table: If the KIK step does not converge, ask the team to bet on the projects — 5 for strong invest, 3 for keep, 1 for low invest, and 0 for kill. A clearer picture will emerge.

Table 10   Risk vs. Benefit/Potential vs. Cost

High Potential projects	Highly desirable projects, cash cows, or rare new ideas	Risk should be assessed, and only few projects should be accepted
Low-potential projects	Projects not worthy of attention	Undesirable projects
	Low Cost	**High Cost**

From Operational Strategy to Plan-of-Record

We have completed a round of decisions and now we have to organize all actions in a plan-of-record. We add the missing element, i.e., timeline, and record the actions, milestones, resources, and ownership. The level of detail should be just enough for owners of the actions to know how to translate them into work plans. We review and revise the operational strategy every two quarters, and the plan-of-record more frequently, for example, quarterly.

Periodic updates of the plan-of-record are shorter compared to the long analysis of the operational strategy. The benefits of these reviews are tremendous. Everything you want from your team is reinforced in this process — motivation, ownership, deep engagement, mutual understanding and respect, and collaboration.

For one of my clients, we stretched and contracted the process a couple of times before we arrived at the right format. We took 3 days to do the operational strategy for the first time. We developed a common language and learned the concepts. Then, we summarized the results into a three-quarter roadmap, which we called the matrix. In the second cycle, we spent just one day to review the matrix, but felt it wasn't enough. The business conditions were shifting, and we needed to be more thorough, so the following iteration was the extended matrix that took 2 days to review — it was just the right size for them.

What to Expect from the Operational Strategy Process

Building the operational strategy (Table 11) and plan-of-record has a powerful unifying effect on the leadership team, and it provides the alignment structure for all managers, down to the last team lead. Sometimes the results are beyond expectation, i.e., the focused team dynamics stretch the boundaries; what you thought impossible transforms into a reality right in front of you. Here are some examples from my clients.

Table 11   Operational Strategy — Plan-of-Record

Operational Strategy/Plan-of-Record	
Step 1 — Identify value streams	Combinations: Product–method–market Decision groups
Step 2 — Drilldown analysis for each value stream	Present: Vital signs SWOT Past: Relevant history What worked — what didn't? Future: Value-stream potential Actions Cost–benefit assessment
Step 3 — Portfolio view	Cost–risk–benefit comparisons Keep–invest–kill decisions Plan-of-record

HIGHER FORECAST

This client of mine is a pan-European manufacturer and distributor of consumer goods. During the analysis of the revenue streams, the leadership team solved a supply bottleneck that affected several regions. They solved the problem by doing a time-share agreement on a key piece of equipment and increased the supply of a product that was hot in the market at that time. The owner of the equipment, the head of one of the business regions, could see that loaning it to other regions would increase sales in the entire company more than it would hurt his own business. The forecast of the company increased by 10% for the year — an amazing result for a traditional consumer goods company. Without analyzing and sharing the revenue streams of all regions as one team, the bottleneck would still be there.

EFFICIENCY GAIN

Software and services companies often acquire technologies, or a small team with technology, that theoretically create an advantage for their portfolio of products. More often than not, however, no matter how good the idea is, putting it in practice takes more effort in engineering and marketing than originally anticipated. When I started working with this client, they had just completed such an acquisition. Field teams all over the company were so enthusiastic that they were pushing the new product to their customer base — everyone wanted to be the hero that would start the success roll. Unfortunately, however, these first attempts were not successful. Customers were receptive to the cool technology, but extracting value out of it was difficult — the evaluations extended without conclusive sales. Frustration started to build up in the corners of the company.

Six months after the acquisition, we had the operational strategy session where we understood, for the first time in this company, the following points:

- The new revenue stream wasn't ready for across-the-board sales; much more work and investment were needed.
- Too many people invested time in parallel efforts without collaborating, resulting in wasted company resources.
- The new revenue stream needed a focused effort with enough resources, rather than under-critical-mass attempts all over the company.

The leadership team decided to concentrate all efforts in one place and empowered the expert in the field to own the project. Without having the entire leadership team clearly seeing the complete picture, these small attempts to create quick premature wins would have continued, with futile, and possibly damaging, outcomes.

BUYING PRECIOUS TIME

Around 2010, selling advertisements on Facebook was easy — it was made easy on purpose. FB subscriber numbers were growing very fast. They had the traffic, but the monetization of this traffic was still under-penetrated. Some quick-on-their-wits online media companies started to generate nice revenues and very nice profits.

Facebook was in the process of building an entire ecosystem. They observed the trends and planned their strategy step by step as all metrics were working in their favor. In 2012, Facebook announced that within one year they would expose the prices of their advertisement space. It was the first calculated move in a series of steps to raise their prices and squeeze margins from their distribution channel, i.e., the online advertising agencies. The move initially lowered the total cost to advertisers, making FB more attractive compared to other media sources. At the same time, the agencies could no longer charge their customers the premium prices, as their cost structure was now exposed. Gross margins for agencies were dropping from 40% highs to the 15% market normal levels.

My client was one of those quick agencies to ride the FB wave and build a decent business around it. The results were so fruitful that they were moving resources to this new revenue stream even after the FB announcement. Their older, non-FB revenue stream with 15% margin lost focus and was now in decline. Their plan was as follows: one year of high profits on FB would outweigh the decline in the older revenue stream. In the meantime, they were working feverishly on new technology and revenue stream called self-serve which lets customers run their online FB advertising by themselves, with similar results. Within one year, they would restructure their business on FB with lower margins, and on the new self-serve.

(Continued)

(Continued)

This was a very high-risk plan. The clock was already ticking on the health of the winning horse; regardless, they were willing to gradually kill a good old workhorse, because it was obstinate and difficult to work with, for the hope that the winning horse would last one more year, and that in less than 1 year the untried colt would grow to win races.

Luckily, we were building an operational strategy at that time. The leadership team could see that it was not logical to risk the entire company on this plan, i.e., too many assumptions had to be correct, all at the same time.

The way the story unfolded in the following year showed that all the assumptions, in fact, were incorrect. The good news was that the old revenue stream was not such an old horse after all, once we put our attitudes aside and gave it proper analysis, we saw that it was still good with potential for growth. With renewed focus, it tripled its revenue and the margins improved from 15% to 20%. The bad news was that the FB announcement created the price pressure in the market a lot faster than expected. As customers demanded cost visibility from their suppliers, prices and margins were deteriorating rapidly. To top it off, the new technology self-serve proved to be a non-winner — customers preferred to pay a 15% fee for the service rather than doing it by themselves on a platform that charged a 5% usage fee.

Overall, we averted three bad decisions, and the more mature approach to growing a business won. Executives in the company said later that the operational strategy process *bought us time and saved the company.*

With these three examples of the additional benefits of the operational strategy we conclude the discussion on the third pillar of the manager's job. (Table 12)

Table 12   Five Pillars of the Manager's Job

Manager and Leader	Ecosystem and Constituencies	Operational and Business Strategy*	Work and People	Managerial Relationships
✓	✓	✓		
Manager's Job Definition				

* More on Business Strategy in Part IV.

Work Management and People Management

9

Work management and people management can be discussed forever. A lot has been said and written about these topics, but I still continue to see managers who prefer to use personal common sense, that is based only on their limited experience, and deny themselves the vast accumulated knowledge of enormous research. Despite the inspiring absolute truths and the latest findings, the application in the work environment is evidently *not that simple.*

Many years ago, one of my employees told me that I always say the obvious — he did clarify that he meant it as a compliment. In this chapter, I review the obvious, i.e., simple principles, methods, and tools that anyone with determination could use. These concepts were helpful to me for many years, and are now useful to my clients, as I've reengineered them to their modern and simplest versions.

Work management and people management are yin and yang, i.e., you organize work around the basic psychology in the workplace and think constantly about effectiveness and efficiency. Work management and people management are central to a manager's role, but you don't have to be a master planner or a psychologist to do it well.

Correct Load, Overload, Context Switching

Employees can either be more productive with lower quality, or less productive with higher quality. In high pressure environments, you have to ask yourself from time to time — what is the combination of quality and quantity that produces the best value? If we could assign weight points to tasks and rate quality, we would multiply them and find that combination of best value. In fact, the SCRUM method in software development is doing just that. However, although most knowledge-based work cannot be measured scientifically, you could look out for the symptoms at the extremes — what does it look like when the work is too little or too much?

You want your team to be effective — produce the best work — and efficient — produce the most work. But these concepts are inherently conflicting. I found a model in a *Harvard Business Review* article that illustrates the basic concept well. Productivity, the combination of effectiveness and efficiency, increases when you load the employee with more simultaneous tasks, up to an extent, and then it starts to decline (see figure below).

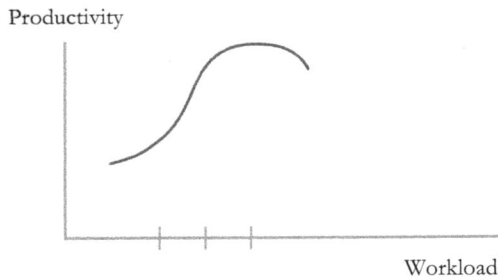

Productivity vs. Workload

For tasks that are more than mechanical steps in a process, you need to think, plan, and coordinate with other people. Productivity increases when you work on one task while waiting for an action to complete on another task. However, each start or stop wastes an amount of overhead time to get into the new task and out of the old task. With too many simultaneous tasks, this overhead per task becomes longer, as it's difficult

to switch from one context to another. The model shows that with too much *context switching* the accumulated overhead causes productivity to reach a breaking point.

I would not advise anyone to draw his team's loading profile — it's for the lab. But let's see what it might look like in your environment — a case of too little and a case of too much. Too little work is harder to spot because it's less obvious at first sight. Too much work, however, is very much in your face.

The Case of Too Little

In the ever-increasing globalization of the knowledge economy, you often see split teams working on shared projects at multiple locations. At least in principle, the wonderful collaboration technologies make it easy.

A common problem occurs when portions of work switch hands and location. Usually, the original owners of the work decide on the transition plan, i.e., the parts that move and the sequence they move in. They also prepare training and other hand-over activities. What comes next, typically, is disappointment from the quality and productivity results of the receiving side.

To fix the problem, the original owners do more training and add verification steps that did not exist before. They write procedures and define the interactions between the two locations. The receiving group is now relegated to following procedures. It should be simpler now, but it's not — productivity is not improved and neither is quality.

I see this scenario often in software development, where one team uses another remote team to do testing or sustaining engineering (fixing bugs). It also happens with corporate and field functions that do the same kind of work, e.g., a corporate marketing team develops sales materials and sends them to the field marketing team to adapt to local needs. A lot of back and forth wasteful work could have been saved if the corporate team just sent the high-level corporate messaging and left the local team to create their materials.

This problem starts with the wrong attitude of the original owners of the work, i.e., *we know how to do it and we will show you; just follow our instructions.* However, this is not how people work at their best, and it doesn't matter which part of the globe they are on. If you restrict the other team more, you actually drive them farther from the goal of assuming the responsibility for the work. Procedures could never cover all the cases they encounter — the receiving team waits for further instructions and productivity goes down.

The lesson from the HBR model is that the *correct load* results from giving *more* responsibility to the receiving team, allowing them to own the work and the transition plan, while giving them the time to digest and learn. Let *them* say what they need in order to assume the responsibility, and they should write down their own procedures. Own more — it's like giving a child responsibility and enough independence to grow, instead of leaving him behind with behaviors that are no longer suitable for his age.

Turning the responsibility table around and giving more of the work to the remote team, in software development, marketing, or any other similar situation, will produce better results faster. But it requires trust in the remote units that the original owners of the work usually find hard to embrace.

The Case of Too Much

Overload and excessive context switching can be found everywhere, just look around you. This entire book is about making work more manageable, achieving intended results in efficient ways and reducing chaos and stress. As a manager you have to pay attention to the symptoms and address them. However, managers themselves are so overstressed that if you go back to the HBR graph you have to wonder about *their* quality of work.

How many times do you send people to do the same work again because it wasn't good enough and did not achieve what was intended? How many times have I heard managers encouraging their teams to quickly respond to emails? People with a high sense of responsibility often take more work even though they are already overloaded. Managers can be less available to

support their teams, but then, you can also find them dabbling in the work of their teams.

These breakage points and symptoms are not easy to address. There is no magic pill or effective talk therapy. You have to put each piece where it belongs, remove clutter, simplify, and reduce the context switching of overloaded employees and managers. When you see the symptoms, know that they affect the entire team; the damage is usually larger than what it seems at first.

Time Management, Urgent vs. Important

Have you ever played rocks–pebbles–sand? Try to fit them into a container. Put the sand in first, pebbles next, and there's no room left for the rocks. Reverse the order, and everything fits fine, you see? You have to plan tasks in the correct sequence. Also, you have to process them efficiently, e.g., clear your dishwasher with two hands and you would save half of the times you bend your back — *that's* parallel processing!

Organizing work is important — do not let the work organize you!

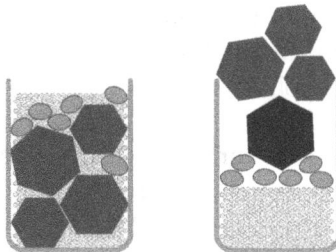

Rocks - Pebbles - Sand

If you make it a habit to check incoming mail as the first thing you do each morning, you are taking the sand first. Urgent and important items should come first, i.e., the rocks and pebbles. In the old paper days, a colleague of mine, Tom from Minneapolis, used to pile incoming mail to two feet high, and then cut the tower in two and trash the bottom half. He never read any of it. To anyone who asked, he would say that if any of it were important or urgent, people would call to his office anyway. Here was a successful manager who never read incoming mail. I am curious how he does it now.

Try hard to avoid:

- Letting incoming mail dictate how you organize your work
- Using social networking as a way to communicate
- Reading communication threads on mass-chat tools
- Spending your time on tasks as they arrive, instead of organizing them according to priority

With strong will and educating your team, you *can* develop new habits, i.e., master the tools instead of being their slave. The three clues for time management are *do less, reduce chaos,* and follow your *calendar as higher authority.*

Limit mail time to skimming the inbox and picking the important and urgent items; block time on your calendar for doing it, same time every day. Keep urgent and important items as *unread* and don't hesitate to mark all the less important items as *read.* Do it in bulk and you would already feel less stressed. Your to-do list is in the unread emails. Send emails to yourself for the missing items, and then, treat all the read items as my old friend Tom from Minneapolis used to do.

Urgent items should be done early or quickly. Always prefer to work on them with someone else, i.e., in pairs it can take less time, and, at the very least, the other person learns and will help in future urgencies.

An *important* item can wait, but it cannot be delayed until it becomes less important or irrelevant. Use common sense — there's nothing smarter to say about it. With an important item, first, I acknowledge to the sender that I received the action and I commit to doing it; then, I schedule it on my calendar as a meeting with myself, and set it as a daily repeated meeting with no end date. When it's done, I cancel all the future instances of the meeting.

I use different colors to differentiate real meetings from tasks — blue for meetings and blocked time, gray for business tasks, red for personal tasks, purple for travel, green for workout, and yellow for other reminders. I also use layered calendars for each color, so that I could share one of them with my team. For example, my purple travel calendar is shared and my team knows where I am. My calendar screen is a kaleidoscope, but I prefer it over maintaining task lists or covering my desk or computer screen with notes. The calendar and the inbox are my only task organizing tools. I never forget anything and I never deliver anything late. I must admit, though, I do delay some tasks so much that they eventually fall off. After all, I *am* human like all of us.

Group similar tasks and reduce *context switching* in your life. For example, while reviewing plans, it's easier and faster to review one after the other while you are at it, instead of reviewing one, switching to a sales call, and then coming back to review another plan. If your team knows your regular time for plan reviews, they will do their work with less context switching as well, i.e., you save time for yourself and for your team. For example, in the office of one of my clients, people worked like one giant team, i.e., anybody could talk to anybody anytime. Their habits led to so much context switching that we had to declare an official quiet-time rule *No Interruptions 9–12*. I offered one hour, but they decided on three. Everyone could now organize their tasks and work on them and that was a tremendous improvement in productivity. If you hear anyone in your office saying, *I get a lot done early in the morning before others arrive*, think of creating a quiet-time window for everybody. You could call it a *happy productivity hour*.

When you disregard the unimportant, you *do less;* attack context switching and you *reduce chaos*. And then, you turn to *higher authority,* and that's your calendar which helps you enforce all of this.

One calendar in particular can be the most disruptive, on one hand, or the organizational healer, on the other — that's the calendar of the boss. For better and worse, the higher you are in the organization's hierarchy, the more effect your calendar has on the organization. A very busy manager with a lot of schedule changes can cause many people to spend time making adjustments in their own schedules. Hyperactive managers can throw their organization into massive context switching without even realizing it. Keep your schedule as stable and as regular as it can be. Think twice before calling for an ad hoc meeting. Could it possibly wait for the next weekly? The golden rule is: refrain from adding to chaos.

SCRUM Is Great

These work management principles are the basis for the SCRUM process that was developed in the software engineering community where the adoption of the method is high. It's an elaborate process with its own terminology — a component of the larger school of methods — *Agile Software Development*. The principles of SCRUM, however, are universal and suitable for any type of complex and continuous work. SCRUM is like democracy — law, order, justice, common goals, joint efforts, and member equality — a lot of goodness when it works. And it does work, for small teams with long and complex projects.

In SCRUM, you assume that your ultimate goal is very far away, and that it's not possible to know all the steps in advance to get there. In fact, this is the reality of many complex projects. But you do know the next steps in the general direction of the goal. Therefore, you divide a project into periods of 2–3 weeks called *sprints*. Each sprint period has goals, and the completed tasks of the sprint demonstrate that these goals were achieved. No work is done outside the planned tasks of the sprints i.e., work is lean all the way through. Normally, only 2 sprints are defined, the current and the next. The team acts very democratically; it owns the sprints collectively and shares the responsibility to achieve the preset goals. The *Daily SCRUM Meeting* is the main enforcer of the entire process where the team addresses all obstacles and allocates the tasks. The shared ownership encourages team members to help each other. The daily meeting is a short 15-min meeting. Sprint design, sprint review, and sprint reflection are longer meetings that happen at the beginning and end of the period.

The main support that the SCRUM team needs is not to disrupt or interfere with the process, which means that they hang a *do-not-disturb* sign on the

door, and that any work request to the team has to go into a queue and wait for the next sprint for a chance to get done. That is the discipline and you cannot break it.

SCRUM gives the team independence to work and a very rigid framework which is self-correcting. Normally, quality and productivity increase after a small number of sprints, once the team is accustomed to the method. The team works together on the project in the most interactive way, usually with high team spirit and morale. However, despite all the benefits, managers have to relinquish command-and-control authority, and therein lies the Achilles heel of this method.

SCRUM is great because it fulfills all three principles of effective and efficient time management and productivity: it is lean, i.e., *doing less*; it is organized, i.e., *low context switching*; and it works with a *rigid higher authority*, i.e., calendar of dailies, sprint reviews, sprint designs, and reflection meetings. Every piece fits perfectly in its place.

People Management

You can model the employees' needs in a three-layer Maslow-like pyramid.

In the broad basis, employees need their manager's involvement to ensure that the work can be done, tools are available, help is available when needed, salary is adequate, and the entire *system is programmed to help the employee do a good job.*

Employees also want the opportunity to shine, to stand out of the crowd, to show something out of the ordinary, and to be *recognized by the larger team and by management.* Work should give them this opportunity.

For the most part, work also satisfies social needs; such as school is for children, work is for adults. You don't need to be the social center of your team, but it *is* your job to create opportunities for social connections and to let the social bubbles float, i.e., team outings, family days, hackathons (Fig. 1).

Social
Connections

Recognition by larger
team and management

System programmed to help the
employee do a good job

Figure 1   Maslow-Like Employee Needs Pyramid

Your daily toolbox for managing people has many simple manual tools, they are not electrical power tools. Doing the right thing is not difficult, but analyzing after the fact what went wrong, however, may require a psychologist.

What are the compartments in your people management toolbox?

- Expectations and skills
- Employee performance and development
- Promoting excellence: recognize, nurture, motivate
- Information and influence
- Recruitment, hiring, and assimilation

Expectations and Skills, Performance and Development

Common practice in organizations — mostly large, but also small — is to manage employee expectations and skills in annual performance reviews. If you have done a round of those, you know that the task is onerous and that the general feeling is that you aren't so sure why you're doing it. So, if the glove doesn't fit, you must quit using it.

You feel this way because of the following reasons:

- In constantly evolving work environments, one year is too long to stop and make assessments of any kind. What was done a year ago has very little bearing on the present and the future.

- Annual reviews are usually connected to salary raises — you do one and you think of the other — you cannot shake it off. Raises, however, depend on many other factors and their link to performance distorts the assessment. You know in advance that some excellent employees will be dissatisfied, as they would think *If I was so great, how come I received only 5%?* These are the employees you care about the most; you want to hear their opinions, and yet, you cannot have an annual conversation with them and disassociate it from the money aspect. And that's a problem.

- The annual review process is so burdensome that many managers and organizations pass the responsibility to the employees — *do your own self-assessment and I will review it.* In the following meeting, the employee wants to know what the manager really thinks of his work; instead, he receives a critique session on how he did his self-evaluation. Even if they agree, the employee is unsatisfied by the process — *he just told me that I am right in my assessment, and that's not much help!* Performance assessment is perhaps the only task that the manager should *never* delegate.

As an alternative to annual reviews, we should have a simpler process with higher frequency — a process that will achieve the following:

- Manage expectations frequently.
- Monitor skill improvements.
- Maintain manager's awareness of his employees' expectations.
- Develop mutual respect.
- Focus on the work itself, not generalities.
- Create self-correcting mechanisms.
- Focus on the future.
- Provide valuable assessments and not grades or rankings.

I recommend using a simple form that both manager and employee fill separately and discuss every quarter. The mini-reviews always consider the *next* three months. With separate filling of the form, the assessments are unbiased and well-thought-through. Your discussion with the employee has a focus on what to change, not in a year, but in the next 3 months. If HR policies require you to do an annual review, take four quarterly mini-reviews, add a grade, and it's done.

The form I use includes the most important assessment areas, i.e., skills, motivation, teamwork, commitment, and main projects. For each category, you enter a statement of the status and the expectations for the next review cycle.

Let's look at the example of the mini-review of a new financial controller and operations manager. He was preparing to replace the sitting controller, who was being promoted to CFO. Here, the assessment was also an assimilation plan for the new manager.

We wanted to ensure that the new manager knew the hard and soft skills that he would need in order to perform well in this job. Because he was expected to be a role model for the rest of the department, we helped him with specific goals that everyone could see and recognize (Table 1).

If you have the good habit of interacting with your team all the time, you might think that you don't need the quarterly mini-assessments. However, you would be wrong. The picture from inside the trenches is very different from the one from above ground. You need to give the employees the respect they need. You owe it to them to stop periodically and reflect on their work, one team member at a time.

The annual review still has a place in the organizational processes as an anchor to renew the mental contract with the employees and to discuss salary raises. With this in focus, you can explain the rules for raises, and how the budget is pooled and distributed to build morale throughout. Everyone, including excellent employees, will be less frustrated once they understand the system. It can be a process to kick-off the year with renewed energy, while the quarterly mini-reviews will focus on performance.

Table 1 Quarterly Assessment for a New Financial Controller and Operations Manager

Assessment Area	Current Status	Expectations, Development
Hard skills and soft skills	Very good: proactive, result-oriented, process, risk taker Good service orientation Quick and accurate Needs to accept failure with less frustration New to the company's systems	Mature handling of failure and difficult situations Proficient on all financial systems Basic interactions with other groups Understanding integration — financial and operational
Motivation	Learning fast all job functions Fear of making key decisions Still follower, needs more entrepreneurial spirit	Own and lead the team Less hesitant to take risk Accepted by the team as leader
Teamwork, internal and cross-functional	Not enough teamwork in his team Not enough integration with peer groups	Develop teamwork and social practices More interactions with other groups
Noticeable accomplishments	Setting up accounting infrastructure in remote office	Open a second new country, accounting and facilities
General goals	Resize the team Needs assessment for finance and operations Cash-flow and tax planning Guidance to sales in large deals	Resized team for growth Increase involvement with regional sales management Upper management decisions

Nonperformance

Performance management processes work well for performing employees. One of the most common failures of managers is when they treat problematic employees in the same manner they treat good employees. Managing nonperformance is different.

The problematic employee needs tighter supervision and clearer conditional messages such as *if you don't improve, then....* As a manager, you cannot overlook the reasons that created the nonperformance situation; after all, you created the same working conditions for everybody, and yet, one employee is problematic where others are not.

If you delay the action or neglect the performance problem, you are doing a disservice to your team. Any open and unresolved case lowers morale, quality, and productivity of the good people.

The problem can be behavioral, wrong skill-set, or lack of commitment to the job. Either way, it's not fun to handle, since as the manager of the situation you are out of your comfort zone. While your management skills are sharpened to drive growth, improvements, and get the most from your team, here you are exposed to conditions that are beyond that. Problematic employees have their own interpretations that will often surprise you. You have to set aside all discomfort and handle these situations professionally.

If there's no hope to fix the problem, first you have to be brave enough to admit it, and then ask HR to help you with the process of termination.

But if there *is* a reasonable expectation to reverse the situation, the *performance improvement plan (PIP)* is the most effective way. It is the last stop before termination. PIP is a formal process with six components:

- Short description of the problem in unequivocal words
- A statement that the problem will cause termination if unresolved
- Test period of typically 1–3 months
- Clear and specific criteria for the test period
- Clear and specific review process
- Acceptance signature

From my experience, about half of the employees on PIP take it as a wake-up call and pass the test period successfully. Others cannot or simply are not ready to try. The PIP should be genuine, i.e., you use it only when the intent is to help the employees pass it. It should never be set-up as a trap with intent to fail someone; such cases should move straight to termination without foul play.

Variations on the Theme of Nonperformance

Corporate politics or wrong company policies could interfere with the practice of managing cases of nonperformance correctly.

In large companies, *nonperformance* lives and stays in the house as background noise. Top-level managers know that about 5% of their workforce is not contributing their fair share. The symptom is known as *deadwood*. The degrees of separation between top and middle managers make it harder to pinpoint, i.e., 5% seems to be tolerable or ignorable. To correct this, organizations commonly do periodical *workforce reductions* such that *all managers have to cut 5% of their positions*. If you are a good manager taking care of all performance cases continually, you are penalized because you have no 5% deadwood margin. But good managers are also quick learners; many of them adopt an unofficial counter-policy of *non-management*. You build a buffer that will shield you when the storm comes. It's a common phenomenon; yet, I have not seen a good corporate policy solution or even a discussion about it.

Some time ago, I lived through an extreme example of this. My company assigned me to manage a remote engineering unit of 115 employees, mostly software developers. The group was working on a new product that had significant market success, i.e., customers were buying and the install base was growing fast. However, the head of the business unit was unhappy with the remote engineering group. He sent me there with a clear mission to fix the situation, prepare a new local manager and transition out, or plan and execute a transfer of the work to the headquarters' engineering unit.

Once I settled into my job after a couple of months, the employees were already comfortable with my open style. They were then quick to expose six blatant cases of extreme nonperformance, exactly 5% of the group. After a short investigation, I discovered that these problems had been there for years. One programmer refused to learn the new programming language that the group had adopted; he was content with his diminishing workload on old software. Another had psychological issues; you couldn't place him in a team. Yet another was working on wonderful tools that no one was using; he was convinced that the day would come when they would understand the value of his work.

When I questioned the HR manager, who had the understanding of the history of the place, she replied that my predecessor didn't like to fire people, *he didn't believe in that*, she said. Obviously, each case had its complexities, but when I addressed all six of them, the real effect of these problems became clear and awesome. The rest of the employees saw that I was serious about removing all obstacles to good work, and the group started blooming with creative ideas and renewed energy. We observed a complete sea change in productivity and quality.

This chicken-and-egg dilemma between managing non-performance and waiting for layoffs drives organizations to settle on low quality and productivity. Good managers suffer from aftershocks that come after general layoffs, as I did in the later chapter of this story.

We certainly need better workforce management policies that are flexible in their mandates in large organizations. We can only hope that smaller companies do not fall into the same traps.

Promoting Excellence

Positive reinforcement is the most effective people management tool in your toolbox because it generates momentum for improvement. In practice, most managers do positive reinforcement only when they happen to be in a good mood, therefore, inconsistently. Yet, it's so simple to create a process across the entire organization — a process to extract the best in human spirit, right there, at work.

I learned the power of special bonuses a long time ago when I was heading an organization of 17 groups, about 400 employees. The manager above me, the head of the department, assigned quarterly bonus budgets, *do with it what you think is good for the company*, he said. My peers followed the

process and awarded special bonuses in their organizations quarterly. I chose to spread my budget and award bonuses 12 times a year. Once a month, I sent a call for special bonuses to my 17 managers. They submitted requests with short justifications, and with few exceptions I approved them. After that we invited each of the selected employees to a quick stand-up meeting with the direct manager and me. We followed a routine — introduction, handshake, handing over an envelope with a check, and watching how the employee left my office very proud, with an envelope in his back pocket.

These little celebrations instilled a culture of excellence in my organization and they were precious. The managers had to stop for a few minutes once a month to think about what it meant to do an excellent job. The system was open and fair. Every employee, not managers, could receive a special bonus if they stood out of the crowd, made a special effort, or achieved an excellent result.

After several years of doing this practice, as long as I had the budget, I learned the lesson that a special bonus budget is a powerful tool — a rare management luxury. Table 2 explains how you could set up the program to *promote excellence* in your organization.

Table 2   System to Promote Excellence — Special Bonuses

System and Process
— Annual budget dedicated to special bonuses.
— Monthly calendar reminder to all managers to submit requests.
— Shared spreadsheet (G-Drive) to submit requests and justifications.
— Requests are for high, medium, or low bonuses.
— Once approved, HR prepares personalized recognition letters.
— Managers use the letters for one-to-one recognition celebrations.

Rules
— Excellence bonuses are for employees, not managers.
— You can give multiple awards but not in consecutive months.
— About 20% of employees receive awards during the year.
— Visibility to all managers to ensure integrity in using the process.
— Gift certificates are as good as cash awards.
— Do not pay attention to people who are offended by not receiving a special bonus; this process recognizes excellent performance.

Information and Influencing Employees

As managers we do a lot of talking to our employees. But can we think about how to do it professionally, the channels we use for each type of information, and the content we deliver?

The first lesson, though, is to communicate regularly. Just think of how lack of communication affects you, and commit to communicate to others profusely. No communication or superficial communication is a powerful enemy of organizations.

A communication vacuum can be disastrous, as can be observed from the following case. A client of mine delivers fee-based online services to its clients. In this business model, you have to watch the numbers constantly and make adjustments in the systems, just as you'd imagine traders do in online stock trading. The company was later acquired and the buyers decided to replace the CEO right after that. For 6 weeks, until the new manager arrived, no one talked in earnest to the middle managers. With the confusion that ensued from the communication vacuum, revenue and profits dropped by 30%, just like that. There was no change in the work, clients, or market conditions, just confusion that disrupted the focus.

With every change of manager, promotion from within or assignment from without, everyone in the immediate environment interprets the event as they wish and they immediately think of how it would affect them. People start talking and create versions of the story that might even leak to customers and partners, with damaging effects. We need to plug the hole with clear and sensible messages before it grows and becomes hard to contain. And if the new manager is also new to the organization, you cannot leave him alone to plug that hole. It needs to be a management team effort.

Communication is a hot topic for employees. Companies that survey their workforce on satisfaction and motivation always find *inadequate communication* as one of the top findings of the survey. The company might be doing a good job of internal communication, but the employees want more. When they get more, however, their attention is often reduced.

Regardless, you have to treat it as a constant unmet need, as if it were a communication vacuum, even though you didn't create one.

As the manager of your team, you are their source of information, the conveyor and the facilitator. Whether communication is easy for you or difficult, the best option is to create a routine. If you are an introvert, you should force yourself into this routine; if you're an extrovert, you'd do well to restrict yourself to the routine.

Communication Pyramid

One of those routines is the communication pyramid. If you're leading a team of managers, you should have open communication lines with employees, on one hand, while backing the managers below you, on the other, making sure you don't go around them. Employees should feel that their voice and opinions have a place and not just through formal upward communication channels.

Inflow of raw information from subordinates is also essential for good decisions; without it, you only have filtered or interpreted information. In his famous book *Only the Paranoid Survive,* Andy Grove, then the CEO of the large Intel Corporation, describes how he stayed in touch with people all over the company. He created a small network with higher-than-usual enthusiasts, the ones who often held divergent opinions. *People in the trenches are usually in touch with impending changes early*, as he said, referring to his personal advisory.

One of my role models instituted a nightly group dinner for all employees who stayed late. That's how he stayed in touch with raw information from the most dedicated employees.

What does a personal advisory network look like? It is a productive natural network that connects around 150 people organically. Malcolm Gladwell describes it in *The Tipping Point* and Paul Adams explains it in *Grouped, How small groups of friends are the key to influence on the social web.* Christakis and Fowler quote it in *Connected: The Surprising Power of Our Social Networks and How They Shape Our Lives.* And I can also attest to it from my experience of growing with organizations. You can regularly stay in touch and maintain productive connections with about 150–200 people — it's both feasible and powerful.

Let's look at an organization from the top position down to four layers of management, i.e., executives, directors, senior managers, and managers. The pyramid of regular one-to-one meetings could be: weekly with executives, monthly with directors, and 2 hours per week for a selection of people from the rest of the organization, up to 150 people that you would touch in a cycle of 3 months. Once the organization is used to the pyramid and people feel safe to communicate openly, some will occasionally ask to skip the line, and that is how you get important information in raw format.

In addition to the weeklies with direct reports that most managers do, you would add about 20 hours per month to maintain the pyramid as a routine. You'd invest 10% of your time to gain unfettered understanding of the organization, build transparency as a value, and have the opportunity to influence all the way to the remote corners. Crossing the formal lines is very powerful when it's employed with respect for people and managers in the organization.

Information that Employees Want

Employees want to receive from their manager information and explanations beyond what's available in their immediate work-group circle. Periodic informational emails are not a good substitute for meetings, virtual or physical; you have to get out from behind the screen and keyboard and be visible. But it's not only about what *they want*; it is also about the directives of the company's management that *you want* them to know.

If you do a good job of internal marketing, selling the company to the employees and building trust in the leadership, the employees will take these messages as cues and sell the company outside. Table 3 gives a checklist of content for company meetings, annual kickoffs, and quarterly or monthly department meetings. The checklist comes directly from the five pillars of the manager's role.

Table 3 Checklist for Company Meetings

Manager and Leader (Be a source of external information)
— Industry trends and competitive landscape — Our position vs. the competition
Ecosystem and Constituencies
— Highlights from other departments, key customers, key partners — Business trends affecting our key customers and key partners
Operational Strategy
— Market segmentation and target segments — Buying priorities and patterns of key customers — Offering portfolio update per target markets — Our operational strategy — Plan-of-record — Company achievements relative to the goals — Improvement initiatives
Work Management and People Management
— New projects, improvements in methods, new systems — Quality policy, benchmarks, and standards — Celebrate success and wins, recognition, awards — Welcome new hires — Response to broad-based employee issues
Managerial Relationships
— Organizational updates — Promotions and expansions of responsibility

Recruitment, Hiring and Assimilation

In the entire process of recruitment, the part that needs serious revision is the *interview*. It is the key mechanism to review candidates and select new employees, and yet, we have to live with the inconvenient fact that *interviews are very poor predictors of successful hiring*. A one-hour interview could hardly simulate the complexity of real work environments, even if we repeat it with several interviews. That's why internal referrals are more successful; the referring employee is familiar with both sides — the candidate and the company; therefore, a successful hiring is more likely.

So many executives and managers are convinced that they are good at judging and selecting the best people that you have to wonder why poor and ineffective management is so pervasive, or where all the average people come from.

Interviews

We would like the interview to tell us whether the candidate is:

- A good person to incorporate in our team
- A good employee that executes and pays attention to priorities
- A candidate that has the skills and experience to do the job

Yes, that's what we would like the interview to do for us. Unfortunately, despite our honest wishes, an interview cannot do all of that. After studying the book *Thinking Fast and Slow*, by the Nobel Laureate Daniel Kahneman, and examining my long experience with interviews and hiring, I am convinced that no matter how much effort we put into perfecting the interview process, we will still fail to predict these three fit criteria.

We, the interviewers, are normal human beings and that is why our judgment is tainted by *cross-biases and the halo effect* (see in Kahneman's book) — we cannot avoid it. It means that we wouldn't judge the answers of the candidate cleanly, not by intent, by our nature. Add to it the fact that we could never simulate real-life scenarios perfectly, and the interview looks like a very miserable tool, indeed. Professor Kahneman also describes the research that shows no correlation between the predictions of very long interviews, sometimes lasting for days, and the real-life performance of hired individuals afterward. It is a fascinating read.

We continue to use interviews because we have no better alternative. On Kahneman's recommendations, I chose to adopt the following criteria for good interviewing:

- Focus the interview on hard skills, which can be tested.
- Document your impression of each answer immediately.
- Forget about interviewing for soft skills — the test is not valid.

Hard skills are the minimum requirements for the job, without them the person is not suitable; for example, required language skills, programming techniques, specific knowledge areas, experience in certain types of projects, and thorough understanding of specific concepts. Any one of these hard skills can be tested, both in writing and orally.

Soft skills are the ones that we would like to test, but unfortunately cannot. Will this candidate be a good team player and go out of his way to help others? Will he be committed to his work and thorough? Will he play politics and antagonize people? Is there a social fit with our environment? Can this candidate be a leader?

Interviewers normally believe that they have good questions to ask about the soft skills. That may be so, but their judgment of the answers and the relevance of these answers to future performance are proven to be false. Many good candidates are dismissed because of this wrong impression-based judgment, and many bad candidates are accepted because we tested the hard skills inadequately. Kahneman goes so far as recommending that, if we dare do it, we should test, not interview, the hard skills, and base our decision solely on the results of the tests. He promises that, statistically, we will make better choices and invest less effort in making these hiring decisions.

Two incidents that happened recently with two of my clients are the perfect examples for what Kahneman teaches us. My client was interviewing candidates for the position of head of sales. After seeing a few candidates, one of them was selected. He seemed to have the correct experience with similar products, and the interview team liked him more than they liked the others.

I happened to be in their office when this candidate came to close the deal of his hiring. The CEO of the company decided on the spur of the moment to include me in the interview cycle, but only because I happened to be there at the time.

Now, the absolute must-have hard skill for a sales person is to be able to present the value proposition to a prospective customer and convince him that the offer is worth the price and effort. This candidate's marquee accomplishment was the sale of a complex technology system to the city of Singapore. I asked him to present to me how he sold this system. After a few rounds of evasive conversation, each round starting with my attempt to refocus the candidate on the question, I finally understood that I would not get a straight answer. The candidate could not explain the system that he was so proud of selling, neither could he show the value that it had brought to the city of Singapore, supposedly.

I was confused; how can I tell my client that the entire interview team did such a poor job in interviewing? I chose to let them see it for themselves; I proposed that the candidate would be invited for one more group interview in which he would have to show us how he sold the system to the city of Singapore. This sounded like a fair suggestion, so a few days later we all gathered in a room. And I did not say a word; I just watched how it played out.

After the group meeting with the candidate, the entire team was in shock, jaws dropped; *how could it possibly be that we all missed the simple fact that this person cannot sell?* I proceeded to tell them about hard skills and soft skills, judgment cross-biases, and the halo effect. Yes, he was a very likeable person, but he couldn't sell.

The second case was with another client but a similar situation, i.e., hiring for head of sales for enterprise telecomm customers. This story ended with less drama. I only needed to show to the CEO the whiteboard, where the candidate had attempted to draw a high-level schematic of the system that he had sold previously to Verizon. He could not draw the schematic, could not explain the system, and he was not hired, even though he had passed multiple interviews and got to the CEO level for final interview.

Keeping in mind that the interview should focus on hard skills, I compiled a few good-practice techniques to guide us in conducting interviews.

Plan Before the Interview

Prepare a list of hard skills that are *must have* for the job, and a list of hard skills that are *nice to have*. These will help to compare candidates. Ensure that the candidates are relevant with phone or video call screenings. Ask them if they have those skills and the required experience, and ensure that their expectation for compensation is reasonable and within the range. Do not ask why the candidate is leaving his prior position; first, because it's not relevant, and second, because you'll hardly ever get the full story.

Review the CV prior to the face-to-face interview, mark areas for drilldown (hooks), and prepare a list of anchor questions.

Hooks, Anchor Questions, and Drilldowns

An anchor is the first question that opens a drilldown thread of more questions. The additional questions in the thread proceed from the candidate's answers. For example, for Java programming skill, the anchor question could be: *what did you program in Java in your last job?* Or, *what was the best program you did in Java, ever?* With such an opening question we could continue to drill deeper and wider, and assess the candidate's proficiency with questions that proceed from his answer. *Demonstrate how you did this* and *what were the main reasons? In what circumstances would this method be appropriate? What are the risks in doing it this way? What alternatives did you consider?*

Or as another example, if the candidate is supposed to have public speaking as his skill, the anchor question could be *Where did you speak and on what subjects?* We could then proceed with, *what were the main messages? Show us how you delivered them? Why did you do it this way?*

Prepare the anchor questions from the hooks inside the candidate's CV. These are the areas that give you the possibility to do a drill-down on his skills, experience, and breadth (Table 4).

Table 4   Anchor Questions and Drilldown Questions in an Interview

Anchor Questions
— What was project X? What was your part in it?
— What systems did you use?
— How did your experience develop from job to job?
— What are your main skills; rate them relative to the experts you know.
— What was your most complex job? Explain.
— What are the dependencies in this role?
— What were the main challenges in your role? Who was involved?
Drilldown Questions
— Describe all the steps.
— Demonstrate how you did it; draw a diagram; and show me a design of your program.
— Present the value of your project.
— How was it different from another project? What was the project plan?
— What are your best skills? Show me why you consider them to be good?
— Explain what the competition is doing?
— How is it different from your company's offering or technology?

Open Questions

All questions, anchor or drilldown, should be as open as possible, giving the candidate the opportunity to think, reflect, and share opinions. A good question is short and it triggers a long answer. The interviewer listens attentively to what is said in response, and to what is missing from it.

Listening Skills

Employees in customer-facing roles need to have a good listening skill. It's a critical skill and you can test for it. The interviewer could switch subjects, jump from one to another back and forth, interrupt an answer, or show some angst during an answer. The candidate's reaction will demonstrate how well he listens and whether he can attend to the needs of his audience. This technique is a simulation of stressful situations, which are generally not valid as tests, but in this case, they are somewhat valid — it could be done. An alternative would be to ask many questions about the needs of

others and do a limited drilldown on them. It could indicate the candidate's openness and attention to others.

Situational Interviewing

A common practice, which should not be used, is to present a case to the candidate, and ask questions like *how would you handle this problem*? It is an unfair question and generally irrelevant as a test of proficiency. The candidate could never know all the circumstances and history associated with the case. It's a hypothetical situation for him. The interviewer, on the other hand, is highly familiar with the problem, and therefore expects specific answers. *How Would You* questions should be avoided entirely. The anchor and drill-down questions are on the candidate's *experience* with relevant situations, the ones from his past that he is supposed to know much about. Use *How Did You* questions instead. In the same vein, puzzles and quizzes of all sorts are not contributing to getting to know the candidate beyond his sleight of mind in solving riddles under pressure.

Time Management in an Interview

The interview is for listening to the candidate, not for the interviewer to hear himself talking. Use the airtime to ask short questions and extract long answers. If the candidate is eventually hired, you'll have enough time later to discuss opinions and share experiences. Reserve the last few minutes for answering the candidate's questions, and don't read too much into it if he is too exhausted to ask any, or did not prepare any questions. Take copious notes immediately after or during every thread of questions, while the evidence is fresh and comes directly from the candidate's answers without cross-biases and the halo effect.

Selling the Company to the Candidate

Whether the candidate does well in the interview or not, it's good to sell the company to him in the last few minutes. Obviously, we invest more in selling the company to the suitable candidate. Now that we know him better, we could tailor our messages to his context and knowledge.

Candidates should hear why this company is good to work for. It keeps a positive atmosphere and every bit of publicity can help.

Simultaneous Interviews

Two or three people interviewing a candidate together is a good practice, as long as the interview team follows strict rules such as, not interfering with each other, allowing the drill-downs to conclude, agreeing in advance on the line of questioning, who asks what, and how to share the time. Each of the interviewers takes notes separately, otherwise we would have a multi-dimensional halo effect that is even worse than the regular halo effect that we are naturally subject to. More listening ears in the room could create a better assessment. The candidate, on the other hand, is sure to feel more pressure as it's harder to appeal to several people at once.

Atmosphere in the Interview

As much as the method of anchor and drill-down questions sounds like an interrogation, the atmosphere should still be positive, calm, and professional. Interview time is quality time and should not be interrupted by phone calls or any other disruptive technology. Remember that the time spent with a candidate in the interview room is short, and that you make very important decisions based on it.

Selection

The right candidate is the one who has the best *potential contribution* to the future. Good and quick learners are better than someone who is likely to cut and paste what they did before in a different place.

Hiring Process

Sourcing, finding suitable candidates, is the biggest hiring problem for knowledge-based jobs. With my clients I see a lot of work waiting for someone's availability, projects that wait for new employees, or work that is suboptimal because the hiring process is too slow. If we wait for the HR requisition to be defined and approved, we are delayed. Approved requisitions, usually, are for current needs to solve execution problems. We tend to execute the hiring process only on approved requisitions because

we want to protect the budget, but that is like solving one problem by creating another one. As with any process that starts with a bottleneck, we need a wider funnel.

The entire hiring process should be forward-looking and set to work on future needs rather than react too late to current requirements. In the case of knowledge workers, 4–6 months is a good horizon for planning. Hiring for future needs also guarantees better candidates and selections, because there's less pressure in making the hiring decisions, and therefore, fewer compromises.

We could solve the budget issue by adding a standard budget item as a hiring buffer. Think of how much you could have saved in the past 12 months if you didn't make hasty hiring decisions. All those hires that did not stick, the ones that are just OK despite the promise they showed at first. You could save more than the cost of the hiring buffer and, just like in high growth periods, you'd attract talent because you see the potential, and not just react to immediate needs.

Assimilation

The assimilation process escorts and supports the employee during the first 3 months. The process helps achieve two goals:

- Full productivity in the most effective and efficient ways
- Integration with the environment and the team

During assimilation the new employee typically needs more supervision. Regardless, we should break at least once a month to reflect on progress and adjust the plan. We can use the same form that we use for quarterly assessments; only for this purpose we do it with monthly reviews instead of quarterly. Table 5 below is a sample of productivity criteria and integration expectations, and activities to use in assimilation plans for individual contributors in technical positions.

With the main aspects of work and people management we have concluded the discussion of the fourth pillar of the manager's role. (Table 6)

Table 5 Assimilation Example: Productivity and Integration for technical positions

Productivity Criteria to Develop and Review
— Proficient in systems, tools, specific code, area of knowledge.
— Familiar with infrastructure — software, process and systems.
— Code a feature according to specification.
— Design a feature.
— Pass code review with minimal comments.
— Execute project according to plan.
— Revise presentation.
— Present core value to the team.
Integration Expectations
— Gather information for a task from other team members.
— Coordinate a project plan and communicate to others.
— Write a specification with product management.
— Write code that works with other people's code.
— Other group members are aware of your work.
— Social interactions are observed during breaks.

Table 6 Five Pillars of the Manager's Job

Manager and Leader	Ecosystem and Constituencies	Operational and Business Strategy	Work and People	Managerial Relationships
✓	✓	✓	✓	
Manager's Job Definition				

Managerial Relationships

10

Human relationships develop over time; we expect them to mature into more trust and higher productivity. As time passes, the manager and subordinate should increase their productivity and quality as they learn from each other what they can do individually and as a team. A stagnated relationship, that has the same division of responsibility over time, stymies personal growth and leads to frustration.

You might be hearing yourself thinking about one employee or a manager in your organization whom you consider as: *he is good, but I believe he could do more, if only he would…be/act/want/understand more….* I would advise you to stop for a moment, and examine your relationship with this person, which in many cases is a fixated symbiosis — both of you follow the same behavioral patterns conveniently and are comfortable with this stalled relationship.

If that's the case, *you* could be the one to restart the maturing process. Rather than *you need to be more of this or do that,* take the team approach of *how do we improve together?* For example, during a quarterly assessment, if an employee asks for more independence and opportunity to fail and learn, or vice versa, for more training and supervision, you could agree to involve the employee in certain actions, or try new activities together. The focus is on *manager–employee relationship*, where it takes two to tango.

There's no right or wrong in assessing relationships — only subjective perceptions — it's about what one does to the other and vice versa.

The situational leadership model helps to understand the work relationships and how to adapt them to the situation. With the assessment tool following it, you can appraise your current relationships and decide on the corrective actions to release them from stagnation.

There are four types of work relationships in the model — *supervise, coach, consult*, and *delegate*. Each one is a step toward more maturity, and that is the general direction in which we want to develop the relationship. If the work or its scope changes for the employee or the manager, the relationship could go backward to lower maturity. For example, if the manager is assigned more responsibility, he needs to transfer some of his own work to his team. He will first supervise the transition and then delegate the responsibility for the transferred work (see Table 1).

Buddhist monks would say that when you define something, it loses its essence. We can certainly define four stations in a relationship, but the essence is in all the shades in between them.

Table 1   Situational Leadership Model

4 **Delegate** — Discuss/agree budget, scope, boundaries — Full delegation inside the boundaries — Scheduled interaction	1 **Supervise** — What to do and how — Check quality — High-frequency interaction
3 **Consult** — Discuss: what, how, etc. — Rough agreement — Discuss scope — Swap ideas — Scheduled interaction	2 **Coach** — What to do — Analyze — Discuss and agree on how — Medium–high frequency

In *supervisor relationship*, the manager interacts frequently with the employee to oversee each action. The manager states what to do and how to do it. He also checks the quality and productivity. He may have started by managing all the work by himself, but as the workload increased he hired people and became the manager.

The *supervisor* has complete control, responsibility, and authority, but he has limited scope to grow. You cannot grow to be a well-balanced manager and leader while watching every step of your team members. The employees in the team are also confined to a narrow scope of work. The advantages of this relationship are in the present; the disadvantages are in limiting the future. Depending on the complexity of the work, a manager could supervise five to nine employees.

The *coaching relationship* is a more mature station. Think of a basketball coach. He may not necessarily be tall or as good as the players in shooting hoops. However, he is expert in analyzing moves, plays, and the weaknesses of the competitive team — he knows what to do but he would not necessarily be able to do it himself. He calls the moves, but agrees with the players on how to achieve them.

The employee and his *manager-coach* iterate in cycles of actions, analyses, and ways to achieve goals. Though some of the responsibility shifts to the employee, the full authority is still with the manager. The employee has more independence and room for personal growth, and the manager could now do more. When he is not watching the team, he could be working on process improvements or on strengthening his leadership of the team.

The next station, *consulting relationship*, gives more responsibility and authority to the employee. Their agreements are rough and are not necessarily binding. The manager relies on the knowledge and expertise of the employee; they will swap ideas on possible actions. They still interact regularly though not frequently, i.e., the manager is no longer tied to the employee's work. With authority to make decisions the employee is, in effect, a manager in training.

The ultimate goal of managerial relationships is to *delegate* full responsibility and full authority within certain boundaries. *This area is yours, you know it better than I do, make decisions and act as you see fit; you don't need my approval as long as you stay inside the budget, and inside your area.* The manager and the employee in a *delegate* relationship discuss and agree on boundaries such as budget, territory, goals, or specific project. For example, head of sales in a territory has full authority as long as he is within 5% of the agreed sales targets. He can hire, invest in training, approve discounts, execute marketing programs, and commit to customers. When he meets his manager, they discuss the economy of the territory, customers buying trends, lessons from other territories, and then reinforce their agreements on the boundaries of authority.

Each relationship is unique to its participants, i.e., it's not a manager's style alone. The same manager can coach one employee and delegate to another. Modern work environments are too fluid to declare yourself *I am a delegating manager*, or, *I like to stay close to my employees and coach them.* Each situation and relationship has the right balance of involvement, responsibility, and authority.

As the relationships mature with time, from station to station, and going through the shades in between, the manager needs to develop his leadership skills as the relationships are sustained more by influence than by directives.

Table 2 demonstrates the *situational leadership assessment tool.* You can appraise the relationship and mark X where you think the relationship is now, and O where you want it to be in 3 or 6 months. Both manager and employee fill separate forms. Then you can compare, discuss, and agree upon the actions to move the relationship forward. Use this tool to discuss with the employee about your mutual behaviors, and how to change them to make the relationship more mature and productive.

You could use the tool also in the opposite direction, to drive a change in the relationship between you and the manager above you. Managing-up is a sensitive subject that we usually hesitate to raise. The tool will help focus the discussion on facts, save it from general statements, and keep it more neutral.

For example a COO chose to assess his relationships with three managers in his organization: OEM manager, new financial controller/operations manager, and the HR manager. In Table 2, note that Alexander has three major functions, each with its own assessment and actions.

The analysis of the five pillars of the manager role are now complete. (Table 3). In the next chapter we assemble the job from its pieces into one coherent tool.

Table 2 Situational Leadership Assessment Tool

COO Direct Reports	Situational Leadership Model				6 Months' Actions
	Supervise	Coach	Consult	Delegate	
Violet — OEM Manager	- - - - - - - - - - - - - - - - - - - X → O - - - -				Own negotiations with OEM partner
Alexander					
— Fin. controller	- X → O - - - - -				Skip COO review of financial reports
— Operations	- - - - - - - - - - - - X - - - →O - - - - - - - - -				Decide up to $5,000, review weekly
— Business	- - - - - - X - - - - →O - - - - - - - - - - - - -				Tour remote offices
Laura HR Manager	- - - - - - - - - - - - - - X - - → O - - - - - - -				Skip COO reviews for non-manager positions

Table 3 Five Pillars of the Manager's Job

Manager and Leader	Ecosystem and Constituencies	Operational and Business Strategy	Work and People	Managerial Relationships
✓	✓	✓	✓	✓

Manager's Job Definition

The Whole Job and Nothing But the Job

11

We have analyzed all five pillars of the manager's job. However, we cannot apply any of these analyses directly to work as it would only result in a very long definition of a job.

Rather, we need to consider all the desired behaviors and actions — all the information collected in the tables of the previous chapters — and construct a simple and useful tool. First we should take a *functional* perspective, i.e., what we actually do as managers and how we track it.

We start with a two-column functional job definition (functions and metrics in columns A and B, respectively) and then add 2 more columns for goals and tracking (columns C and D) as shown in the below figure. Since the analysis from the previous chapters is complete now, all the insights will find their place in this tool and it will be our only tool.

A Functions	B Metrics	C Goals	D Tracking

Column A — Functions

The number of functions in a managerial job depends on the position: a team lead has at least three functions; managers, four or more; directors, about six; and CEO, seven to nine. We will follow the process with the example of a CEO in a small $60M company. The seven functions in the CEO's role can be identified as follows:

1. Set the company's direction.
2. Deliver revenue and profit according to targets.
3. Develop and maintain a skilled and motivated workforce.
4. Develop the young and inexperienced team to be more scalable and strategic.
5. Have relationships with outside world such as strategic partners, key-customers, and main go-to-market channels.
6. Have continuous improvement (CI) goals to improve productivity, process, and quality.
7. Manage the board of directors, and other key stakeholders.

Column A of the CEO's job is straightforward, i.e., almost generic (Table 1).

Column B — Metrics

Column B answers the question, *what does it mean to do a good job? Well, …if for each function in column A, I do all these activities, and I take*

Table 1 CEO Role Definition — Column A

A Functions
1. Strategic direction and market position
2. Execution, revenue, and profit
3. Develop and maintain skilled, and motivated workforce
4. Develop leadership team — scalable management skills, executive characteristics and strategy
5. Relationships — strategic partners, customers, main go-to-market channels
6. Continuous improvement — productivity, process, quality
7. Manage the board and be the company's representative in the holding company

steps to reach these long-term goals, and I use these metrics to measure my progress... then, I can safely say that I am doing a good job... column B adds content and meaning to the functions in column A.

We fill column B with these specific details and review the tables from the job analysis (Chapters 6–10) to ensure that we have covered everything. Column B includes:

- Break-down of the function from column A into different types of activities
- Long-term goals, gold standards, and benchmarks
- Types of metrics, such as numbers, surveys, and self-assessments
- Actions from the analysis tables

How do I know that I do a good job? In the CEO example, we break down the first function — strategic direction and market position — to: vision, industry presence, and operational strategy. Each type of activity has its long-term goals, and the kind of metrics to measure progress (Table 2).

Table 2   CEO Columns A and B — First Function

A Functions	B Activity, Metrics, Long-term Goal

1. Strategic direction and Market position	**Vision**
	— Create and communicate vision — outbound and inbound
	— Metrics: brand recognition, customer satisfaction ratings, website hits
	— Goal: In one year:
	   — 100% improvement; all metrics
	   — All employees can present the vision
	Industry presence
	— Comeback plan: conferences, media, product awards
	— Metrics: brand recognition, customer satisfaction rating, website hits
	— Numbers of new customers and returning customers
	Operational Strategy
	— Idea pipeline: products and go-to-market
	— Strategy quarterly reviews; new rev. stream every 12 mo.
	— 10% budget allocation for strategic experiments
	— No losses in existing revenue streams

The second function of the CEO is: execution, revenue, and profit. We divide it into targets-and-plans, products, and go-to-market (Table 3).

In general, finding the right metrics can be challenging; after all, not everything can be measured with numbers and scales. Therefore, you could use quantitative or qualitative metrics. For example:

- Hard numbers — for revenue and profit
- Benchmarks — our bug rate relative to industry standard
- Ranking on an external scale — our market position is third
- Self-assessment — our quality of service is two out of five

Several iterations are required to complete column B by going back and forth to the job analysis tables until it's settled. Column A needs an update only if the job changes; while column B should be reviewed at

Table 3   CEO Columns A and B — Second Function

A Functions	B Activity, Metrics, Long-term Goals
2. Execution, Revenue, Profit	**Targets and plans** — Set revenue and profit targets + plans — Deliver revenue and EBITDA results — 5% forecast accuracy in one year — 17% annual growth **Products** — Focus on the right products — Smooth new product introductions in the field — Marketing to support new products — Quarterly reviews: in one year — prod. and rev. mix — 20% new — Offering portfolio — pipeline of alternative products **Go-to-market** — Segmentation and addressing long-tail problems — Widen penetration into existing customers — increase wallet share; 20% more revenue from top 50 accounts in one year — Quarterly review of partnering value proposition — Marketing for each target segment

least twice a year to update it with any new insight on execution, i.e., how we do the job and how we measure it.

Filling column B takes time and effort; however, you only need to do it once and enjoy it for the rest of your time in the managerial the role. The investment pays off when the team sees how their collective efforts add up to a complete picture, which is the job of their manager.

The Manager's role is fully defined with all of its intents and details once columns A and B are filled (Table 4). We can now use it in the next chapter as a *checklist for goal setting* — Column C.

Table 4   Five Pillars of the Manager's Job

Manager and Leader	Ecosystem and Constituencies	Operational and Business Strategy	Work and People	Managerial Relationships
✓	✓	✓	✓	✓
✓ Manager's Job Definition				

Setting and Achieving Goals

PART III

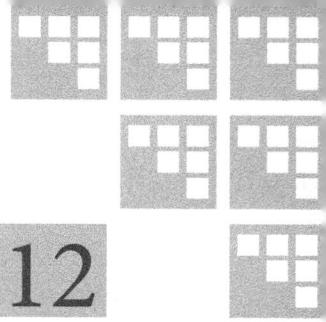

Setting Quarterly Goals

12

In general, in most companies we regularly set and adjust goals every quarter. But we don't pick them at random — anything we do is a step to achieve the long-term goals, which are now well defined in column B as a checklist (see example in Table 1). The quarterly goals are listed in column C.

The quarterly goals in column C are like road signs along the way that help us navigate to our final destination, and achieve the long term goals of Column B.

Quarterly Plan

Column C specifies all the work that should be done in the quarter, including the details of dates, milestones, and targets. Also listed are all the details of the actions and the expected outcomes. The focus is now on results and how to achieve them — we should use numbers wherever possible. The goals in column C are realistic; the place for dreams, hopes, and long-term intentions was in column B.

The content of Column C is your contract with the company to deliver the expected results. It's also your plan, therefore, it should be realistic and manageable, and include only doable actions, specified with all the resources identified and coordinated with all involved.

The principles of column C resemble the known goal–management processes, MBO, OKR, and other versions. The main difference lies in column B, which we use as a checklist to select the right goals for column C and to provide continuity from one quarter to another.

There are *no stretch goals* in column C. By definition, stretch goals convey the message that it's *OK to Fail* and I don't subscribe to the idea of planning to fail. You have to *plan for success*, else you won't be successful. If it's OK to fail, rest assured that you will mostly fail. With stretch goals, you might also start a cat-and-mouse chase between you, as manager, and the employee who is the owner of the goal — one of you tries to avoid committing to extras, and the other tries to stretch them. Over-achievement, by definition, cannot be planned, as much as winning a lottery cannot be planned.

In the following example (Table 1), we take the column A function of *operations and product development* from the job definition of a VP of products and systems, and break it down to seven activities. For each activity, we define the long-term goals and metrics, and enter them into column B. From these entries we extract specific quarterly (Q4) goals and put them in column C.

For example, let's take the last activity *product and operations roadmap*. We want to create and maintain a roadmap with a visibility of four quarters. The metrics and long-term goals in column B would be of two types, stability and balance:

■ Roadmap stability — churn of ideas:

How many of the ideas that we discussed, deliberated, and entered into the roadmap, passed the test of time, and stayed in the roadmap.

Today we churn 25% of our roadmap; long term we want it to be at 10%

■ Roadmap balance between operations and product:

The roadmap includes product tasks that generate revenue and operations tasks for the development of our internal systems. We want to achieve the correct balance between them.

Today, finished products wait for fixes in our installation tracking systems; long term we want both product and systems to be ready together.

In column C we commit to the following actions for this quarter (Q4):

- Create the roadmap for next year
- Engineering focus to reduce backlog of operational tasks by 30%

The seven activities are listed in column B, Table 1. If there's no current action, the activity would still stay in our job definition, but not for this quarter, therefore, we enter TBD in column C.

Table 1   Example: Operations and Product Development — Column B + Column C

B Activity, Metrics, Long-Term Goals	C Q4 Goals
Products meet business needs — Publisher recruitment — Sales growth Long-term goals + metrics: 1. Completeness of offering — 90% delivered, 10% pending requests 2. No deal lost on missing features	Create a standard to measure and assess current and future offerings Rank all existing and planned products on a scale of 1–5 according to the standard
Inbound communication Procedures, information sessions, training Long-term goals + metrics: 1. All collateral ready upon release 2. All training complete upon release	Procedures: inquiries, requisitions, proposals, sales orders, execution follow-ups, billing, internal communication Procedure templates; Training Q4, Compliance Q1
Outbound communication Sales — Media, Product; Media — Product Long-term goals + metrics: 1. All users informed — 2 months from release 2. Partner users — within 1 month from release	Capture all Q4 use-cases and create a baseline for marketing and rollout calendar in Q1. Review use-cases EOQ4.

(Continued)

Table 1 (*Continued*)

B Activity, Metrics, Long-Term Goals	C Q4 Goals
Knowledgebase for international offices Long-term goals + metrics: 1. Unified information and document repository for all global departments 2. User satisfaction > 90%	TBD — next year
Product and operational innovation Long-term goals + metrics: 1. User innovation ideas > 2per quarterly. 2. Customer satisfaction > 90% 3. Partner satisfaction rating > 80%	Capture current ideas of new products and business and start a review process Build a process for the entire company
Keep–invest–kill decisions Long-term goals + metrics: 1. New offerings contribute > 5% of GP at 3 months from release 2. 15% budget allocation for new ideas	Deferred to Q1 strategy session
Prod. and ops Roadmap — 4 Q visibility Long-term goals + metrics: 1. RM Stability — churn <10% down from 25% 2. RM balance ops vs. prod. = support departments ready upon release	First release of next year roadmap Reduce delivery backlog of operational requests by 30%

Achieving Goals —
GS/MR Process

13

Some managers believe that goals will be achieved if money is attached to them. For them, quarterly goals turn into *quarterly bonuses*. This link, however, is both a blessing and a curse.

Since you cannot award bonuses to all employees all the time, organizations commonly impose a bell curve on the achievement levels. But that's just like changing the meaning of the goals to *stretch goals*. When people know in advance that not all of them can achieve 100% all the time, they will adopt an attitude of *win some–lose some*. And that is, as we discussed previously, counterproductive. These artificial preset bell curves distort the purpose of managing work, which is to focus on achieving goals and not to maneuver them to fit a preset statistical tool.

Bonuses, on the other hand, give credence to goals — you take them seriously if your money depends on them. Regardless, I prefer to use good management practices to enforce goals, and not to count on the bonus system to do it. The company needs to be philosophically ready to pay 100% bonus to all employees — even though it never happens in reality. With such a policy, as the manager, you would focus your efforts on helping your team accomplish the goals and get full bonus payments. It is truer to the core of what management means, and your employees' motivation will improve. They will also be more inclined to admit to failure when a goal is not fully achieved, if they see the system as fair and balanced.

Tracking Progress — Monthly Report

Column D, the last column of the job-tracking sheet, is the corrective process that helps track progress and make adjustments. You update it monthly or more frequently, and use it as a *monthly report*.

Column D entries are status statements with only enough details to be informative. Complete details of the action item are not necessary. Anyone who needs more detail can ask for it or find it in other documents. Examples of column D status statements are in Table 1.

Avoid generic status phrases such as: done, ongoing, in progress, postponed, delayed, and working toward goal. These have too little information in them. Whenever a programmer tells me that his task is done, I always turn to the user to ask if he also thinks it's done. Usually, the answer is, "well, I am testing it now." The true informative status in this case would have been "programming is done, now being tested." Always think of the next step and include enough information.

Table 1   Sample of Status Statements

Type	Status Statements
Level of completion	— Phase 2 complete — phase 3 started — 25% done — on track to finish on time
Changes to priority and the reasons	— Project B deferred to next quarter Project A now has higher priority
Changes to due dates	— Need 2 more months due to changed architecture Stalled — waiting for product management input
Change of requirement	— Cancelled — business has no need — Delayed to TBD — investigation required
Rollout	— Released; now active with 2 customers

We continue with our previous example and add column D status statements (Table 2) to the function *operations and product development*.

If your job has many components, column D will be long, because it accounts for all quarterly tasks and their status. If you use it as a monthly report and if your relationship with the manager above you is *consult* or *delegate*, the details might be too much for your manager, in which case

Table 2   Operations and Product Development — Column C + Column D

C Q4 Goals	D November Tracking: Monthly Report
Create a standard to measure and assess current and future offerings	Draft in last round of approval
Rank all existing and planned products on a scale of 1–5 according to the standard	Criteria awaiting approval; will be done in December
Procedures: inquiries, requisitions, proposals, sales orders, execution follow-ups, billing, internal communication	Complete and approved for: inquiries, requisitions, and proposals; rollout. Others — deferred to next quarter
Procedure templates; Training Q4, compliance Q1	Enforcing templates for inquiries, requisitions, and proposals; collecting field feedback
Capture all Q4 use-cases and create a baseline for marketing and rollout calendar in Q1 Review use-cases EOQ4	We have 20 documented use-cases; an estimate of 10 more to complete
Knowledgebase — TBD — next year	Scheduled discussion with stake holders in mid- December
Capture current ideas of new products and business and start a review process Build a process for the entire company	Missing update — will report next month
KIK decisions. Deferred to Q1 strategy session	Deferred to Q1 strategy session
First release of next year roadmap	Still collecting inputs — deferred to early Q1
Reduce delivery backlog of operational requests by 30%	Reduced 10% — will get to 20% by end of Qtr.

you could add a summary version that includes only the essence of the monthly report — *highlights, lowlights,* and *need help* items.

- *Highlights* are no more than three positive monthly notes on events or accomplishments; they motivate and instill a winning culture and reinforce it. Always put a couple of *highlights* in your monthly report.

- *Lowlights* are the disappointments — only if you have them; there's no need to report lowlights if they are not worth mentioning.

- *Need help* items are the ones at a dead end, or waiting too long for an action from someone else — these are red flags. Obviously, you don't wait for your monthly report to raise red flags, but it's your chance to go on record; here are items that are stuck and you need help to jolt them free.

We followed the example of the same $60M business CEO (see Chapter 11), through columns A–D. The summary — *highlights, lowlights, need help* — reflects an enthusiastic up-beat CEO, ready to *charge and drive*. With this mindset, he is the best motivator to his leadership team and organization. The points in *lowlights* and *need help* show a CEO with a hand on the pulse of the organization, realistic and focused on execution (Table 3).

Table 3 CEO Summary of the Monthly Report

Highlights	Continuing previous quarter momentum; beating monthly revenue and profit targets by 10%; great energy and optimism around the office from the positive trends; happy with the coming office move
	Renewed focus on metrics that drive the business
	Four key positions filled with great hires — PM, BI Engineer, BI analyst, and UI developer
Lowlights	Outsourcing project moving slower than planned, affecting our focus on new products
	Minor organization adjustments needed in engineering — should have been done as part of our recent re-org
Need help	No dependencies at the moment; holding off bigger plans to focus on business momentum

Setting and Achieving Goals — Full Process

Doing the monthly report, column D and its summary, is analogous to going outside the trenches and seeing the entire picture before diving back into next month's activities.

The full report with all four columns serves several important purposes:

- *Hierarchical engagement and control*: The Column A–D structure makes it easy to find information that's suitable for the different levels in the organization. Strategy is in column B, execution in column C and in column D. Upper management will read these reports, because the details are just at the right level. Escalations are also exactly where you'd expect them to be — in the *need help* segment.

- *Synchronization*: Column D translates into a to-do list for synchronization with other departments, customers, or suppliers. With consistent use of column D you'd avoid many cross-functional communication breaks.

- *Teamwork*: Shared goals and a unified picture is the basis for all teamwork. The four-column report is all you need for the monthly staff meeting.

I like to call the entire process GS/MR (goal sheet/monthly report). We started with a full analysis, but the purpose was to get to the goals, and how to track them in *plan–act–review* cycles, which is your full GS/MR tool.

Simpler GS/MR

If you want to skip the long analysis of the five pillars for now, you could still build the GS/MR by doing it in reverse order. With this shorter approach, the resulting GS/MR is good for setting and tracking goals, but it lacks the analysis that makes the goals deep and strategic.

Start with column C, listing everything that you do as a manager. Gather all the actions from your calendar, to-do lists, and any other tracking sheet, and consolidate them into column C. Then, classify and organize the activities into functions and build column A. From this high-level/low-level view of columns C and A, you can approach the big question, "how do I know that I do a good job?" Think of long-term goals and metrics and iterate a few times until you have built column B. The quarterly and monthly cycles of columns C and D would be the same as before.

With this simpler GS/MR you could train the team to work in cycles of plan–act–review, and achieve the teamwork effects as you revise it with them. The tool will serve as a good starting point for the full five-pillar analysis that you should do at least once a year.

Global Company Strategy

PART IV

Starting with a Hax

14

Strategy is a big word that answers a short question: *what should the company do in the long run?* But where is that horizon? Is it 5 years, or 18 months? Traditionally, the strategies of enterprise computer hardware companies have a 5-year view. Now that cloud technologies compete on the same customer budgets, the pace of new developments has changed dramatically — a lot of twists and turns could happen in a story in 5 years. On the other extreme, if you're a small company doing business on the capricious Internet, you are swept by swift hurricane storms. Waves are so massive and fast that they could change everything for you within a day.

Larger players on the Internet have to reinvent their strategies every few years because they play the big game among themselves. Initially, Amazon was the ultimate bookstore, then the everything-store, and now the datacenter of the world. If you are an SMB, your datacenter is on Amazon and the other computer companies lost your business. Google was for search and advertising, and now it is competing head to head with the ubiquitous Microsoft Office suite. Lastly, Facebook hatched into the Internet ecosystem as a benevolent phenomenon using the power of masses to do good in the world. After the IPO went through, however, it turned purely commercial, while still dissembling as its good old self. All four giants compete for their share of customers' wallets. The small companies have to continuously search for orbits around them for their survival.

The Internet, mobile trends, and globalization push all strategies from several directions, i.e., they move fast and we have to match their pace. *Global Company Strategy* that looks farther into the future is now much closer to *Operational Strategy*. In fact, they partially overlap — operational strategy is obviously influenced by the global strategy, but the reverse is also true. In order to change your global strategy, you have to consider the following: *can the budget support the investment? Do we need external investment? Do we have the right skills? Will we lose market share during the transition? Should we develop or look for an acquisition?*

Start with the Hax Delta Model

We start building the global strategy with our position in the market. We could be a startup focused on a differentiating product for a niche market or a startup with a customer base that needs to expand. A more mature company may need to decide which of their possible expansions to choose.

Arnoldo Hax of MIT Sloan developed the Delta Model that raises the right position questions — a strategy, according to the model, is about moving from one position to another. When you understand your position, you can build a strategy.

According to the Delta Model, a company starts its life with a *product centric strategy*, i.e., differentiating product, service, or offering (package, bundle). Whether it's unique, better, or cheaper, the company is focused on the product. The strategy is simple with a single thread — all resources are focused on penetrating the target market and developing features to maintain the advantage. If customers value the product enough to pay premium prices, the company protects the high margins by embracing the customers with excellent service, free of charge. Customers who love the product and the company are less likely to look elsewhere.

The *product centric strategy*, however, cannot last for long. If the company is successful, and if there's demand, the competition would not take long to arrive at the scene. Inevitably, direct competition leads to price wars, margins are under pressure, and the entire strategy collapses. With serious

competition, the strategy of *best product–high margins–hug the customer* no longer works.

A proactive approach to strategy widens the scope and reduces this risk. In the same market segment, you could offer complementary products, or sell services associated with the main product. You use your relationships with customers to make life easier for them; they will benefit from dealing with fewer vendors and from stronger buying power. The life time value (LTV) of the customer increases because you sell them larger packages.

Another way to expand the scope of the strategy, albeit more risky, is to address a new market segment — affiliated, adjacent, or with similar needs. For example, a software product for the telecomm industry might also have differentiating value in banking.

With a wider scope, the company strategy has several threads — it's a *portfolio of offerings*. Ease of doing business is the main differentiating value that is often more important than a new feature. Steady customers trust their vendors to close any feature gap; for them, waiting is less costly than switching to a different vendor. With the portfolio strategy, the company can slow its product release cycles as a single feature no longer wins the customer, total customer experience (TCE) does. The innovation pump continues to run, but the releases are in bigger chunks. A *portfolio strategy* is a higher level of mutual commitment between the vendor and its customers.

Most companies strengthen their portfolio strategies over a long period and stay in this position forever. A few companies, however, manage to break through the ceiling and create an entire solar system around them. Apple, for example, with its i-series — Pod, Tunes, Phone, Pad — is such a company-system. A huge number of satellite companies develop applications and use-cases for Apple; they exist by enhancing Apple's products and making Apple invincible. For Apple, and other companies in similar position, the customer LTV is now even larger. You know it from experience, an Apple customer never leaves. The Internet giants — Amazon, Microsoft, Google, and Facebook — are all centers of such solar systems, but since they operate in the same galaxy, we can expect serious cosmic clashes in the future.

Hax calls this powerful state of existence *system lock-in* — the giant company has an entire industry locked into them, and they call the shots. *Dominant exchanges* — NASDAQ, Chicago Mercantile, and eBay — also built a position of system lock-in. The Internet is full of companies that try to be dominant exchanges in travel, entertainment, home services, and gaming. However, with the ever-evolving new features from Google, they are at risk of being overshadowed by this meta-exchange of everything. A small company that orbits in one solar system has a risky existence. Larger companies that operate in a few of them diversify their risk, but they pay for it dearly with high operational costs.

Companies with strong portfolio strategies make strategic moves to climb in the direction of system lock in; however, only few will get there.

When considering strategic moves, think of the Hax Delta Model (see Figure 1) and the right questions will emerge.

- Move from the product corner toward portfolio:
    - Have we considered the added complexity?
    - What are the organizational and infrastructure costs?
    - Are we diluting our resources to under-critical-mass?

- Expanding the portfolio to address another segment:
    - What are the prospects of new competitive situations?
    - Are we disrupting our partners and risking current revenue?

- Moving too fast:
    - Are we skipping necessary steps?
    - Could we test our idea before making investments?
    - Is our portfolio strong enough to support steps toward industry lock-in?

Strategic moves need a new budget from external investment or by competing internally with existing projects. Strategic moves are never

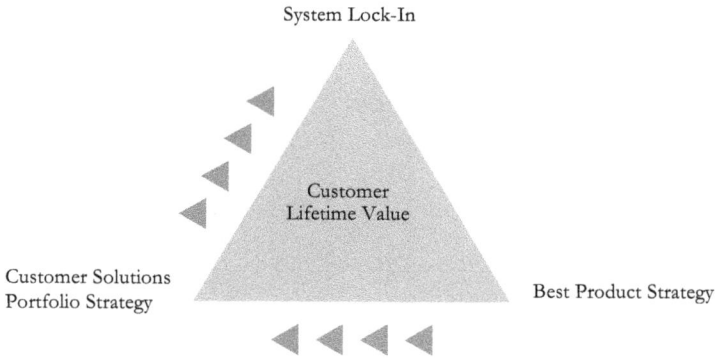

Figure 1 Hax-Delta Model

considered in isolation. In most cases you have to remove something from the existing strategy before you add to it.

Building a global strategy for the company is a heavy lifting exercise. You *put-it-all-together and break-it-apart* in repeated cycles until you have exhausted all new thoughts and insights. In the course of a year you should do two to three revisions, and extract from them the necessary adjustments to the operational strategy.

New Ingredients in the Pot

15

A major disadvantage of new ideas is that they come without a history to analyze. The next best thing to do in this case is to use someone else's experience. Hax helped us understand why we want to change the mix in our strategy, but now we need to see how, and examine the effects of each of the new components on our strategy.

As we've seen, we examine revenue and value streams by analyzing their present, past, and hypothetical future. But, with no real present and past, we need to answer the following three alternative main questions:

- *What if* we already had it?
- How do *they* do it?
- What would *other people* think?

What If We Already Had It?

The environment we know best is our own environment. If we need to analyze and guess the effects of a new idea, the best place to start is in our own backyard. Let's imagine that we had the new idea fully executed a year ago; how would we look at it today — all the good and all the bad? When we understand the hypothetical past, we could be more accurate with our projections.

Table 1 Hypothetical Present and Past Questions

Hypothetical Present and Past Questions	
Vital signs	Metrics to measure the success of this idea
	Where would we be today on these metrics?
Go-to-market SWOT of our idea compared with competitive ideas	Direct competitive products — where are they today?
	Alternative spending: what did customers buy?
Relevant history of competitive products	What do we know about their actions?
	How well did these actions work for them?
Potential years 1, 2, and 3	From our hypothetical position today, where would we be next?
	What actions can we expect from the competition?
	What is the projection for them?
Proposed actions and risk assessment	From our hypothetical position today, what are the next actions?
	What are the costs, risks, and dependencies of these actions?

But, first we have to agree on the definition of the idea — what's in it and what's out. With a view to the first phase of the hypothetical past, we define all the parameters such as target market, product, price range, geography, promotion, GTM channels, key value proposition, technology, critical partnerships, and dependencies.

Then we examine the idea from as many angles as possible, looking constantly at competitive products. We also look at the complementary competition — other options that customers have to spend their money on. We examine our hypothetical present and past with an idea that we could have had. Table 1 is a sample of questions to raise on the new idea as if it had already been part of our strategy for some time.

We should also do this analysis for projects and ideas that are in their beginning phases of execution. If nothing else, we would understand the road ahead and prepare in advance for potential surprises — good opportunities or bad roadblocks.

Table 2   Questions on Our New Idea vs. Existing Competition

Compare Our New Idea to Existing Competition
Why are they successful? Root-cause analysis as deep as it makes sense
How will we take market share from them?
What phase are they in? Start-up? Growth?
What is their momentum?
Do they already have a network effect?
They are not successful — how are we different from them?

How Do They Do It?

The grass is always greener on the other side of the fence. But, what if they use a non-ecofriendly fertilizer? What is their monthly water bill? Should we still be jealous?

If the existing competitors to our new idea are successful, we want to understand why and assess our chances of also being successful. If they are not, we want to convince ourselves that we have a better chance. Table 2 is a sample of questions we want to ask about the competition.

Portfolio View

We have vetted our ideas — some are better than others. As we did in the operational strategy, we combine all of our existing and new ideas and compare them. We look at the picture with the realistic glasses of cost–risk–benefit and clean the strategy with the KIK brush. Now we are ready to get out of the building, as Steve Blank says, and test the new strategy.

Testing the Strategy

16

One of the questions that's left unanswered from the previous chapter is — *what would other people think*? Most of the time however, you cannot ask the people that you really want to ask. You couldn't survey the neighborhood if you plan to use a non-eco-friendly fertilizer, could you? You could ask them if they'd prefer greener grass on your lawn, but you already know the answer, so it's not helpful. As an alternative, you turn to statistics, consumer reports, and anything else you can find that people said about your idea. In the information age, people say a lot and you can learn from it.

Your strategy competes for customers and their money. The strategy lives in the larger space outside the building. Test your strategy as a whole, inside and outside the building, at least with the following tools:

- Risk analysis
- Voting and betting tables
- Bottom-up vs. top-down vs. inside-out
- Gartner's magic quadrant
- Reality check — consolidated roadmap

Risk Analysis

How much risk for the company does your strategy represent? Is the company strong enough to operate with this level of risk? Take all existing and potential projects and place them on a cost-risk vs. benefit chart. The cost of an existing project that you need to consider is the incremental cost to continue with it from now and into the future — the sunk costs of the past are no longer relevant to making decisions. Now that we have done the analysis of the hypothetical past, we have more realistic estimates on the costs of the new ideas, as they are well understood in relation to our own environment.

Table 1   Cost Risk vs. Benefit

The projects in the top right corner of the table (Table 1 above) have the strategic potential, but they are also the ones that could stall the company. You have to be very choosy and keep only the best, as too many of them amount to too much risk. Risky projects also take a lot of management attention; therefore, too many of them will make other areas of the company suffer from lack of it.

If the financial strength to support the strategy depends on future cash flows from existing projects, consider their stability. Startups and online businesses have to be very careful because their revenues are not stable; therefore, they can't support with confidence high-risk projects with dependence on future income.

Low-potential and low-risk projects have a right to exist only as experiments for a future purpose; otherwise, they're defocusing noise.

Low-potential and high-risk projects are probably expensive tests. Otherwise they don't make sense. If you have such projects, think of cheaper alternatives to test ideas.

High-potential and low-risk projects are the tried and tested moneymakers of the company. Ensure that your strategy decisions don't starve them of the funds that they need to continue.

Voting and Betting Tables

As normal human beings, we get attached to our ideas and projects and hence it's so difficult to make *Yes* and *No* choices. We especially don't like to say *No* when we need to reverse previous decisions or to overcome vested interests. Whenever we say *Yes* to invest, we should also ask how much to invest in this specific choice. To capture how the strategy team members think in relative terms, ask them to vote on a scale of 1–5. A clearer picture of their choices will emerge, sometimes saving a lot of discussions on ideas that people support, but not so much (Table 2).

If the strategy picture is still fuzzy after voting, or has too many components, ask them to bet their money. Each participant gets 100 virtual coins to

Table 2   Voting Table

Projects	Voter 1	Voter 2	Voter 3	Voter 4	Voter 5
A	Invest 4	Invest 4	Invest 5	Invest 3	Invest 5
B	Invest 2	Invest 2	Invest 1	Invest 4	Kill
C	Invest 5	Invest 5	Invest 4	Invest 5	Invest 4
D	Keep	Keep	Invest 1	Invest 2	Keep
E	Invest 1	Invest 3	Invest 2	Invest 1	Invest 3
F	Keep	Keep	Kill	Keep	Keep
G	Keep	Keep	Kill	Keep	Keep

bet on the projects. Betting with fixed budgets of coins will force the participants to think harder in relative terms; therefore, the picture will become clearer still.

Bottom-Up vs. Top-Down vs. Inside-Out

My approach to building a strategy is from the *inside-out*. We examine everything we know and have, and then reach outside to expand this space. We vet the ideas and we plow through the execution aspects. The vision of the company is calculated from this inside-out view; therefore, it represents the lowest possible risk.

The common *vision-mission* approach is very different. Here you start from the market and make assumptions on its future technologies, buying patterns, etc. You paint a picture of the future, carve a piece of it, and call it *our vision*. The execution plan comes next with a phase-by-phase iterative approach. The strategy, which is the combination of vision and execution plan, is done *top-down*. The vision stays rigid and the execution bends around it, because that's how we built it in the first place. Since it's hard to admit execution weaknesses and the vision is fixed, strategies are often compromised and become weaker with time. Try to search on Google for the phrase: *strategy execution 90%* — it is a hot topic. You will find many quotes and discussions around ...*an astounding 90% of well-formulated strategies fail due to poor execution...*

For startups, however, the inside-out approach is mostly irrelevant as they start from scratch and have no history. Steve Blank's *Lean Methodology for Startups* is a blend of the two approaches. You start from a vision and then build and accumulate history step-by-step. You make plans only for the next step. Blank lets both the vision and the execution plan float and adjust to the findings of the step-by-step experiments.

The lean methodology for startups uses a strategy canvas that documents all the starting assumptions in nine categories: key partners, customer segments, customer relationships, revenue streams, cost structure, value proposition, key resources, key activities, and carriers. Every assumption

is tested *outside the building* with real customers, suppliers, partners, etc. Most of the effort is invested in how to test, and what the test results mean. The assumptions on the canvas are either validated or changed. The process is *lean* because you only risk the costs of the next iteration. He builds it piece by piece with a *bottom-up* approach.

Gartner's Magic Quadrant

Success is 10% strategy and 90% execution. A strategy that cannot be executed is like setting the bar too high. There's no practical use for it.

Gartner's Magic Quadrant considers both strategy and execution, and compares companies that operate in the same space (Table 3). In this model, Gartner assesses companies based on *completeness of vision* and *ability to execute.* For example:

- Your vision is to have a complete portfolio of products for your market segment, so that your customers need not go elsewhere for products in your category. How complete is your vision? Do you have all the products? Are you offering them to your customers? Are you still working on them?

- You created this vision so that customers would not go elsewhere for products in your category. What is the reality though? Are they buying into your vision or do they continue to buy these products from other vendors? How well do you execute this vision?

The model identifies four types of companies that operate in the same space:

- *Leaders* score high on completeness of vision and their ability to execute. They are financially conservative and strong. They can develop or buy technology, and they satisfy the customers' buying preferences. All the industry lock-in companies are here.

- *Visionaries* understand where the market is going, or how to influence buying patterns and technology adoption. Their messages resonate well with customers, their vision is *complete.* However,

Table 3 Gartner's Magic Quadrant Model

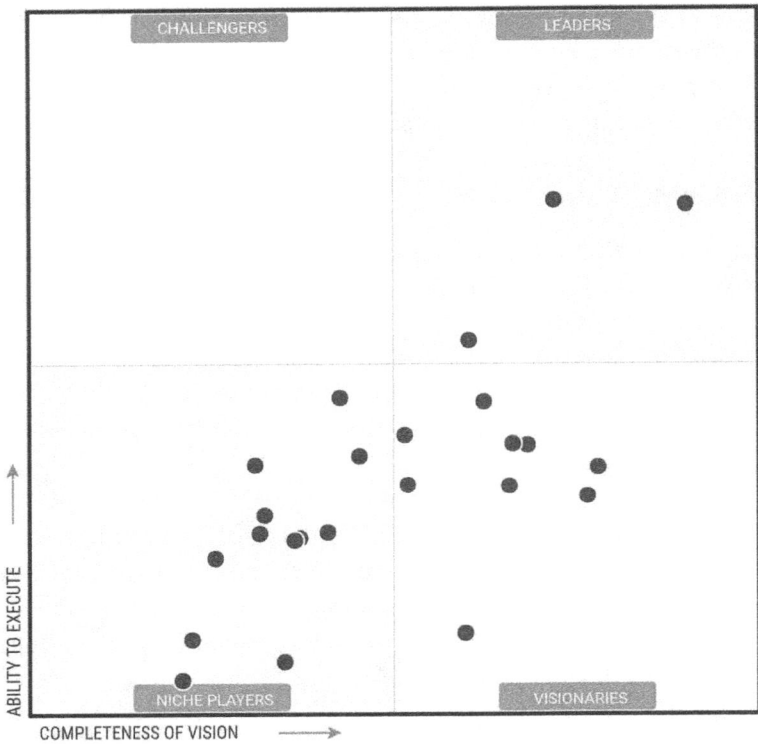

execution is weak on: technology, finances, services, organization, or leadership. These companies are often targets for acquisition.

- *Niche Players* have a narrow vision. They execute successfully in a small segment. Successful startups are here.

- *Challengers* have a narrow vision that's wide enough to address a large market segment. They might be riding an industry wave and executing very well in it. With their narrow focus they are learning quickly how to operate on a big scale. The key to their success — large yet narrow — is also the Achilles heel of their strategy. Think of all the famous companies that executed very well and then disappeared. Challengers are the best candidates to become leaders.

Use the Gartner Magic Quadrant model to assess your position relative to other companies in your competitive landscape. It will open your eyes — are your ideas less realistic, now that you've seen the position of the competition? Or perhaps they are too conservative, now that you realize that the competition aren't doing much with these ideas, and you're convinced that you could do better.

Reality Check — Consolidated Roadmap

Just before you leave the strategy session, do another reality check. Put everything into roadmaps with high-level actions for each function of the company. Make sure nothing is left outside the roadmap; short-term and long-term actions are included in one consolidated picture. Check that everybody is in agreement and ready to do their parts until the next strategy-revision session.

17

Strategy —
Do's and Don'ts

Every strategy has its appropriate currency to measure results. Top and bottom line numbers and value to shareholders are the metrics for business strategy. Third sector organizations — NGOs and not-for-profits — have different currencies to measure the value they produce. For example, for an organization that is dedicated to improving education in third world countries, the currency is education level and the profit is the achieved improvement. The value streams, in this case, are the different ways they generate the value, for example, teachers' education programs and children's nutrition programs. The competition is when other organizations follow the same goals, except that they can collaborate and it would not be considered as collusion. Strategy is important for every organization, and the concepts are the same. If you spread the budget too thin, you cannot achieve results, since you're operating below critical-mass; and if you continue with a project despite the poor results, you're violating the sunk cost principle.

Especially in large business organizations, it would be a valuable exercise for internal departments to produce an operational strategy with the value streams of their work. However, attempts to attach revenue and profit as a metric for their results are likely to be futile. Obviously, every action that internal departments do eventually leads to revenue and profits; however, the linkages are so indirect, sometimes, that the measurement is invalid. It's like making ROI decisions on sending your child to a specific enrichment class because eventually he'd earn a higher income as an adult; such linkages to money are too flimsy.

I've seen feature requests with promised revenue value attached to them. I've also seen a trip to a conference justified by leads multiplied by conversion rate to calculate the potential increased revenue. If you think linearly, you'd be disappointed by the results — there are too many other factors in-between. The correct alternative metrics in such cases could be descriptive or numeric, but not generated money. Every situation has its appropriate *value currency*.

Critical Mass

When you measure strategy execution with numbers — money or other KPI's — and the numbers don't move, ask if the investment is too little to make a difference, i.e., it's below critical mass. However, when you measure results with descriptive qualitative assessments, it's harder to detect; you'd often find a sign on the door that says: Sorry — Too Late.

BELOW CRITICAL MASS

I was once asked to look at the marketing plan of a small company that wanted to penetrate the US market. The marketing planner created a program with a budget of one million dollars. The CEO reacted to the plan and said that he only had half a million to spend. After examining the plan and seeing that it was minimal already, I told the CEO that America is a big place, and that half a million dollars is too much money to throw away. Working below critical mass is like throwing the money away.

That's why it's so important to watch for the symptoms and consult with others.

Sunk Costs

I already mentioned the concept of sunk cost several times in the book, but, I see it so often that I have to describe it here as part of the strategy considerations. *Sunk Cost* is the single concept that confuses us the most. Psychologically, it's very difficult to separate from something that we've already invested in, especially if we have invested a lot — money or effort — and we own it. Many projects continue for no other reason than ...*we have come so far...* or, as many books on investment strategies point out, we tend to hold a stock until we recover at least the cost of buying it, even when there are obvious better options.

Read about the subject of *loss aversion* from the works of Prof. Daniel Kahneman or Prof. Dan Ariely and you will be as convinced as I am about how the *sunk cost fallacy* plays on us as human decision makers. In business we always have more than one option — we should choose the one that has the best ROI measured from now, and not from a point in the past. The fact that we've invested in something up until now has nothing to do with whether we should keep investing in it — the past investment is sunk cost that cannot be recovered. Always keep in mind the *relative contribution* to the bottom line of the available options; and *always forget* — as much as it's emotionally difficult — the sunk costs.

Stability of The Strategy

Unless you're starting from the scratch, you revise the strategy regularly, and you don't pivot too often. *Strategy Vacillation* puts the execution in danger; it's as if you'd be hitting your own team with overhand attacks, making it impossible for them to keep the volleyball in the air.

If you keep changing it, how could you possibly know if the strategy is good? The bottom-up and inside-out approaches make the strategy and vision last longer, and their strategic moves are stable evolutionary steps.

There are two types of companies — the quick and the dead, is a famous Andy Grove quote. A stable strategy does not make a company slow; quite the opposite, multiple incremental strategic moves make it fast.

Strategy Do's and Don'ts
— Value is not always expressed in money.
— Do not force an artificial metric where it does not fit.
— Learn how to do the value stream analysis.
— Avoid decisions of: too little — too late.
— Divorce yourself from attachment to sunk costs.
— Vacillation is destructive.

As the Rabbi Said...

18

The Jewish Passover Haggadah quotes Raban Gamliel, the leading Elder of the 1st. century Sanhedrin, who said:

> One who has not said these three things in the Passover Seder has not fulfilled his obligation, and these are **Pesach, Matza and Marror**.

- **Pesach**, because our lord passed over our homes in Egypt and saved us from the most horrible plague.
- **Matza**, because our ancestors were fed by miracles along the way and were saved from Egypt.
- **Marror**, because they suffered in Egypt and therefore need to be thankful for being saved.

And these three words sum the entire history of an ancient people, to be recited each year to fulfill the obligation.

*

And those people who have not said and done these three things — *Dissect, Analyze, and Test* — as they were sitting around a strategy table, have not fulfilled their obligation.

- *Dissect*, because strategy is a complex picture, and you cannot understand it as a whole unless the pieces are clear.

- *Analyze*, because there are many ways and shades to look at business and operations.
- *Test*, because you cannot assume that you know the future, and neither can you assume that you know better than others.

There are no shortcuts. You have to sit through the entire Haggadah. Unfortunately.

Communication
Technocrat

Fundamentals

19

One's speech should lead to harmony among beings, it should be kind and pleasant and it should be truthful and beneficial

— Aung San Suu Kyi

Bring Aung San Suu Khi's assertion into the context of business and organization, and it would mean *respect*. Most organizations today are culturally diverse or act globally — with clients, suppliers, or employees. Let me point out the obvious: communication with *respect* could prevent and resolve many problems. Respect the situation of the listener, audience, or reader, and you will engage him to go along with you.

Communication is the first tool in the manager's toolbox. As with any other tool, you use the one that's right for the job — hammer for a nail, and plane for a rough piece of wood. If you want to achieve the intended outcome, you will use different communication techniques for one-on-one synchronization meetings, negotiations, emails, or group meetings.

At the atomic level, communication is effective when the *message is clear* and the audience *retains* it. In business, *action* is the third key component of the formula — action that's called for explicitly or implicitly. It's the audience's job to understand the message, retain it, and act accordingly; therefore, you need to start with understanding the audience.

141

Table 1   Communication Formula — 3 Components

Effective Communication
— Message delivered
— Retention
— Action

The audience, however, doesn't want to listen. That is human nature — we are created lazy. It takes an effort to focus on new information — seldom are we fully attentive, completely clean from wandering in other lands of thought. In written text, if the message isn't served to us right at the beginning, our brain wanders elsewhere, as we read, and re-read, and lose interest altogether. Oral communication is worse, we cannot push the replay button; therefore, it's even harder to follow and focus.

As communicators, unfortunately, we cannot create an audience to our liking; we are bound to work with what we have — an audience with natural listening flaws. Our job is to make it as easy as possible, so that more gets through and is retained, and the stage is ready for action. The formula is simple — the techniques require practice (Table 1).

Message Delivered

How many times do you need to read an email before you understand why it was written and what it meant to say? It should be just once. During live presentations, the presenter should tell you a story that develops from chapter to chapter so that it's easy to follow; however, I see many presenters that lose the audience without even noticing it. The first component of the formula, the message, is the hook that catches the audience and engages them to listen or read. If you don't have a message, don't communicate.

Now that you do have a message, the job is to make sure the audience has it too — that they heard, understood, and internalized it. You start with *delivering* the context and then the message without beating around the bush. If it's done well, the audience is interested in the story that comes afterwards and in the proofs of your arguments. Refrain from jargon as much as possible — simple words are easier to digest. If you were a

storyteller, you'd build your story layer by layer, with tension and anticipation that the audience enjoys; but in business the audience wants to know first why they have to listen. If they are going to pay with their effort to listen, they want to know the value; and your message should be that value.

Retention

In a presentation you want your audience to act; in an email you want them to react. But in both cases, first they need to understand what you are saying; the parcel that you delivered to their door should be brought inside and opened, else it has no use. Because human nature predisposes them to be lazy, you need to help them with the effort. After the message, and if it's not already obvious from the message itself, you provide supporting statements, i.e., details, proofs, evidence, logical arguments, graphic illustrations, or analogies — all with a *direct mental connection* to the message. Deliver the story in its shortest version and don't dilute the focus on the message — it should be easy for the audience to *retain* it.

Action

No Action–No Email is one of my hard principles. Even if your email is *for information only,* think of why you want the recipients to be informed, and ensure that your text says it — explicitly, implicitly, suggestively, or even ordered, as long as it's clear. Reduce your informational email broadcasts and ensure that when you do one, it has value for the audience — the messages are simple and it's clear what you want them to do. For example, do you want to rally the troops? Tell them the story that you want to tell, but also finish with how you expect them to change.

*

Message delivery, *retention,* and *action* are the three musketeer bullets that will make your communication not only effective but also efficient. We will use them everywhere in communication, such as in emails, presentations, meetings, chat, chat-on-steroids, and even in social media tools.

Email Madness

20

I like to raise the subject of emails with managers. I like watching their reaction even more, i.e., a big sigh of frustration and a face of ... *I know what you mean* ... So I wonder, "how did we manage to take a wonderful tool and system, and turn it into such a source of waste?"

In many emails, we tap around an issue instead of hitting it on its head. Sometimes we use it as if we were in therapy — sawing an issue back and forth until we get cuts and bleed. We send long reports over email. Or, we attempt to fix an entire system by sending a single email. We use it like a power tool to fasten one screw after the other. Or sometimes as a sledgehammer that shakes the entire neighborhood with one of those *Hello everyone* mailers.

Email is not omnipotent. It's a very effective and efficient tool when used properly. Recently, out of frustration, some workgroups started using chat systems instead of email, but that doesn't solve the organizational communication problem either. Instead, it makes it worse.

Let's look at two examples to see how one writer addresses the reader with a *service orientation*, and another who makes it easy on himself, but not to the reader. My *{embedded notes}* in the below emails highlight what I want you to see.

I recently received the following almost-perfect email:

To Our Clients and Friends:

*As we approach year-end {**context**}, it's again time to focus on last-minute moves you can make to save taxes — both on your current return and in future years {**message**}.*

*To get you started, we've included a few money-saving ideas here that you may want to put in action before the end of the year {**action**}. Contact us if you have questions about which ideas may be appropriate for you or if you want to discuss other tax-saving strategies {**service orientation**}.*

This email continued with the tax-saving ideas, each with a title and a brief description. I could easily skim over the ideas and select the ones to read. The structure helped me go over the text without needing to read the entire email.

*

I also received an email from a different tax firm around the same time. I assumed it had similar content, but I read it only because it was a good example for this book. I received it as an attachment — the email itself was a greeting — and it didn't tell me why I should open it. The attachment started with an introduction about the prospects of changes in tax laws, with their election year flavors, followed by the general recommendation that

*… long-cherished maneuvers that could help many taxpayers — such as accelerating deductions and postponing income — might not be a smart idea for large numbers of people … {**and here it had more long text about more ideas that we might not want to use**} … The best strategy for many taxpayers this year may be simply to procrastinate;*

Despite these major question marks, many Americans may benefit from a few ideas, including what not to do. Here are a few from tax advisers:

I scrolled to the end of the document that had 3 full pages of loaded text and I had no idea what I might or might not do.

Table 1 Business Email

Business Email Standard Structure
Clear subject

— Greeting
— Context
— Message
— Supporting arguments — proofs, details
  — Point 1
  — Point 2
  — Point 3
— Action
— Signoff

Same information was delivered in two very different ways. The first was quick, easy to read and use as reference. The second had copious adjectives (long-cherished), circuitous arguments and counter-recommendations (despite these major question marks), and numerous quotes and names — it was long-winded and tiresome.

*

Table 1 gives a standard structure for business email writing.

Email Focus and Purpose

A good email has *focus and purpose* — just one set. Before you write, ask yourself, *what* does the reader need to know? And w*hat* do I want to say? Only then compose the email with the right context, message, and action, and save a lot of time for yourself and the reader.

Brevity

Be brief and don't add clutter to the email as it's not environmentally friendly. If you happen to think that *brevity* is impolite, think of how appreciative your readers would be. With a short and structured email, you are also likely to receive a short and structured answer. Wouldn't you appreciate it? Also think of all the back-and-forth clarification emails that you'd save. A good email begets more good emails, while a bad one begets waste.

Expressing Emotions

Email is not the right place for emotions — any emotions, explicit or implicit. If you show *enthusiasm* or deliver *compliments* over email, bear in mind that they could be ridiculed or offensive to other people. Better refrain from overstatements and stay factual, subtle, and polite — say no more than *good job*. At all cost, avoid *arguing* over email; just think of the time it would take for the other side to craft the argument to beat your argument. It's an utter waste. You also have no control over forwards and interpretations of your email; it can backfire and turn into office gossip. Overcome the urge to send a loaded email. Write it and send it to yourself instead; it's therapeutic.

Supporting Arguments

Use points and bullets where each piece of text stands on its own. The reader will have the option to skip or repeat items without having to look for the right place. Never bundle two points into one bullet. If you have many points, add a summary at the end to get the reader back to the main message, right before the explicit action statement.

If your supporting points are long, you can divide the email into two sections. On the top, form the bullet points as *executive summary* texts. Add a dividing line below and call the section *further details*. You could also use an attachment. Most readers will be happy with the short summary, and you will be satisfied that you've recorded everything.

Reports on Email

Reports should not be in the email's core text. Send an attachment instead, where you could preserve the standard structure of the report. If it's a very short report, you could create a section at the bottom of the email text, as long as it has a repeatable structure. In the top part, address the readers and help them with a summary in three parts:

- Highlights — positive extracts from the report
- Lowlights — negative extracts from the report
- Need help — red flags and warnings

The highlights and lowlights are the *key messages*, and the need help is the *action*. Now you have a perfect email.

Email Threads

No reader should be forced to go deep into a series of back-and-forth emails to find the context, message, and action. The most irksome example is a forwarded email thread with only an *FYI* message. Why should I have to read and decipher everything that you, the sender, have (hopefully) already read? Tell me briefly what you saw in the material and why you think I should be interested in it. Remember, the reader is the lazy character in this play; the writer is the hard-working one who does more than FYI.

Long-threaded discussions transform quickly into dreaded discussions. If you receive one, see if you can cut the chain, call a meeting, or restart the communication with a new thread and a summary of where we are.

Distribution and Frequency

With anything that's related to email, think small — shortest texts, fewer occurrences, and smaller distribution circles. The arteries of the organization are already clogged — we need a serious diet to save ourselves from big trouble. Inundating people with words isn't the way to keep them informed. If you lead a project, for example, and many people need to be continuously informed on the progress, create a standard report that you send regularly to all of them. Definitely do not keep them on a large distribution circle of the project's correspondence. With a regular report, your audience would not think you're keeping them in the dark, and the project's correspondence can be kept within the close circle of the project's team.

Audience Consideration

21

You cannot sell products without thinking of the prospective buyers. In communication the buyer is our audience — the content consumer. When you want your audience to consume the information, always start with what occupies their minds at that time. If you overlook their preoccupations you miss the opportunity to engage them, and missed communication reflects badly on you — the messenger.

We examine three common scenarios in business environments where we see how to take the audience into consideration, and how their mindsets guide us on the content and format of delivery. The scenarios are:

- Reinforcing leadership
- Getting agreements
- Tracking progress

Reinforcing Leadership

We do All-Hands or Town Hall Meetings to rally the troops, increase morale, and instill purpose — that's what we, the communicators, are thinking about. The audience, on the other hand, wonders about whether the leaders know where they are leading. In the back of their minds, they're concerned with the quality of the leadership, and with any recent changes in employment policies or reorganizations that affect them. Think of the gap between the two mindsets. The presentation needs to be the bridge — reinforcing the leadership and addressing these audience concerns.

The audience is pre-staged to judge the leadership also in conferences with customers and investors or in board meetings. On the surface, the audience shows interest in the strategy of the company, but the deeper thoughts are on the quality of the leaders. You present the strategy, but you need to remember that it's only a proof point — the strategy shows how good you are as a leader. You stress the points that make your case, and use the rest as background. As a credible leader, you have to cover any recent change that is visible outside. You cannot leave the audience without answers to preoccupations, such as " ... *yes, but what about the recent foray into China?*"

The audience expects their leaders to know more than they do — show your knowledge with confidence, and they will trust you more. Select the strongest points and don't try to cover everything. Too much detail could derail the main message and weaken their opinion of you.

Another situation where you consider how the audience absorbs information is board meetings, where you have to use spreadsheets. Spreadsheets in presentations violate every rule of good technique. The audience cannot absorb all the details, and you don't want them to. But they trust spreadsheets, so you have to use them. Think of the points that you do want them to notice in the information that's on the spreadsheet, and build the story by putting circles around these points. The audience will follow you from point to point, and will view the rest of the spreadsheet as shaded background. For example, if you want to show that you are conservative with money, show the steep increase in the cash reserves. You want to show you are excellent in operations, point to three consecutive quarters of reduction in inventory levels.

Getting Agreements

Agreements owe their success or failure to communication, and how well you can think of the others, i.e., your audience. In agreements, regardless

of seniority and knowledge, all sides have to agree. They're of equal stature even though some have more to give than others and some show their cards while others hide them. The principle of stature equality applies to all agreements — negotiations, work sharing, exploring business cooperation, or any plan that affects multiple stakeholders.

George Orwell said that ... *political speech and writing are largely the defense of the indefensible ... thus political language has to consist largely of euphemism, question-begging and sheer cloudy vagueness ...* In business, however, we assume that the positions are defensible; therefore, we should avoid any political speech and fuzz. If you want an agreement that's good for you, first think of them. Collect as much information beforehand and put yourself in their position — that's how you'll know better what to offer and how much to concede. In a negotiation meeting, leave the airwaves to the other side as much as possible, apply the Mickey Mouse approach: big ears, small mouth.

This is how the big ears work: people have a tendency to talk; when they walk into silence they'll fill it. Therefore, use short and open questions, small mouth, and leave a lot of room for long answers; this is the best way to know more about the other side's position; they will talk more and expose more. If you take the airwaves, on the other hand, you lose precious time to collect information. Come prepared for several scenarios. As you collect information during the meeting, you choose carefully what to say, and that's how you perfect your position. Active listening — short questions that solicit long answers — is the art of negotiating agreements. Think of it as Mickey with radar antenna ears.

Watch Mickey's shadow as the story unfolds in the following example.

INTERNET/SOFTWARE COMPANY — STARTING A NEGOTIATION

A client of mine received an inquiry from another company to check the possibility of cooperation. They saw a fit for our product in their broad market reach. As we prepared for the first call we weren't sure why they had approached us as they already had a competitive offering. We thought of several possible reasons and scenarios, and

(Continued)

(Continued)

deliberated them until we could see a clear business model for the potential partnership.

This was the outline of our preparation for the meeting (Table 1):

Table 1   Standard Preparation for Negotiation

Preparation for First Negotiation Call	
Assumption	They want to be our channel partner
Benefit to them	Our product makes their offering more friendly to users compared with their current product
Business models	License per user, license per server
Benefits and value to us	Upsell opportunity to their clients, co-marketing, monetization, new target market, new revenue stream, improve our brand
Negative aspects to us	Cannibalization of our existing revenue stream, engineering distraction
Value to them	More complete portfolio, grow their user base, press release with our brand name
Negative effects to them	None

We then decided on the approach for the meeting:

- Clarify and validate value to us and value to them. {Gather information}
- If promising, get agreement for another meeting. {Buy time to plan our moves}
- Ask open questions and listen. {Preparing Mickey for action}
- Answer all their questions with respect. {Build credibility and trust}

In the meeting we asked the following open questions:

- *How do you see the partnership working?*
- *What is the value to you?*

(Continued)

(Continued)

- *How do you see the value to us?*
- *How do you see us making money?*
- *And you?*
- *Is monetization a possibility?*

They responded as expected, with a lot of information. We gleaned the following:

- They agreed that we monetize their users.
  {Even before discussing commercial terms}
- Their existing product failed because of weak features. It was from one of our competitors.
  {Competitive information}
- They tested our product on their users and knew it's better than their existing product.
  {They really want our product}
- They count on our engineering strength to make it successful.
  {We have a good reputation}
- It is an important part of their overall strategy.
  {They really (!) want our product}
- They are comfortable to let the business grow to $18–25M per year without adjusting the agreement.
  {Almost pure profit, excellent ROI on engineering effort}
- They prefer a longer approach to avoid failures.
  {We will have time to fix our product and make it a success}

To their questions, we reinforced the advantages of our product and the strength of our engineering team. We agreed to another meeting in a week to discuss the principles of the partnership and make the first plan.

We came out of the meeting so much richer with important information; that is how well this Mickey mouse works.

Internal agreements are not like negotiations though. The right approach is collaboration between parties who share the same interest — here is what we will do, and that's what we need you to do. In collaboration people seek fairness and recognition, so if you come with open cards, you build trust that will last even beyond the current agreement. It's the simplest way to reach a good internal agreement.

Tracking Progress

Why is audience consideration important in communicating about progress tracking? Think of your project meetings, staff meetings, and cross-functional coordination. Is everyone paying attention to all the details? Should they? Have you noticed how many of the participants are busy with their mobile devices during these meetings and not paying attention? To solve this attention problem, create a structure and protocol for the meeting and make it predictable and repeatable. The participants will know what to expect and won't miss the information that they need.

The purpose of these meetings is to share updates, they are not for discussions. When the updates are complete, the meeting ends. The meeting leader enforces the protocol and ensures that the meeting doesn't derail into discussions, as so often happens.

In tracking progress, the topics don't change much from meeting to meeting; therefore, it's best to put them in a table format with topics and update columns. Use document-sharing tools, like Google sheets, to eliminate the need for meeting notes. Everyone, including remote participants, can see the updates on the shared document as the meeting progresses. To ensure that the participants prepare well for the meeting, they should enter their updates beforehand. Any last minute update is done on the fly. You freeze the document after the meeting to keep the history, and make a copy to be used as the draft tracking sheet of the next meeting.

Project leaders who use task-management tools to track dependencies, e.g., MS Project, Jira, Trello, Asana, should limit their use to the project team.

These tools are too complex and very hard to follow during coordination meetings with a broader audience.

Remote participants will especially appreciate the structured meeting format. It overcomes some of the difficulties of being remote, such as language barriers, quality of sound, and poor video equipment. The online document, shared live as the meeting goes on, helps them follow the meeting and they don't miss anything, as they can see the same information as the local participants.

Presentations

22

If there is anything worse than the emails that run through our inbox, it's the presentations. Let's get straight to the core of the problem — most of them are neither effective nor efficient. In one word, they are wasteful. However, they are ubiquitous and unavoidable, therefore, we cannot ignore them. Presentations are boring, unfocused, rambling, and even lacking purpose. People in the room are often busy with their mobile devices, which presenters pretend not to notice. If one person from the audience takes the presenter off course, the rest take a break, and never resume listening. Too many times that's what I see. Do you see that too?

If we prepare the presentation with the audience in mind, we have a better chance to engage them. Remember that the audience is *born to run,* not to sit and listen. Their preoccupations are a serious obstacle. Though they're physically captive in the meeting room, their minds are roaming like free-range chickens.

Think of a typical room where presentations takes place — a nice, darkened room with comfortable chairs and a constant hum from the projector. Your mind is already sleepy just by reading my description. That's where the audience is; busy slides will not wake them up.

Focusing on the audience doesn't mean that we disregard our needs. The presentation is a bridge between us and them — a solid bridge with two solid columns. To wake them up from the stupor and convince them, we need to understand them as much as we understand ourselves.

But let's make sure that we first understand ourselves clearly, before we try to convince them. The helpful keyword is *sell*. You sell your idea, project, or product, and they pay with continued confidence in you, with support, increased motivation and dedication, money, agreement, etc.

The material for the construction of this bridge lies with the department of: *how I advance their state of mind with what I am selling*. It's more than a value proposition. For example, you try to sell an operational efficiency project by presenting the potential savings — now that's selling with the use of a value proposition. But, if your audience is constantly in fire-fighting mode, chances are that you won't be able to convince them to take on yet another project. The most you could get from them is *some other time, maybe*. Instead, if you focus on how your project improves their fire-fighting existence, you might have a better chance because you'd be talking directly to their main preoccupation.

The *delivery* is no less important than the content, and that means you — the presenter. Think of a hypothetical experiment: in a live presentation you let the audience read the slides while you are just clicking them forward. They will understand little and retain a vague idea, at best. But, if you interact with the slides and the audience, it's a different story. You could improve their experience and retention even more if you use their examples. Better still, if they are responsible for passing the information to others, they will *own* the information that you delivered to them.

Let's see how we use the three principles — message delivered, retention, and action — to build *content* with its consumers in mind, while the *flow* and *format* follow the logical and mental associations of the audience. We remove distractions as much as we can or at least we don't add any.

Content and Flow

With the following simple structure, you can build a *story that sticks* with any audience in business, operations, and organizations. It works every time. Think of what you'd save if you practice it a few times. You use a formula

Table 1 Presentation Standard Storyboard

Build a Presentation
Title — promise
Resolution of the promise
Value statement Evidence and supporting arguments
Reinforcement of value and promise
Actions, next steps

instead of sifting through your thoughts and material, and selecting what to say, what not to say, and in which order. It's a storyboarding technique for business (Table 1).

Slide presentations are the most common tool — we use it here as well. Any tool that's more dynamic or innovative takes the attention away from the presenter and focuses the audience on the tool itself, which is another distraction to be prevented.

Title — Promise

People will listen if you promise them something that's meaningful to them. Curiosity will open their listening channels and will make them ready to absorb new content. Generally, when they enter the conference room their mind is locked. The title of the presentation should be capable of unlocking it. The title is an *opening statement* — it's important and it needs to *hit home*. A good title is like the frame of the bridge that you can already walk on. If there's no bridge from you to the audience, and you try to walk, you can only fall.

For example, let's consider a quarterly presentation to upper management or board. The outline of the content is: *here is what we do and why, and these are the results and our future plans*. But what you want them to understand is the underlying storyline: *you should continue to trust us because we are trustworthy*. You cannot bluntly tell them *Trust Us*, but your opening statement should convey that to them as an underlying message. Try the title: *Continuing to Grow Quarter over Quarter*, or if you need to use boardroom speak you could say *Q/Q Momentum*. Such titles have the flavor of promise — we are doing well and will continue to do well. If, however, your quarterly results are nothing to brag about, you want to convince them that you're in control of the situation. Try for example, *Cost Control Is Working*. Either way, you definitely don't want to title your presentation *Quarterly Review* — it's neither promising nor does it do anything to help open the listening channel of your audience.

Finding the right promise isn't that straightforward. You'd find the answer if you think of questions such as: *how can my product ease your pain? How can my service help you fulfill your potential? How can my leadership motivate you? How can I convince you to invest in my idea?*

But be careful — your statement shouldn't be a bridge too far. Your credibility will be hurt if the audience thinks that the promise is detached from reality. Also, your opening statement shouldn't overreach; you cannot promise to a CEO that you'll make him more money — that's his job. However, you could say that your product will open a new market. To him it means the same, but you stayed within the limits of safe reach and respect for his position.

Resolution of the Promise

Imagine listening to music with tones that go on higher and higher, you'd be eagerly waiting for the low ta-ta at the end. The composer uses clever ways to create the suspense; when he finally resolves it, you feel the drama and the release from tension.

In business presentations, however, we do not welcome prolonged suspense and drama. You made a promise, and you cannot leave it hanging — your credibility is on the line. You need to resolve the promise immediately to a state where we, the audience, are ready to imagine and believe that it's feasible *in our own context*. If you leave it open for long, the flame you ignited with that promise will be quenched immediately.

The best resolutions place the audience in the reality of their improved state, i.e., before and after views. For example, following the *Q/Q Momentum*

promise in a board meeting, show them right away the great numbers and your forecast for the next Q. The board will accept the good news and listen to what you did to achieve these numbers and how you plan to achieve the forecast, which is the rest of your presentation. In a technical presentation that promises better system performance, for example, show a conceptual block diagram of the old and new architecture, highlighting the change that will make the difference. Now that you showed the audience how your proposal would affect them, they are ready to listen. Simple illustrations, in no more than two slides, are the best for showing the resolution of the promise.

Value Statement, Evidence, and Supporting Arguments

With a promise and a resolution, the audience knows what you are selling and what it means to them, and they believe that it's possible. But you haven't convinced them yet — your promises might be empty, after all.

The audience is conditioned, however, to accept the proof; in fact, they are interested to see it.

The best proofs are references. The story of your fat neighbor that turned into a fit marathon runner could easily convince you to use the same personal trainer. But there are other forms of evidence that work just as well: numbers and graphs that build to a supportive argument, facts that are logically connected to the promise, and analogies that claim that what worked there can also work here.

Select only the strongest *proofs* and don't overdo it. When you present several arguments, you go from the strongest to the weakest. As you spend more time on the weaker secondary points, the *halo effect* makes your initial stronger points fade and become weaker (Daniel Kahneman — *Thinking Fast and Slow*). That's why it's best to limit yourself to three strong points. We like to think in threes, and to take action because of three reasons, because in our minds, three is neither too little nor too much.

Presenting the proof points and their elaborated details shifts the audience's focus from point to point; therefore, you first need to present a menu that serves as the big picture *value statement*.

Here's our BoD presentation example. To this point, the storyboard with the menu of value statements is: *We are in a Q/Q Momentum. I showed you the numbers and forecast and we are going to see how we are doing it: {menu of 3 value points} Strong Pipeline in New Market, Good Trends in Traditional Segments, Effective Training program.*

Table 2 shows another storyboard example of a video accelerating solution for internet service providers. Table 2 includes the first four parts of the presentation: promise, resolution, value proposition menu, and proofs.

Table 2   Presentation Storyboard: Promise–Resolution–Value Statement–Proofs

Video Acceleration for Internet Service Providers			
Promise	**Higher Speed — Same Cost**		
Higher speed of video serving over the Internet without additional costs. The audience is constantly thinking about how to increase revenue from existing customers — faster video to customers means more business.			
⬇			
Resolution	**Conceptual Diagram**: Video accelerator in the customer's video data flow.		
This diagram is of their environment, before and after the accelerator. It should also show the concept of the acceleration.			
⬇			
Value proposition menu	**Better Product + Lower Costs = Better Business** — Video-streaming acceleration 10X — 10% operational savings — 5% increased business in 1 year		
The three strongest points are the ones that concern this audience the most — more revenue and less cost			
⬇			
Proofs	**10X Reference customer**	**Operational cost calculator**	**Quote from industry analyst**
The first two proofs are graphs, diagrams, and numbers. The third proof is a lighter weight quote.			

Reinforcement of Value and Promise

As you present the proofs, the story line splits into several branches; the audience that's been following you from proof to proof might lose the main message at this point, and they cannot scroll back as it's a live presentation. The technique to bring them back to the message is to *repeat* it. You started presenting proofs with a menu, as in *I will show you* these three proofs; next, you were *showing* them the three proofs, one by one. Now, in case they forgot where they are in the story, you say *I showed you the three proofs and here they are*. You present the menu again, but in different words, to *reinforce the value statement* and to validate with the audience that they understood the full picture. With the reinforcement, you've already told your story three times from different angles and the chances are higher that they will retain it.

The story now is complete. What is left is to say what you want them to do, i.e., the action.

Actions, Next Steps

The presentation doesn't end without explicitly discussing actions with the audience.

To stimulate this discussion, list a few options. In a sales presentation you could ask: *who else needs to hear the proposed solution; do they need a more technical presentation? Are you ready to test the solution?* In a review meeting you could ask: *what would you like to see next time? Do you have more ideas? Do you agree with the proposed program?*

The last slide with the options for the *next steps* stays on until the last person leaves the room. Leave it there, because that's what you want them to remember.

Slide Mechanics

You built a presentation according to the storyboarding technique. Keep the slides in draft mode, because you are going to attack them with axe, knife, and scissors, to remove all distractions and help the audience focus on you.

*

Other than the free-range thoughts of the people in the audience, which you cannot control, the main distractors are the *slides* and the *presenter*. Most of the presenters and slides that I see work against their own interests. Instead of helping the audience to listen and engage, they create additional distractions that do the opposite.

The presenter is the central figure in a presentation event — you don't want the slides to draw the attention away from you. You do want the slides to help the audience follow what you say — that's their function. I am sure you have seen slides that are full of words; here's what happens to the audience when you present and a busy slide is projected:

- They read the slide and they don't listen to you.
- Or, they try to listen to you, and they work hard to avoid the slide.
- Or, they jump back and forth and they cannot focus on either.
- Or, they try hard to do both, but they get tired fast.

The slides should never compete with you for the attention of the audience. *You* need to be interesting — the slides should be boring and let you shine. Let's review rules that will keep your slides free from the blame of stealing the attention from you.

- *Avoid*, at all cost, any *interesting presentation* of information: animation, kaleidoscopic graphics, and long texts.
- *Use colors* sparingly, soft to the eye, and consistent from beginning to end. If green is your color for money, don't make it orange later. Avoid yellow, you cannot see it on the projected screen.
- *Avoid* busy slides, simplify your illustrations and schematics. Build them up in layers if they have more than three squares, two circles, and two arrows; never more than seven elements in a slide.

- *Don't* let your creative graphic designers decide for you.
- *Avoid full sentences,* your bullet points are titles, keywords, or very short phrases, like the titles of newspaper articles, or as I did for the titles throughout this book.
- *Keep it short,* if the audience needs to read the words, it's too long. The audience is focused on you; there's nothing interesting on the screen, just a few keywords. As you use a keyword, they just glance at it. It helps them understand your explanation and remember it.
- *Simple schematics*, if the audience needs to study a diagram, it's too complex. Guide them through the schematic as you explain; for example ... *look at the third layer of the triangle; it's the last component of the program ...*
- *Symbols,* use the ones that the audience recognizes and that everybody else is using. Don't be creative.
- *Don't change the order,* follow your explanations from point to point as they are listed on the slide. Try hard not to go back to previous slides, else you'd be breaking the line of the story.
- *Handout samples?* Don't pass anything from hand to hand during presentation, not a photo, not a sample. Any toy that's passed around takes the audience's focus away and you'll lose them. Samples don't prove any point, anyway; if you like to show the real product, show it after the presentation. Don't tell them you have samples as they might ask you to show.
- 2 *minutes per slide, including the title slide* is a good average. The presentation is not a slide clicking show. Now that the words on the slides are sparse, you and your story have plenty of space.

Demonstrations

Software demos can be a good thing. I prefer scripted demos though.

First, be sure you can transition in and out of the demo smoothly. Test it in the room before the presentation, and make sure your computer fits the projection screen like a rectangle not a trapezoid. Don't count on an internet connection, test it.

To do the demo session, use the technique that I described before — *I will show you — I am showing you — I showed you*. Prepare a few scripts of the most common activities that users do with your software. For each of the scripts, create a slide that lists the steps of these activities, five clicks at the most.

Show the slide and explain the steps. Then slowly show it live. Summarize what they saw and pause. Give your audience a chance to breath and then move to the next script.

The Presenter

A good presenter interacts with the audience. Maintain eye contact and tell them a story. You hardly ever turn your face away from them, because the slides are on the computer in front of you, while the projected screen is for the audience.

Talk to the audience during your presentation. Ask them if they have experienced what you just described. If they ask a question, answer it, but if it derails your story, act with confidence and promise to answer later. Show your knowledge and enthusiasm for the subject, don't be dry. When someone contradicts you, promise to check, but assure everyone in the room that your point is based on your experience. Take control over everything that happens in the room — it is your show.

Show a winning attitude. You are convinced that the story is valid to them. But stay humble, friendly, and attentive.

Any sign of nervousness is a killer of a presentation. That's why it's best to have nothing in your hands. And God-forbid, no shaking of coins in the pants pockets — I have seen those; and no turning your back to the audience — you have seen those, too.

If you have a foreign accent, don't panic, you are not alone. If you're new to this audience, you should spend the first couple of minutes on small talk, let them get over the accent hump and adjust their ears to listening to you. You could say where you're from, many people like to know that. Any

comment that reduces the curiosity factor will help you focus the audience on what you say later in the presentation.

Diverse Audience

If you have vegetarians and carnivores over for dinner, you make sure there's enough for everyone. That is also what you do with a mixed audience in a presentation. You can explain your slides twice, if necessary. For example ... *for the marketing people here, the feature I just showed to the engineers creates new options for solutions to position in the market...* In this case you can use two sets of vocabulary: software stacks language for the engineers and positioning speak for the marketing people. Divide the proof points to have enough for both of them. Work the entire room, do not neglect anybody.

Feedback in Communication

23

S table organizations have their own ways of detecting when something is off target and then correcting it to get closer to that target. Knowing that something is off is the *feedback* that triggers the corrective mechanisms. In unstable and dysfunctional organizations, however, we see the following symptoms: projects that don't end, delayed decisions, prolonged discussions, procrastination, conflicts among and within the teams, consistently missed goals, lots of wasted time, or just plain nonproductive competition between units. These symptoms point to lack of feedback and failing corrective mechanisms. That's why you often hear the phrases *what you don't measure, you don't know* and *what you don't know, you cannot fix.*

Feedback can be quantitative, like revenue and profit that the accounting system measures. More often, though, feedback is qualitative, assessed and communicated by people; we'd call it *human feedback.* Human feedback is not scientific. The giver and the receiver of feedback add their interpretations, which are often productive, but as often nonproductive, or even destructive. Some feedback is explicit, as in *Good work! We are 5% from target,* but it can also be implicit, or even passive, for example, *the gap from now to the goal* is taken as feedback to act upon — it's implied or understood. Because feedback is the trigger of the corrective mechanisms, it's important to identify all its forms, and use them profusely.

Organizational behavior research shows that positivity is directly correlated to productivity (Lozada Zone). Well-performing organizations have a ratio of about 5–6 times more *positive feedback* in their human interactions than the amount of *negative feedback*. Marginally performing organizations have a ratio of 2 to 1, while any organization with higher negativity than positivity performs far from its potential — in other words, it's failing.

Based on this research and our personal experience of organizational behavior, we can conclude that all human feedback, which can be controlled, should be positive, to counterbalance the negative feedback already coming from external sources, such as competitive position, clients, unfavorable results, etc.

But, is positive feedback enough to get us the best results? If the bar is set too high, we see it as negative feedback, as in ... *I am not good enough to jump that high...* But if it's too low, we laugh at it, cross-over, and don't even try to jump as high as we could. If the vision statement of the company is too visionary, will it generate positive feedback from customers and employees? Or will it be counterproductive and seen as unrealistic or detached? Which type of feedback will give us the best results?

By definition, *positive feedback* encourages us to continue the current behavior, or to pursue a planned action, whereas *negative feedback* encourages us to stop the behavior, or to avoid doing the planned action. In the workplace, we should be able to tell someone to stop or avoid doing something without worrying too much about contributing to general negativity or harming productivity. In this chapter, we review a few common scenarios and learn techniques that increase the positivity of positive feedback and reduce the negativity of negative feedback.

*

The bigger problem with feedback, though, is *lack of feedback*, irrespective of it being positive or negative. Think of what happens when you don't receive a response to your email? As soon as you notice the delay the negativity

starts building up. *Didn't the receiver see the importance and urgency? How do they work over there that they don't respond? Was I too pushy? Am I not important in their eyes? How come they don't take me seriously?* Meanwhile, you keep checking your inbox and consider calling them, but you are not sure about it. You are also not sure what to do with the task, should you wait another day or continue without their input? We could stretch this simple example for much longer, as you would in a farcical satire, and build up anxiety, disrupt plans, hurt confidence, and contribute immensely to dysfunction and waste. On the other hand, if the receiver of the email responded with ... *I am sorry I won't have time to address your concern before tomorrow* ... the task would still not get done right away, but all the collateral damage that hurts productivity would have been saved. Now, multiply this story to all the emails in the organization where an action is delayed because it's waiting for an answer, and you can clearly see how a simple rule of organizational behavior could save a lot of waste.

This *lack of feedback* scenario is called *dead-time* in systems theory; it's a major source of dysfunction and is *the enemy of stability*. A period in which nothing happens, or when one side is waiting for the other without knowing the state of things, is dead-time that causes instability. Unanswered emails are just the most common sources of dead-time, but so are prolonged discussions, delayed decisions, or complex projects without enough synchronization points along the way. Dead-time caused by delayed feedback generates a lot of unnecessary rework and waste.

SCRUM and lean methodologies go to the extreme of solving the dead-time problem by creating mechanisms of constant feedback. Since I would always advocate more feedback than less — I am leaning on the side of *lean.*

As in *lean,* coordination meetings that are structured and predictable are key components of creating the feedback that the organization needs. However, as soon as the routine is disrupted — meeting cancelations, change of meeting time or agenda — dead-time enters the scene, waste starts to accumulate and affect the organization as a whole.

Every organization, in any size, should design, revise, and stabilize its communication processes and not assume that the right balance happens by default. Each type of feedback has its appropriate cadence. Lots of casual communication is not a good replacement for established communication processes — it's like leaving the door open for the dead-time enemy to settle in.

In small organizations the communication processes revolve around one or a few dominant people who are also the busiest in the organization. If they change meeting schedules frequently, they become the main source of disruption and cause a lot of dead-time. The most important people in the organization are also the biggest potential disruptors. With time their organizations become less efficient, and as a result of it the busy people become even busier. It's a vicious cycle. As the leader of the organization, you need to give up the right to call any meeting any time, and that requires willpower.

In large organizations, you also need to be cautious about *communication stovepipes*. With any change or a new reality, you need to revise the cross-functional communication processes to prevent the departments from driving in different directions. The case of Sony, the dominant company for decades in electronic entertainment, shows us how destructive it can be. Sony had all the ingredients for the revolution in cloud-based digital entertainment, and yet, by its own admission, it allowed Apple to take the lead. Stovepipe communication was so entrenched in the company that the departments did not cooperate. In 2005 they hired an outsider CEO, Sir Howard Stringer, to overcome the cultural stovepipe barriers. He attempted to create new cross-functional communication processes; however, the sins of the past had already gone too far at that point.

Positive or negative feedback — what should we use? A *consultative approach to giving feedback* can transform almost any negative feedback to a somewhat positive one. Instead of ... *I don't want you to do this* ... you can offer ... *I see how you have done this — let's examine other options* ... Or, you could change a statement of ... *the result is unsatisfactory* to ... *it is a step in the right direction; let's examine the next steps* ... The behavior of the

manager in giving feedback could make a huge difference, one feedback at a time.

This consultative approach to giving feedback may seem like giving a marketing spin to the reality, but we can't deny the psychology of people in how they react to negative feedback. When we add to negativity we hurt productivity, and that is a well-established fact. It's not about being right; it's a matter of being smart. *Consultative feedback is constructive feedback.* The only exception is when you deal with a case of misconduct; here the message needs to be loud and clear … *stop doing that, or else …*

Moreover, in group meetings, be extremely careful with any negative feedback as it may cause shaming — an environment with shamed employees doesn't function very well at all.

Righteousness is the *communication Achilles heel* of many otherwise very good managers and leaders. When speaking from a position of absolutism of any kind — righteousness or purism — any well-meaning feedback can be totally spoiled and work opposite to the intent. When there's no absolute reason to adopt an absolute principle, it's much more productive to use the logic of psychology and apply the principles of motivation and effective communication.

ABSOLUTISM STORY AND DESTRUCTIVE FEEDBACK

I once worked with a business line where the leader had absolute principles, especially in sales and in achieving the quarterly forecasts. At that time, the sales of the new business line were slightly overachieving the targets, and since the leader believed in pure sales management practices, he raised the targets. His team kept warning that the new product was not ready for all applications, and that the

(Continued)

(Continued)

target market should be limited to where the product functioned well, but he didn't want to change the targets — a goal is a goal, and he expected his team to reach it. With the raised targets engineering had to create customized solutions to allow sales to reach beyond the product's *comfort zone*. Sales reps convinced prospective customers to accept customized versions of the product, and the sales of that quarter reached 95% of the raised goal.

The principled leader declared it as a total failure of all involved, engineering and sales together. The failure, however, was in sticking to the unrealistic goals, quite obviously. The damage was more than missing the goal; customized solutions required later customized service and that's both costly and a burden to productivity. Even more damaging to the morale were the messages coming from his purist's view ... *we missed the quarterly goal and that's all that matters...* We all knew that the goal was an arbitrary number that represented the wishful thinking of an overzealous leader who wanted to impress himself and the investors.

This leader's communication practices, always purist and totalitarian, were so notorious that his leadership team and managers would follow behind him after every one of his forays around the company, to ensure that the employees were not too upset to continue to work.

*

In exceptional situations not giving feedback is the strongest and most effective feedback of them all, as you'll see in the following story.

ARRIVED LIKE A LION AND LEFT LIKE A LAMB

Several times in my career as an executive, I was parachuted in from the outside — hired to replace someone, or assigned a newly created position. Being an outsider put me in the suspicion zone initially. Managers and employees had to adjust to the reality of a new executive with a bit of a foreign accent from the less commonly seen gender. Other people had to overcome their disappointment in being passed over for the position I was hired to fill.

This specific story started when the announcement of my appointment went over email to my employees who were spread in a few countries. Mostly, I received congratulatory and welcoming emails in reaction to the announcement, but there was one email, particularly long, that spelled out a litany of requirements that I had to fulfill in order for the sender to be able to work for me.

Well! This was my first day on the new job; I had not even been through the first reality test. In its text, this email didn't really say much beyond the list of requirements, but *between* the lines I could hear the real message loud and clear. This was my dilemma — how could I respond to a message that existed only between the lines?

Despite my strict rule of not letting anyone wait for an answer, I decided to let this one simmer for a while. After a few days, I suggested a short call with the intent to propose a one-on-one meeting in a neutral location — neither his office, nor mine. We then scheduled an afternoon meeting with no time limit. Two weeks had passed since his email; when we finally met, the visual effect of the first few minutes added a comical streak to the situation; the man was huge — twice my size.

(Continued)

(*Continued*)

I decided not to react to the email at all, and after a few pleasantries I moved directly to discuss his area of responsibility, the challenges that he sees, some of the thoughts he had for improving things in his job and mine. We spent three hours in consultative interactions and concluded the meeting with an action plan that included only a sprinkle of new ideas from me; the bulk of it was his.

Before leaving for the day, he said openly that he appreciated the time I took to review his role and that he saw that he could learn a lot from me; he hoped to be able to work with me for a long time.

A few days later when my boss, apparently from hearing some rumblings in his office, asked me about our meeting, I responded … *the gentleman arrived like a lion and left like a lamb* … And that is how I like to tell this story.

Obviously, any reaction to his email — positive or negative — especially if I had retorted a *response in kind*, could not have ended in a productive result. The delayed meeting was the right response. We started a very productive and mutually beneficial work relationship, which lasted as long as I was there. Holding back, and not providing feedback, in this very special case, was a very strong and effective feedback indeed.

Sensitive Meetings

24

Company success is *10% strategy* and *90% execution* and this is also the correct balance of information exchanged in most meetings. We set meetings to discuss operational strategy subjects — plans, coordination, adjustments, information sharing — and also to reinforce the company's global strategy — industry, competitive landscape, and strategic moves. The meeting is usually about what to do and how; and referring to the elements of the global strategy reminds the participants of the reasons why.

As discussed in Chapter 21, a meeting to discuss sensitive information requires more than the general practice of audience consideration. As a manager, you will have to deal with *adverse situations*, or discuss *uncomfortable topics*; it's an essential and crucial part of the job.

Some sensitive meetings such as ending someone's employment, or putting an employee on warning follow a strict protocol. Such meetings are unpleasant, but not difficult to deliver because the messages are clear, and the protocol dictates the method of delivery. In these meetings, the manager talks and the employee listens; the protocol doesn't leave room for discussion.

In less extreme situations, however, the *intent* of communicating sensitive information should be to *extract good from the bad* and to mitigate the collateral damage. For example, if the manager needs to tell the employees that there will be no annual raise (bad news), he would want to extract a commitment from them to work on improving the future (the good), despite the bad news.

Sensitive situations and conditions require techniques that are more refined — keeping in mind possible scenarios and planning what to say. Use and practice the following rules; they apply in most scenarios.

Let the Facts Do the Talking

People would be more logical if they are presented with the evidence, even when they are affected emotionally. However, you have to ensure that you don't twist the evidence into criticism. For example, if you say ...*the fact is that you refused to do it...* the employee might think otherwise ...*the fact is that you don't know what's possible — I didn't refuse, I just couldn't...* Staying factual means that you speak about whether it was done or not, without accusation, as in ...*let's agree that it needs to be done and let's see how...* As opposed to judgments, facts are devoid of emotions, and that's why they are more effective.

Open Discussion

Emotionally charged meetings are complex. The emotional layers are usually not fully exposed, and the meeting is set to find a solution to the main problem and not to address the emotions, even though they play a role. Time is a great healer of bad emotions and that's why it's so important not to rush such a meeting to conclusion once the solution is found. Allow all sides to express themselves fully; your role is to create the open and respectful environment for the discussion and extinguish any sign of disrespect.

Oral Communication vs. Written

Refrain as much as possible from writing about sensitive topics. Discuss, present, but don't write. Never trust that your email is confidential and is not circulating without your control. I've seen embarrassing situations that started with a careless forwarding of an email, not to mention when the

forwarding is done intentionally, or IT leaks it from behind the scene. With sensitive information communicate face to face, by phone, or by video calling — nothing in writing unless it's a formal warning.

Shaming

Shaming is disrespectful. Never use shaming intentionally or unintentionally. All managers who still live in the past (I've met a few) and intentionally embarrass individuals in front others, because ...*that's the only way they will learn...*, should listen to the research that proves that fear and intimidation don't work. Human knowledge and motivation are the most essential raw materials of today's factories — shaming kills motivation and harms how the knowledge is applied.

Listen More than You Talk

Better managers listen more and speak less, in general. With sensitive information and situations, it's even more important to listen. Active listening — short and open questions that solicit long answers — allows you to know more about what the other thinks, and then you can select just the right words and arguments. The skill of active listening requires time, patience, practice, and discipline, but it's worth the effort and investment.

Beware of Emotions

Emotions are mostly hidden; but you should be constantly aware that they play an active role in all human activity. Negative emotions are the reasons for intractable behaviors, employee performance issues, prolonged discussions with no resolution, and customers or suppliers who are too quiet. As a manager, you need to recognize the symptoms, and respect and address the emotional sides even when it's not explicitly shown.

A powerful technique directed at the brain's chemistry is to elevate the discussion and talk about the concepts. It's easier to talk about concepts because they create a distance from the negative emotions. From a higher-level discussion you can lead the conversation to the real issues. But at that point you've already created a better atmosphere for the harder discussion.

Let's review a few common scenarios of sensitive information.

Talking About Compensation

Sales compensation with its significant commission component reflects a direct link between performance and pay. The system is accepted as fair even though there are many conflicts related to territory allocations and commission splits when more than one person claims credit for a deal.

However, other than in sales positions, it's hard to find and accept the fairness. Salaries are usually drawn from market standards, bonuses are subject to rules and limits, and raises and stock options are restricted by company policies. The direct link between performance and pay is lost, and top performers are never paid relative to their contribution.

A compensation conversation with a *top performer,* therefore, is a sensitive discussion, as managers need to overcome the unfairness of the system and explain that their discretion in making compensation decisions is limited to a small percentage of the employee's pay. The burden of communicating about compensation is always a challenge for managers.

Resolving Conflicts

Conflicts happen on all frontlines, i.e., within and between teams, with upper management, clients, or suppliers. Conflicts could be explicit, or implicitly described as *difficulty.* The manager's role is to resolve conflicts and find the middle ground that the sides can live with.

In conflicts, each side believes that their position is justified. Some people tend to be more self-justified than others, and they create more conflict around them. To move the parties from a stalemate to a productive state, you may favor one party, mediate among the parties based on common ground, or find an alternative. Either way, it would be futile and damaging to show to the losing side that they are less justified and

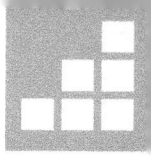

completely noneducational to show to the winning side that they are more right. Always present the resolution as the best solution by emphasizing the facts.

A conflict is inherently fraught with emotions of anger, frustration, threat, fear, shame, and neglect; none are helpful to motivation and productivity. As well as dissolving the entanglement, your role is also to quench these negative emotions, but not by squashing them. It's because of these emotions that conflict resolution takes time and several iterations to ensure that no live embers are left to start the fire again.

The basic technique in resolving conflicts is to focus the sides on their common future. Arguing the past is futile; each side has its reasons, which is why we are in a state of conflict. First, you should give all sides the time to present their positions and justifications fully and genuinely, and then ensure that everyone understands and recognizes them. This baseline is needed so that the emotions take a minor backseat and remain in it. Only then you lead the discussion to the options of the common future; the emotions will play a smaller role and logic will prevail.

Communicating About Missed Expectations

If you're disappointed with your team's results or from insufficient cooperation from other teams, clients, or suppliers, the reason could be that the expectations are unrealistic or the communication is inadequate.

Missed expectations are similar to conflicts. Your expectation is justified, hopefully, and the side that didn't deliver has its own reasons. The emotional overtone is of frustration and helplessness. Communication, however, cannot be perfect all the time; if lack of communication is isolated, it won't develop into a serious problem of missing expectation. However, if a team has a tendency to be disappointed or disappoint others, you need to revisit the communication practices.

For example, annual performance reviews generate a lot of missed expectations. Anyone who doesn't pass with flying colors is a prospective disappointed employee. Usually, you cannot keep up with all the changes that happen in today's work environments, and a year is too long to keep records and review. Because the process is outdated, its discussion about expectations doesn't have a chance to be effective.

The technique to address missed expectations is to let the facts do the talking and not to pass judgment. State the evidence, discuss a corrective plan, and agree on improved communication going forward. If missed expectations persist, it would be fair to conclude that the goals are unrealistic; better communication cannot solve real blocking factors.

Responding to Pushback

When *missed expectation* develops into a *conflict,* it's *pushback.* Below is a rough outline of a pushback:

- *I expected you to do something.*
- *You didn't do it. You missed my expectation.*

And now the pushback:

- *I will not do it, because …*

To address the pushback, first try to transform it from a mini-conflict (with growth potential) to missed expectation, and then discuss facts and solutions, as in the two rough outlines below:

- *I see that you rejected my request, and I understand your reasons, but I request that we meet to present both sides, see the problem and look for solutions jointly.*
- *I see that you rejected my request, and I'm not sure I understand your reasons; regardless, I propose a meeting to…*

Mean Means of Communication

25

Anything on steroids is only a temporary solution, at best. Some of the latest communication phenomena, such as social networks and super chats, are just that — communication on steroids.

Modern life has given a whole new meaning to *Timing is Everything*. We used to say *perfect timing* whenever planning met luck, but now planning has become outdated for some aspects of life, and to meet luck you have to be where luck makes its rounds. It seems to me that you don't even exist unless you are on Facebook; everybody is there, even though Lady Luck doesn't visit.

We want immediacy in communication nowadays; we seem to wait for luck, with our social networks and chat apps antennas in alert mode all the time. Mobile technology makes everything quick; we're constantly in a *praying* position, with our heads down looking at our mobile devices and waiting for luck.

We have new definitions for friends, acquaintances, business contacts, and colleagues. If you add all your connections from email, social networks, chat apps, and virtual communities, you have access to thousands of people. A fiction writer I heard recently said that he regularly spends a few hours per week to chat with his worldwide virtual connections, who are total strangers to him, because that's where he gets the weirdest and most creative ideas for his writing.

The world of work becomes more and more web-based; the advantages and disadvantages of these new means of communication are changing rapidly.

Social Networks for Business

IBM and other companies are pushing social business as the new means of communication, both internally and externally with clients and suppliers. The question that remains open is whether it will generate productivity gains. If we look at the spread of computer technology in business since the 1960s, it took more than 30 years to have a positive effect on productivity at a national level. The Nobel Laureate Robert Solow, who studied economic growth, states in his 1987 *computer paradox*, "...you can see the computer everywhere but in the productivity statistics...".

I predict that social business as a means of communication will take even longer to contribute to productivity, unless we expect a new type of human being who's active socially and is simultaneously more productive as a result of it. With the exception of new businesses that use social networks to make money, such as online media advertising, we have yet to prove that the advantages of this means of communication outweigh the disadvantages.

Social business opens the communication to the connected network and makes it more public. All network members have access to everything currently happening or stored — it's a democratic system. If we control access by categorizing content and authorizing access to subnetworks, the network becomes less social and more like a research repository.

Theoretically, the *power of the crowds* should help members achieve research results faster, as anyone could be an organizer, a reader, an author and a publisher of surveys or discussions. But, if you have ever tried to follow a threaded conversation, you know it's very hard to arrive at any conclusion, even on a task as simple as coordinating an activity. Some networks employ community moderators whose job is to police this type of communication. I still don't see how it could increase the productivity of a business.

Again, theoretically, it's logical to expect advantages from connecting remote members to the center of the action, and provide them with the immediacy they need. However, if you worry about quality and validity of

information, you'll immediately think of limiting social business. And once the network is restricted, it loses the potential advantages, as members will opt for communicating outside.

Many success stories cite the advantages of social communication starting from the release of Web 2.0 technologies. If you allow *crowds to influence the inner workings of your network,* you also have to weigh the risks, as it's difficult to control member behavior inside the network, and impossible when they are outside, on different networks, for example.

Chat and Super-Chat

Setting social business in an organization is a big and irreversible decision that involves risks of losing control. *Chat*, on the other hand, was considered as small decision as long as it was just point to point communication. However, now that mass-chat systems have taken over, many-to-many chats are common and the disadvantages of social communication seep into them. When you encounter names like Jostle, HipChat, Fleep, Contriber, BiTrix24 with Slack leading the pack, you wonder if they were really focusing on productivity of your business. The user testimonials are no more promising, … *I have a feeling of intimacy with co-workers on the other side of the country that's almost fun. That's a big deal, for a job….* Chat is a nice complementary tool for emails and calls; however, constant notifications from multiple chat systems that open simultaneously are already a prevalent annoying disruption.

With one of my clients, the employees were so used to unlimited chatting that we had to declare a closed communication window of 3 hours per day to overcome the constant disruptions. They embraced this aggressive rule and all reported improved focus and productivity.

Chat also disrupts communication threads. Anything that started in email and moved to chat, or vice versa, splits some of the information to multiple locations. Searching and seeing the entire picture are now impossible.

Instead of mass chatting without limits, it could be used productively on *scheduled chat sessions.* As opposed to a meeting, it allows multitasking, and with the right conditions it could add to productivity. I've seen software development teams keep a chat line open while working on the same code from two different countries. The open chat line allowed the two teams to work as one. Another advantage discovered accidentally is that chat, unlike voice, isn't sensitive to foreign accents and less sensitive to language proficiency.

Chat notification features, such as vibration, flash alerts, beeps, pop-up notifications, and the likes are bad for the work environment. For a meeting to be productive, make it a rule that all notifications are off, even the so-called silent ones. Anything that might only be tickling gently in someone's pocket disrupts a participant of the meeting, and therefore, all the others. Let's accept it and enforce true focus!

Modern means of communication are here to stay in the workplace. We need to be selective and consider the effects on productivity of having multiple systems. As the manager, you decide and enforce the appropriate usage and lead by example.

B2B Marketing Basics

PART VI

The Bedrock Under Marketing

... We have to very rapidly establish the world we are transporting them to. That's very easily done by saying ... In a World Where ... You very rapidly set the scene ...

Don LaFontaine, 2007

The late Don LaFontaine created a little business empire simply by matching his deep throaty voice with the half sentence ... *In a World Where*.... Don the *Thunder Throat* recorded five thousand film trailers and hundreds of thousands of promotions, advertisements, and other voiceover acting pieces. He became the de-facto standard for voiceover productions; if you've been to the movies, you'd recognize the voice immediately when you hear it. In a 2007 TV interview, he explained his signature phrase ... *In a World Where* ... and with it summarized the essence of marketing.

We have to very rapidly establish the world we are transporting them to. That's very easily done by saying ...In a World Where... You very rapidly set the scene.

The function of sales in business-to-business (B2B) is to *convince* the customers to buy. Marketing needs to develop the market, to *set the scene* so that sales' work is easier. It isn't simple to sell or market complex offerings, and that's why sales and marketing evolved into more complex organizations and functions. If we want to keep these functions lean, we need to examine these organizations, reduce the auxiliary activity, and set the goals as close as possible to the narrow definitions of selling and setting the scene.

For example, sales people should not spend much time on online CRM systems to create, categorize, and organize data; I've seen tiny companies obsessed with data, spending more time on it than in active communication and prospecting sales opportunities. Obviously, it's the wrong balance of using time. The process and its tools should never dilute the main activity; *sales should sell and marketing should set the scene.*

An old boss of mine once said ... *the trick is how to sell! If you can sell it, I will find someone who can make it* ... Simply put, the goal of the entire business organization is to grow sales and increase profit; all managers in the organization serve these goals collectively, including those in fulfillment, delivery, and administration. Therefore, all managers should understand the basic principles of sales and marketing which are the spearheads of the company.

The Marketing function in the organization produces messages, materials, events, publicity, and information to build the market position of the company, and serve the sales function. However, these activities are not done in a vacuum; they all relate to the environment where the company operates.

It's like building a structure on foundations that are anchored inside bedrock. You have to understand the qualities of the bedrock, or the structure could be overdesigned and wasteful or underdesigned and vulnerable to the elements.

The key layers of this bedrock are evolving stories about everything that influences the work of marketing. Economy, technology, competition, buying preferences, and partnerships are the main themes of these stories as they explain why the company exists. The audience for the stories is diverse, i.e., employees, customers, partners, analysts, and the media.

Messaging in Relation to Global Economy

The high and low tides of the global economies influence the company's strategy. For example, as of 2012, China plans to build 100 airports. This construction boom is a target market and a trigger for new trends in airport-related technologies — security, billboard advertising, navigation, electronic ticketing, electronic identification, etc.

Asian economies, in general, are projected to grow faster than others, but pricing for these markets is considerably lower than in other regions for most products. A typical B2B offering needs versions suitable for these markets, versions that cost less to produce and sell. Any competitive offering that has high sales activity in Asia can cause lower price trickling into your market. In a global economy, everything is linked.

The global economy also affects *buying moods and investment sentiments*. Depending on the prevailing moods, prospective buyers might be sitting on their money and buying only for current needs, or on the other hand, joining in a trend of technology investments for future development.

Government policies and regulations of a dominant country also create new buying trends, and in the current global economy, those trends are likely to extend beyond borders.

A company's most basic marketing story is how it fits in the global picture. It tells how the massive trends of globalization, technology, and Internet affect their product, pricing, and market reach, and how they promote the company and its products. This is a critical story that every manager should be able to tell with confidence.

Messaging in Relation to Local Economy

The *Local Economy* of our target market brings us closer to understanding our B2B customers. Their considerations are our considerations as well. Is their market growing? Are we competing with higher priority items? What are the funding possibilities and how much risk will they tolerate? Do they need to comply with regulations? Will they gain tax benefits? All of these considerations are as important to the customer as the promised ROI.

The local economy of customers affects their buying moods and investment sentiments even more than the global economy; it's closer to the customers' hearts and minds. In a depressed area, the customer is unlikely to pay premium prices for enhanced features — the ROI might be convincing, but the local mood is not supportive. In a booming area, on the other hand, hot and cool features can make the difference between two competitive products.

Every local-economy story fits a specific target market; there's no *one size fits all*. Following the process of *segmentation*, marketing develops the understanding of each local market separately. A very large customer is treated as a local market on its own, and its story is tailored accordingly. The *ultimate segmentation* is done one customer at a time.

In addition to sales and marketing, these local-economy stories also help managers understand the variety of go-to-market strategies and make better decisions when they support field activities. It's also the brief that anyone should study before facing a customer.

Technology Messaging

Depending on how customers see it, the technology inside the product could lift the sales process or hurt it. For a conservative customer, *advanced technology* could be too advanced and delay a purchase, while for an early adopter it can be the reason to buy it. When new technology is the main theme of a sales campaign, the situation is inherently more competitive. Especially when addressing existing customers, the new technology opens their minds to competitive options as well. You are walking a fine line when talking about new technologies to existing customers, but as Clay Christensen's *Innovators Dilemma* explains the disruptive technology cycles, you cannot postpone innovation for too long either.

The power of the technology inside the product is in *feature-to-feature competition*. This could seal a deal in the early adoption phase, when customers buy the product for better features. But when we address the mainstream buyers, other considerations are more important, e.g., product utility, true ROI economics, entry price, and quality of vendor (*Crossing

the Chasm, Geoffrey Moore). Only rarely can a product sell on technology *innovation* repeatedly, and it's usually in the space of consumer products and not in B2B, where purchases are more rational.

A *superior technology* could help or hurt the sales process, but *inferior technology* works only in one way — the product is inherently in a defensive mode that will become indefensible with growing competition. The product might still be price-competitive in certain markets where it's good enough, but continuing profit erosion will eventually kill it. The marketing story that sustains the product for the rest of its sellable life is *good-enough product that is cheap.*

Also tricky to sustain is the startup story of *unique technology*; you might believe it's an advantage when actually it's a disadvantage. Having to *defend uniqueness* continuously wears the company's resources, sometimes all the way to breaking point.

POSITIONING UNIQUE TECHNOLOGY

The story of a company from my past illustrates the problem of positioning unique technology. Their product was an expensive inspection machine that automatically finds defects inside electronic components, before incorporating them into finished products. The company chose a superior technology that gave the best results. Customer adoption was wide despite the high price, as it replaced Sisyphean manual work and the value was justified.

The success of the company brought about competition that offered a good-enough solution with simpler technology. The company had to defend continuously the advantages of the more esoteric technology over the new competitor that was cheaper and much easier to understand. The competition between them developed

(Continued)

(Continued)

into a price war. Our company was limited by higher costs on how far it could lower the price, and the competitor enjoyed the price shelter. Their lower costs allowed them to be cheaper and still gain high margins.

With the price war going on for a while, the profits were no longer enough to sustain our company and the cheaper competitor eventually acquired it and eliminated the competition from this niche market. Very quickly, though, the acquiring company turned around and adopted the more expensive technology, eventually eliminating its original product-line, while raising sales prices to a sustainable level. The best technology eventually won, but the company that created it lost.

Marketing should create the *technology value story in relation to other technologies, and use the simplest conceptual terminology that everyone can understand.* Marketing's job is to position the technology correctly for the variety of sales situations.

The Language of Competition

Marketing develops the understanding of offerings that compete directly or indirectly with the company. Anything that interferes with the sales activity is classified as competition.

One of the most common tools is the *Feature Comparison Table* that shows advantages over competitive products. These comparisons educate sales personnel, but they usually don't work well with customers as a sales tool. It's very likely that competitors present similar lists to them, but with different conclusions. A comparison table could also turn into a trap for a sales person who cannot handle the questions that the

customers raise on the competitive features. As a sales tool, the features alone can never tell the entire story of why one company leads and the other lags.

Other marketing tools that don't work as expected are *kill the enemy* programs. If they manage to damage the competition, it's because the company's *incentive programs* give away too much value for the same price, eventually sacrificing the product's real value for the longer term. Customers perceive incentive programs as weakness, and they quickly learn how to take advantage of them even after the program ends. You could clearly see a little bit of suicide in every *kill the enemy* story. Samson's account wasn't a success — he died together with his enemies (Judges 16).

More than just killing the enemy, the story that sales tells customers has to have true and lasting value that their company is building to gain advantage over the competition. It's the difference between strategic value and price decisions and short-term marketing programs to inflate sales results relative to competitors.

To assess the overall competitive strength of companies that operate in the same space, use Gartner's Magic Quadrant Model (see Chapter 16). This *map of the competitive landscape* divides competitors into leaders, visionaries, challengers, and niche players based on the combination of *completeness of vision* and *ability to execute*. Because the model focuses on companies and not on specific products, the competitive strength is assessed more broadly. Rather than comparing products and deciding which is better, this competitive landscape shows more options that customers have to spend their money and gain the value that they are interested in.

Of these options, a few are *direct competition* of a similar product from a competitor, and others are *indirect competition* of alternative approaches to solve the problem from a competitor. If the customer prefers to *do nothing*, it is yet another form of indirect competition.

Indirect competition could also develop as a negative outcome of a partnering relationship. A company could bring a partner into its target market to enhance the product value, or gain broader market reach. With time, these partners could see a higher gain for themselves by addressing the customers directly with alternatives. The partners might still continue to work together, but since they also work separately in the same target market, the relationship is now *coopetition* which is a *respect-and-suspect* relationship.

A special case of coopetition is internal competition or *cannibalization*, when one of the company's products competes against another. It's usually large companies that cannibalize their own products. When a cheaper competitor enters into the market segment, the company will think more about protecting its future rather than getting maximum profits from a specific deal. Cannibalization often happens during product transitions from one generation to another; the new product offers more for a better price, and the customers might choose it over their prior intent to buy more of the older product.

Product transitions could also develop into *backdoor competition*. When a company lowers its attention on an aging product line because they are successful elsewhere, a competitor might grab this neglected market segment and develop a niche product for it. At first, this new competitor is unnoticed, but then they could follow the company's footsteps and quickly turn into a competitor for the entire portfolio. These competitive developments are usually irreversible; the company that neglected the niche segment is left only with stories of past glory.

The language of competition continues to develop faster and with much more complexity. With the Internet and social connectivity, sales people have less control over information that flows to their customers. The Internet has brought the sales function back to human basics — *it's more about the people and less about the products*; the real differentiators between vendors are *relationships, ease of doing business, and overall quality-of-service*.

Buying Models

Buying models tell us about customers' buying habits. They might prefer complete solutions, or buy best-of-breed products and create in-house solutions. A buying model could also develop into a trend and a separate market segment. For example, *Infrastructure as a Service and SAAS (software as a service)* are prevalent buying models because they let customers avoid building IT infrastructure and buy software in the cloud.

If customers insist on a *must-have feature*, then that feature becomes a buying model, and it doesn't matter if you think that the feature itself has no true value. The following story illustrates it.

THE FEATURE THAT MADE THE DEAL

Before the era of computerized control systems, the managers of large industrial plants used the control rooms of these sites as showrooms. Plant managers of oil refineries and large food factories explained the process to their visitors on a big board that showed the schematic of the plant and the current status, with flashing lights and moving needles on meters. The operators of the plant were constantly moving in the room, monitoring, and adjusting buttons on the instruments of this control panel. For the visitors that was a live show in real time.

Outside the control room, a plant's structure has thousands of interconnected pieces of equipment — pipes, valves, vessels, reactors, rotators, heaters, coolers, etc. Process changes are common, and they require physical changes in the plant's structure as well as in the control room.

(Continued)

(Continued)

These updated changes on the big board control panel often spoiled its esthetics. Then came the product that solved the problem — the mosaic mimic board. This was a Lego-like grid with small plastic squares that also held the instruments. Updating it with the process changes meant buying new pieces and moving pieces on the grid — the esthetics of the board remained intact. But, the board was always waiting for the parts to arrive — it was mostly outdated. The operators had no use for it anyway; they memorized the process and kept up with the changes as they occurred.

Computers changed all of that; even with the technology of the 80s it was easy and fast to make updates, and all the data of the meters, controllers, and buttons was now on computer screens. There was no more need for quivering needles or flashing lights on big boards; the operators were now sitting in comfortable chairs highly focused on the small screens.

Computers made it better for the plant and for the operators, but plant managers lost the show that entertained their visitors, and they did not like it. Throughout the 80s they continued to require the big room with the live mimic board, even though it was completely unnecessary, useless, expensive, and outdated.

As a vendor selling computerized control rooms, you also had to offer a board of plastics if you wanted to be considered for the job; it became a buying model that was more important than the real features.

The modern version of the story happens often with B2B products that deliver better results, but fall short on visual presentation, such as attractive dashboards. The *show-and-tell features* should be treated as a *buying model* that cannot be ignored in the design phase — that's the customers' preference.

Packaging and *Compatibility* also dictate the customers' preferences. A startup product with unique technology might have the best performance, but customers would prefer to buy a portfolio of products for a larger set of problems, and not let a niche product or a niche problem break their technology buying standards.

A common buying model in IT is *products packaged in a service.* During the 1990s, IBM, with the leadership of Lou Gerstner, built most of its B2B revenue around services — their customers bought complete projects, from requirements to functioning systems at the customer site, sometimes including the operation afterwards. They redefined the *turnkey* buying model, and saved IBM at the same time. Much of the high-end IT business — as high as 30% — is done through turnkey projects. All major vendors adapted their offerings to include services while blocking access to small vendors who could not offer full packages.

Pricing models are also a form of buying model. *Pay-as-you-grow*, like SAAS, is such a *usage-based* model that makes the entry-level pricing very low. Internet publishing and advertising offerings come in many variants of *view + click + action*; *pay-per-click* and *pay-per-impression* are the most common.

Newer buying models on the Internet are buyer-friendly *information and experience centers* and *dominant marketplaces*, both for consumer and B2B markets. TripAdvisor, for example, with its rich social networking features is the click-to place for leisure travel; another example are the new browser features that Google releases continually to its users that gradually eliminate the need for other aggregators.

Buying models represent *the way customers want to buy.* Marketing should develop these constantly evolving stories and educate the rest of the organization, because although going against the grain is important for product innovation, buying models are usually very hard to overcome. When buying B2B products, customers examine the options and follow their buying patterns of similar or complementary products. Going against these standards is like expecting a miracle — they do happen, but they are rare.

Complementary Products and Partners

Complementary products and services from other companies enhance the overall value to the customer; they are sometimes necessary to make a deal happen. The preferred partners to work with address the same market with complementary products that don't compete with yours.

The key question to ask when considering a partner is *who is pulling whom*; not in a single deal, but over time and in more market segments. If your startup product doesn't offer sufficient value, you'd prefer a partner that pulls you into their market; you save expenses and validate your product. These advantages, however, diminish over time. As the partner's offering matures, the need for your product decreases, or, the partner downgrades its importance and forces you to reduce the price. If your partner has a strong market presence, you're vulnerable. You could benefit from the partnership for a while, but at the same time you have to invest in the value of the product so that it could stand on its own, or find more ways to reach customers.

If you are the strong side of the partnership, you also face risks. The weaker partner could be too weak to support a successful program, or be a target for acquisition by a competitor and leave you exposed. That's why the strong partners often acquire the weak partners. Such is the case with companies that make *compatibility gateways* that offer a temporary solution to a missing feature. With time, customers exert pressure on the company to enhance the main product and eliminate the need for them — gateways usually have a short lifespan.

A balanced partnership between two equally strong partners has a better chance to survive. However, these tend to develop into coopetition realities; as each partner wants a bigger piece of the pie, they gradually enhance their products and services, and encroach onto each other's space.

Three-way partnerships are especially vulnerable. It is very difficult to balance the relationship of two partners over time — three are almost impossible to sustain. At first, the three-way agreement addresses the current and future interests of the sides, but cracks appear as things

develop, and renegotiation is highly impractical. If this kind of partnership is needed, it's better to form an independent entity with the three partners as its board of directors.

A whole new set of partnership concepts and complementary offerings are an essential part of commercial life on the Internet. Partners collect a few cents from each transaction in which they are involved — it's a volume business. Mostly, these partnerships are completely invisible to the seller or the clicking buyer. Between them there are many interlocking commercial agreements of traffic generation and technology companies that bite into the overall profit of the transaction. It's similar to the world of stock market trading but with a lot less regulation. With time and consolidation of the industry, many of these background players will be absorbed or disappear.

All partnerships carry problems and risks that should be weighed against the benefits. Few companies are as strong as Apple that owns all the customer-visible parts — products, services, stores — to the extent that they can dominate their large partners, i.e., hardware suppliers, and their small partners as well, i.e., application developers. In many B2B scenarios, companies depend on partners to succeed and grow.

Since the *value of partnership changes over time,* you need to evaluate and adjust all the elements of the strategy, one partner at a time, and prepare alternatives in case of breakage (Table 1).

Table 1   Partner Assessment Checklist

Partner Strategy Checklist
Who are the prospective partners that operate in the same market?
What completes my strategy: product, solution, customer reach?
How do they improve my position in the market?
What are the potential developments: technology, M&A?
What assets can I leverage and for how long?
What are the investments to develop a fruitful partnership?
How many alternatives do I need to develop?

Managers from many departments are involved with partners, starting from the administrative perspective to engineering and sales. Marketing is the function that unites all interests. Each partnership is a continuously evolving story that guides all the relevant decisions throughout the company.

Marketing Building Blocks

27

The bedrock stories about economy, technology, competition, buying preferences, and partnerships are the background for the company's strategy. Marketing produces and maintains these stories for use by all employees and especially for managers. They are also the background for marketing's main work — building the company's position and supporting sales. If we skip the development of the background stories, the components of the marketing plan will have to go through many revisions, and much work will be wasted in the process of creating the value proposition, segmentation, events, positioning, messaging, collateral materials, analysis, and publications.

After the bedrock stories, the first step in building the marketing plan is to create its *building blocks*. We develop an understanding of the *target markets* by segmenting them, we create *value propositions* for each segment, and then refine the *messages* that express these value statements. All other components of the marketing plan are methods of delivery of these basic building blocks.

Marketing needs the full participation of sales, senior technologists, and upper management in creating the building blocks. Good marketing material presents vetted ideas that are deliberated, tested, and have broad consensus. Without cross-functional participation the material will be revised again and again, and in many cases just make rounds without conclusion.

A common problem for marketing is that others think that they could do their work better than them. Because we are all consumers of products and information, we have opinions and convictions about marketing deliverables. Senior managers have personal preferences related to their marketing material, and they often influence the marketing outputs without giving enough consideration to the target audience. Therefore, the quality of marketing output is often compromised. A common symptom of this problem is the abundance of very busy slides in presentations — good marketing professionals, who remember their basic education, would never produce such slides.

Reaching agreement and producing high quality marketing building blocks is best done in a *marketing workshop* with full participation of all stakeholders. The workshop resolves differences in opinion, clarifies and crystalizes the main use-cases, themes and messages, and produces the supporting evidence that good marketing material needs.

Marketing Workshop

In a B2B marketing workshop, we profile the target audience and create segments. We then tailor a value proposition to each segment, refine the messages, and select convincing proofs for each value claim.

People's profiles play a major role in their capacity as decision makers. Similar to the marketing of consumer products, we want to know the typical profession, seniority, academic background, experience, and demographics of the consumers of our marketing material — customers, partners, and suppliers.

As an example, the profile of senior medical staff and executives of a large hospital chain is: *accomplished people with medical background, interested in business and operations of healthcare organizations, and in community and social missions.*

The following examples show how to use what we learn from the profiles. The subtleties that are demonstrated here make a big difference in the audience's reaction to us.

- Baseball analogies remind Europeans that they are dealing with foreigners — when we use them, we create distance instead of the closeness that we want.
- Executives — CIOs, CFOs, and CEOs — are interested in technology concepts more than in technical details. Always start with a conceptual diagram and limit the details.
- Europeans find an argument more convincing if the reference is also European; in some cases it needs to be from the same country.

To continue the profiling, we also consider the target audience's *predispositions and job aspects* — their ecosystem, company size, main challenges, and priorities. What's on their minds when they consume our material — is it budget, HR, productivity, or prestige?

Their job aspects could be a selection from this list:

- It's a fast paced job with a lot of pressure.
- The job is repetitive and monotonous.
- Employees need to adjust to a lot of change.
- It's a growth area with time-to-market focus.
- Cost control and savings are a constant focus.
- Employees' skills are lacking.

For example, anything that we would present to the head of engineering in a hi-tech company should consider his usual predispositions: time management, setting priorities, dealing with pressure, closing competitive gaps, shortage of skilled people, tough boss, and tight budgets.

Now that we have captured the personal and job points of view of the target audience, we get closer to the messages by finding ways to connect our offering to their context and highest priorities. Our focus is on how our *product* and *company* can help the prospective customer. For example, our offering would reduce their workload by automating certain processes, or improve productivity by raising working conditions and employee morale.

In the following story, I was assisting the general manager of a business unit in resolving operational bottlenecks. Our main problem could be resolved by the huge service organization of the parent company, but first, they had to be convinced to help. I was struggling to find the correct message that would make our issue a high priority for them. We wanted to convince them to support us despite the fact that our volume of business was negligible for them.

A JOURNEY TO FIND THE RIGHT MESSAGE

This business unit sold a new product with goals to increase revenue from the parent company's existing customer base and to penetrate new market segments.

The original design of the product intended to eliminate the need for on-call service entirely, and limit the service to scheduled annual visits; it was an innovative concept at the time for this kind of product. A low-cost service contractor was hired to do this work.

Sales of the product picked up nicely, and all plans worked fine until the early-adopters gained confidence and started to use the product more intensely. Large IT systems are often exposed to quality and performance issues when they're stressed with heavy use, and that was the case for our product. The problems spread quickly throughout our install base, and business slowed as sales and customers lost their confidence. We also received high volumes of service calls and the service contractor couldn't handle them; engineering personnel had to halt further development and step in to resolve the service issues. At that point, the execution of the entire business unit derailed.

(Continued)

(Continued)

The recovery plan included the redesign of parts of the product and an interim survival program. We had to find another solution to provide service and release engineering to work on this plan.

The parent company had a huge service department and the appropriate personnel, but they were busy to capacity supporting hundreds of thousands of units of other products. How could they be bothered with a couple hundred installations of a new product whose future was uncertain? Even getting their attention was a challenge.

To convince them to adopt this baby, I visited their centers all over the world and campaigned for the cause. I presented the vision of the product and the amazing initial success and promise. I explained the recovery plan and the business problem of having to keep customers happy during the recovery period. I also showed that engineering had to be freed to work on the redesign.

As I developed the story, they found it interesting; gradually, my audience turned into converts who volunteered to save this promising, yet currently sick baby.

Ten years later, the product flourished with thousands of installations, and it was all due to the special care it received during its difficult infancy.

I spoke to their professional pride; I presented the problem, but never told them what they had to do, and that's why I succeeded. The managers of the huge service organization were eager to take care of a little problem, beyond their routine work and main issues, and get a sense of accomplishment from it — I just found the way to connect our problem to their hearts.

Value Propositions, Proofs, and Messages

In the marketing workshop, we select *value propositions* from a generic list of values that our product or service could deliver. The generic list includes: increase productivity, reduce costs, reduce risk, open new markets, attract new business, increase quality, increase safety, create competitive advantage, add innovation, create prestige, increase employee morale, and address regulatory requirements.

Once we customize the value propositions to our product, we take these value propositions and *map them to our customer segments*. We use the language and context of the prospective buyers in each segment to express the value propositions in the simplest way possible. To add validity we prepare *proofs* for each value proposition, such as: references, success stories, analysis, supportive arguments, test results, ROI models, trends, graphs. Even if we use the same proof for two segments, we describe it differently depending on the specific audience profile.

For each segment we now have the *customized building blocks* — value propositions, messages, and proofs — that marketing needs to produce high-quality outputs.

The following is a sample of these building blocks from a marketing workshop of a healthcare informatics company.

EXAMPLE: MARKETING BUILDING BLOCKS

The company offers knowledgebase memberships to hospitals and pharmaceutical companies, where the system matches suitable candidates to clinical trials. The vision of the company is to become a dominant exchange between pharmaceuticals and hospitals, and to cut the matching process from years to days. Hospitals provide unidentified patient profiles, and in return get involved in lucrative

(Continued)

(*Continued*)

and prestigious research. The company charges success fees for the matching service, while the membership itself is free. Their conversations with prospects in hospitals and pharmaceuticals are with their medical and research staff, IT professionals, and regulatory officers. The success of the company depends on creating a patient database that's large and diverse enough to find these matches.

The first set of value propositions is for *hospitals and their medical staff*, and these are: entry-level membership is free; membership automates the search and therefore improves research productivity. It helps stressed budgets. Administrative workload is reduced and medical staff gains valuable time. The system is cloud-based, and therefore has only minimal dependency on IT.

The second set of value propositions targets the top priorities of medical staff and corporate management that are specific to *teaching hospitals*. And these are: increase in volumes of research and revenue, and elevated prestige. The automated validation features of the system also improve risk exposure and compliance with regulations.

More value propositions target the needs of the *IT function* to fulfill their promise to hospital administration to automate business intelligence. *Safety and regulations officers* can gain unprecedented access to cross-referenced information and make decisions based on insights.

For *Pharmaceutical companies*, the value propositions are linked directly to cutting the drug-development cycle by a few years, which is an immense productivity gain.

As *proofs* for these value statements, we created scripted queries that showed on a live system how it does the matching. The

(*Continued*)

(Continued)

audience could see that it was fast and accurate, encrypted to satisfy compliance regulations, and with only minimal requirements on the infrastructure.

In this workshop we built customized value propositions and proofs for each target segment of audiences. From here, the marketing department was able to produce their deliverables — brochures, website content, sales presentations — quickly and with high quality.

Proofs are Crucial

In B2B dealings we have to prove every claim of benefit, and the proofs should be convincing.

Relevant *references* or *success cases* are excellent proofs to provide credibility to our value stories. Of these, the best are quotable references — people who agree in advance to be identified and quoted, or even take calls from prospective buyers. References are so valuable that vendors give away the product or service, sometimes, in exchange for a customer's agreement to be quoted.

When references or success cases are not possible we use other proofs to support the value stories — *market trends, needs analysis, test results, ROI Models, analyst reports, logical conclusions, and analogies.*

Market trends prove a *growing need or a growing adoption* of similar solutions. For example, video content on the Internet is constantly growing; therefore, the *need* for technologies to address the demand must be growing as well. You could use this *growing adoption* to convince prospective investors of the market validity and opportunity.

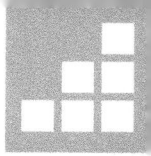

Needs analysis could validate an offering. For example, a prospective customer agrees to an examination of its IT environment, and then to consider technologies that improve productivity. The needs analysis proves the problem, and the customer agrees, in this case, to the implied proposed solutions.

Test results from a lab environment are the closest to real references as possible. When test conditions are close to real environments and customer use-cases, the proofs are accepted as valid.

ROI calculations support value propositions that are explicitly linked to revenue, profit, and cost. The ROI model calculates future cash benefits and compares them to the required investment. ROI models are rarely accurate; they are convincing only when the conclusions are significant, clear, and obvious.

Analyst reports are a strong third-party validation. Even though they're not entirely clear of bias, quoting analysts is a good way to add perspective in support of a point, but it's not strong enough to stand alone as proof.

Logical conclusions and analogies prove that *it must happen here if it happened there*. For example, pharmaceutical safety regulations eventually become a requirement for the food industry. The same government body regulates these industries; it's only logical that the need will be similar in both.

*

In the process of sales of products, services, or ideas, our audience expects to be educated. The proofs are the best way to educate them as closely as possible to our interest. They would not buy unless they understand. An overconfident vendor that assumes that their market position is sufficient, and no further convincing is necessary, will eventually lose. Arrogance always returns as a boomerang to hit the sender.

The lessons from the following story that's taken from my work in the 1980's are still relevant; one overconfident systems integration contractor lost a large public works bid despite being the largest competitor with a huge price advantage.

ONE OVERCONFIDENT VENDOR!

A metropolitan area of three million residents was building a new wastewater treatment facility; it had two main sewage collection plants underground, amidst residential neighborhoods, and a pipeline that pumped the collected sewage to a remote treatment facility in the sand dunes around the city. Above ground were the city's main tourist areas — beaches and important historical sites.

A consortium of municipalities in the metro area owned the project, paid for the construction, and was also responsible for the operation.

The main worry was the possibility of sewage leaks or floods and the potential damage to residential and tourist areas. The control systems had to protect against any possibility of such a disaster. Therefore, the mandatory requirements were strict criteria of triple system redundancy.

Toward the end of construction, the consortium published a bid for the control systems of the entire facility as a turnkey project. The redundancy requirement included duplication of subsystems with automatic transfer of control between them, and using different technologies to prevent any failure in one affecting the other. The required technologies were: analog and digital controllers, computers, wired and wireless communication.

System integration contractors in the area were hungry for projects. Five qualified bidders entered the race with the lowest at $2.2M (real 1980s money) and the highest at $5M. However, three out of the five bidders struggled to comply with some of the bid requirements, so only two bidders remained in the race — the lowest at $2.2M and the one in the middle at $3.8M.

Both bidders knew each other well; employees switched from one to the other regularly. The low bidder was a specialist in public works

(Continued)

(Continued)

clients, where profits are made with cost overruns, while the mid-bidder focused on industrial clients where timely execution is more important. That's why the low bidder could bid so low — they were experts in playing the game of stretching projects and profiting from change-orders.

The low bidder was so confident in their eventual win that they submitted a design, but *provided no evidence* that they could deliver. In addition, their design for the costly redundancy was obfuscated, so much so that the consortium customer requested clarifications from the two remaining bidders.

The mid-bidder had the reputation for fast delivery with high quality, albeit slightly expensive. They followed their normal practice and proposed known components and a proven design that *could be demonstrated.*

The competition manifested as a battle between the promised land and reality. The low bidder continued with overconfident attitude toward the consortium's officials ...*we can deliver – you should trust us...* At the same time the mid-bidder built a demonstration system and invited those officials to watch their system working in simulation, with all the magic of redundancy switching the control from one subsystem to the other.

Even after losing, the low bidder continued with its supercilious attitude when they sued the consortium for unjustifiably favoring a higher bidder. They lost the case again, this time in the courtroom.

With a less haughty attitude, the low bidder could have won the deal; they were a capable contractor, and the price difference was huge. But they didn't focus on the customer's need to have a trustworthy failsafe system against failures. They didn't present a *proven value proposition.*

Collateral Material

28

Marketing collaterals, such as brochures, promotional videos, and whitepapers, come in several formats, with their individual purposes and principles for good design. To develop these collateral materials, the content uses the *building blocks* as main themes, and the *style of delivery* is attuned to the purpose and use.

Though delivery styles might only have slight differences, each difference is significant. For example, in an exhibition hall, you want to *attract relevant audience* to your booth — in the handout flyers you'd use only keywords and simple graphics, such as for an advertisement. The brochure, on the other hand, is meant to support communication with the people who are already engaged with the topic and are there at the booth — it needs to be more detailed.

The most effective style of delivery is storytelling; it makes the flow of content suitable for the audience. People always prefer to follow a story over any form of *corporate speak*. In his 2014 HBR article, *Paul J. Zak* describes his experiments with *storytelling* and how it causes the audiences' brains to release oxytocin — a chemical that makes the story stick with the audience even after it ends. Whenever possible, make text and illustrations look and sound like a story.

Flyers and Landing Pages

A flyer is like an advertisement; its job is to attract attention, bring the readers closer, and make them interested in more information that's available in the brochure. It's a one–two punch device, i.e., one easy message and a pointer to more information. Use simple visuals that can be understood at a glance, or the reader would drop it. Likewise, landing pages are meant to make the viewer click further and deepen the visit on the website.

Brochures and Website Pages

Brochures and website pages are for engaged audiences; they provide more information and technical detail on the value, and are used as reference material. Divide the space and design it in such a way that it's easy and quick for each target audience to find what they want. For example, in medical informatics, we would dedicate separate sections to doctors, administrators, and IT personnel.

Be careful with the graphic design. The effectiveness of brochures and landing pages depends on content brevity, clarity, and quick access — overloaded graphics could deteriorate the quality. On a website, as opposed to printed material, you have more flexibility to design and arrange information in the pages, but the navigation — the clicking tree — needs to be simple with logical connections among texts, illustrations, photos, videos, and demos.

Remote Presentations

A popular form of delivery is to do remote presentations; they save travel time and cost. Video enabled meetings over the Internet are second best to real meeting rooms. With a one-person audience, a computer-to-computer meeting is very productive. With a larger audience, however, you have to consider the limits of common audio and video equipment, and other disruptions that are hard to control from afar. A halfway solution to the problem is the *Webinar* format; it's effective for presentations, but very

limited for interaction. Use them only for training sessions. When designing remote sessions, the material should flow slower than in live meetings, and include pauses to reengage the audience and overcome any monotony that might develop at the remote site.

Demonstrations

Marketing should prepare canned or simulated demos to replace live demos wherever possible. A canned demo is a live demo that follows a strict script; in a simulated demo, on the other hand, we only show how it would look on the system — screenshots of software, for example. Scripted demos, canned or simulated, are more user-friendly than live demos to nontechnical audience, and they don't break the flow of the meeting. Demo scripts should be short, five steps at the most, enough to prove the main point of the demo script, and no more.

Handout Material

Presentations should never be designed as handout material. Handouts have a lot of detail, while presentation slides are as slim as possible. Also, presentation material should never be emailed or left behind. If audiences ask for copies, we engage them in a conversation, understand the real reasons, and then offer proper handouts — a whitepaper or a brochure that tell a success story in context.

Promotional Videos

To produce a promotional video of a technical B2B product, we turn to experienced producers. With their advanced technology and libraries of video, audio, and special effects, they produce dramatic and beautiful films as short as 30 seconds, much like movie promos or television advertisements. Made for TV promos could give us a sense of validation for our product; however, they are effective only with a lot of viewer exposure, i.e., frequent and repeated screenings. Video productions are costly and time-consuming; if you don't see the prospect of your target audience watching them repeatedly, you might as well save the money and effort.

Elevator Pitch

An elevator pitch expresses in lay language what the company does, why it's great, and where it's leading to. It is a short story meant for any unknown audience. Start with an everyday example that anyone could relate to, and continue with the story; for example … *when you go to an ATM machine it gives you cash and the latest data of your account; it's all done by computers talking to computers. We create the software that guarantees that there are no mistakes in the data. That's what we do today. In the future, we will provide similar guarantees to online access of bank accounts. Most banks use our software...*

A good elevator pitch unites all employees on a simple message and turns them into loyal company citizens.

*

More marketing collaterals, such as whitepapers, websites, press releases, conference material, reference sheets, and testimonials, follow the same principles of using the content of the building blocks and designing the delivery according to the purpose and usage. Always use the right tool for the job.

Marketing Events

29

A ny marketing output tied to a date is an event, e.g., conferences, periodical newsletters, seminars, website launches, product launches, and announcements. *Inbound marketing* events strengthen the company's position in the eyes of the employees, while *outbound marketing* events target external audiences, such as current and prospective customers, partners, conference attendees, and analysts.

Producing events with high quality is precision work according to an event calendar that coordinates everyone involved. Managers from all disciplines often contribute to these productions, from setting up and operating the systems, allocating budgets, delivering presentations and demos, and all the marketing work associated with it.

New web and communication technologies enable new event formats. The latest is *virtual social networking events*, as done in the gaming industry. It brings thousands of active virtual participants together to watch broadcasts, interact over social media systems with presenters and other attendees, and participate in challenges and competitions, all from the convenience of their home bases. This type of event is sure to come shortly to a B2B neighborhood near you.

Each type of inbound and outbound marketing event suits its type of audience and purpose. We review a sample of the most common events in B2B and learn how to get the best results from the effort and budget.

Kickoff Conferences

Kickoffs are annual events to re-energize the sales organization and create focus for the year after the intense fourth quarter that just ended. Sales people expect higher goals for the upcoming year and the event needs to convert them into believers that *anything is possible*. The event is oriented on one theme; it's full of success stories and winning attitudes. Any piggyback activity, such as training, that you need to attach to the agenda, should be separated from the main energy-building program as a wedding is from a funeral.

Training, Seminars, Workshops

An agenda that contains only a sequence of presentations cannot be considered as training! Learning happens only with interactions, repetitions, and practice. A one-hour presentation takes up to five times longer to train people how to present it to an audience or how to use the information in it with a product or system.

Training should be done at the right time; well in advance of a new product release, for example, but not too early so that the trainees forget the content by the time they have to use it.

Training sessions that involve travel should take into consideration that trainees are fatigued; training is one type of activity where catch-as-catch-can is a waste of time and effort for all involved.

Town Hall Events

One of the nicest town hall events is the US presidential press conference. The president starts with a few remarks and then members of the press are free to ask any question without limitation. The president answers or declines, as the case may be, all under the gazing eyes of the public. The practice of open press conferences is a sign of strength and confidence that comes with this high-profile office.

Internal town hall meetings in companies keep the employees on the same page; they also address any pent-up frustration or unrest among employees.

These meetings are effective when they work as a slow pressure-release device rather than one big-bang event to solve all problems; therefore, keep the sessions regular and interactive.

Externally with customers and partners, a company is ready to expose itself to the scrutiny of a town hall meeting when their confidence and status are very high. An external town hall meeting is a long-term commitment. Customers and partners, who have the opportunity to question the company directly, and in public, will expect more opportunities to do so. No matter how well the first session turns out, the company cannot renege on the promise.

User-Group Meetings

A user-group meeting is a milder version of the town hall meeting that, once started, cannot be stopped. It's a one to three day event where the company has an opportunity to exchange ideas with its existing customers, and also to allow them to share best practices amongst each other. The atmosphere is usually positive; the facilitator ensures that the meeting doesn't deteriorate into a criticism session. The company is perceived as appreciating the inputs from customers, whatever they are, and any criticism is acknowledged and appreciated, but not rebutted.

The meeting should follow a strict agenda with two to three main themes. The company provides the stage and facilitation, but yields most of the focus to the users. Ideally, participants leave the meeting with an appetite for more and ask for more frequent meetings. To create continuity the session ends with a discussion about ideas for the next session.

Tradeshows

Historically, tradeshows were marketplaces where companies in a specific industry came to trade. Nowadays, it's rare that deals for complex B2B products are consummated during the show itself; the tradeshow is a place for *creating presence, trading information,* and *networking* within the industry.

Creating presence is a slow process that happens by being actively present where everybody else is, i.e., one tradeshow at a time. Tradeshows are also the best place to learn about the competition and technology trends, and for winning best-product awards.

In the preparation phase before the tradeshow, all company participants are trained on the top company messages and how to communicate them. Each participant should have specific goals to collect information and interact with customers and partners. Depending on the conference, speaking opportunities might also be important.

Broadcasts

Video broadcasts to employees, live or recorded, are very common in multinational or large multisite companies; it's the best way to reach remote employees regularly. With customers and partners, however, we limit the broadcasts to written newsletters.

Good newsletter broadcasts take into account that the readers are inundated with information. Their structure should highlight attractive headlines and the rest is clickable content, just like in online news websites. Web analytics and technology can help us optimize the use-cases and increase the effectiveness of the newsletters.

Information and Analysis

30

Business Intelligence (BI) is booming and that's no coincidence. As compared to the days when the phrase originated, today it's even more true that ...*there are only two types of companies: the quick and the dead.* Major macro-forces — population growth, globalization of work and commerce, and technology advancements — mean that companies should make quick decisions and be fast in action. In addition, they also need to be smarter, i.e., make more complex decisions based on analyzed information.

It's marketing's job to stage the company's position on the basis of industry and customer information that they collect and analyze. Information on product usage and adoption patterns is critical to understanding the potential for business expansion. The amount and pace of change require that company managements revise their operational strategies frequently based on marketing's analysis of trends in service, delivery, order fulfillment, and competitive information. More than ever, surviving and thriving companies are genetically obsessed with reviewing information that comes from the outside as well as from the inside.

Competitive Information

We use Gartner's magic quadrant (Chapter 16) as a guide to assess our competitors. We ask questions about *completeness of vision* and *ability to*

Table 1 Competitor's Profile — Vision Checklist

Competitor's Completeness of Vision Checklist
State of their technology relative to trends
Products that they sell now — key features
Products in development — key features
Buying models of their customers
Complementary offerings and how well they partner with them
Success in different market segments — geographies, vertical, size
Their published vision in announcements and articles
Completeness of their portfolio relative to customer preferences

Table 2 Competitor's Profile — Execution Checklist

Competitor's Ability to Execute Checklist
Innovation cycles and their ability to achieve success
Effectiveness of their sales channel, partners, distributors
Success of sales campaigns, stability of pricing
Customer and partner loyalty, total customer experience
Adoption trends of new products
Financial results and their consistency
The company's history of success in M&A activity
Concentration or distribution of their customer base
Success in different market segments — geographies, vertical, size
Dependency on a few large customers
Organizational stability: employee turnover, re-orgs

execute (Tables 1 and 2). The assessment will be deep; a lot more than the usual feature comparison tables that constitute only a partial picture of their threat to us. Clearly, we also do an honest self-evaluation along the same questions, i.e., we should not give ourselves an easy pass.

Customer-Base Information

Business expansion depends on how well we understand our existing customers. We need to drill down and develop complete analyses of the

Table 3   Customer-Base Analysis Checklist

Customer-Base Analysis Checklist
Feature usage patterns
Shelf-ware: purchased products not in use
Adoption dynamics of new features
Value validation
Expansion opportunities
Total customer experience
Satisfaction with the sales process
Satisfaction with the company

customers' environments and buying decisions. Many web-enabled B2B products allow access to the customers' systems for remote service and monitoring, and all SAAS and web services are inherently open to the vendor for research purposes. With these access features, it's easy to collect real data and information, and compile customer-base analyses that are important to marketing. A sample of related questions are listed in the checklist. (Table 3).

Partner-Base Information

We form partnerships to give us technology advantage or market access. If our strategy depends heavily on a partnership, we need to carefully watch all the major developments and adjust our strategy to the moves. Here are a few common partnership scenarios that develop into problems.

- Our key distributor starts offering a product from another vendor directly or indirectly competitive to us. As a result, the rules of the competitive game change entirely, especially the pricing.

- Our product is a layer on top a major industry technology. Any significant change in that technology can cause a wave of compatibility issues and workload, often without any commercial benefit to us.

- Successful partnerships are vulnerable exactly where the success is, i.e., the contact points with customers. As each partner develops its portfolio of offerings, the natural expansion is into the partner's space. The partnership is now a coopetition disguised as *giving customers more choice options.*

- Our technology is inside a mass-produced product sold by a major player in the industry. Large companies don't like to be single sourced — they are probably looking for alternatives that will eliminate their dependency on our product.

These scenarios are just the most common strategic partnership problems. A proactive marketing strategy monitors all aspects of the company's existing and potential partnerships and presents them for discussion at the company's strategy forums.

Building the Company's Position

31

The *B2B company position* is a big puzzle board of all marketing components that we have reviewed so far. Beyond the methodical design of each of these components, we need to ensure that we ask the big picture questions and that as a whole the company positions itself well with all of its constituencies (Table 1).

The company also needs a simple and interesting *image* that generates talk and helps people remember it. For example, Apple's name evokes an image of innovation, clean design, and elegance; Microsoft and IBM, everything you need for business; Facebook, young and social that is doing good in

Table 1 Company Position Checklist

Company Position
The company sells itself to employees as the workplace that is committed to their success and future.
The company sells itself and its offerings to existing and future customers.
The company sells itself to partners to reinforce their interest in and commitment to the partnerships.
The company sells itself to industry analysts and to the press to benefit from publicity.
The company sells itself to the BoD, investors, and market analysts to secure financial support and stock position.

the world; EMC² and Dell, execution machines. With companies as with people, an interesting personality of a winning hero or an innovation geek will generate talk, while a boring image will remain... well, boring.

A company could choose its character and personality, and work over time to build and reinforce it; the image doesn't have to reflect reality right away. Conversely, a company that suffers from a negative image — slow, cumbersome, old, and lacking direction — has to work harder to overcompensate, reverse the image, and catch a new wave to ride on.

Marketing Calendar

32

Marketing is an enormous multidimensional puzzle board where the pieces are not laid-out openly on a flat table; so it's difficult to assemble.

The simplest way to organize the process of finding all the pieces and putting them together is with a coordinated calendar of internal and external marketing events and preparation meetings. Milestones and deadlines should be clear. Every marketing-related activity involving other contributors should be on this calendar, e.g., interview cycles of sales people on customer satisfaction, checking the readiness of demos and testing presentations before events, etc.

The marketing function in the company owns this calendar and all the execution aspects. In small companies, or startups, the CEO will be the one to marshal the combined efforts.

As an example, a recent simple marketing calendar that I created with the marketing team of a small company client included a monthly planner for the whole year with the following details: categories, deliverables, purpose, and tasks as shown in Table 1.

Table 1   Example of Annual Marketing Calendar.

Annual Marketing Planner

Categories	Deliverables	Details, Purpose, Long-Term Goal	Jan Task	...	Aug Task	Dec Task
Value props	VP for direct advertisers	- Dedicated 24/7 service - Strong Media partners - High demand: all verticals and platforms	New Brochure		-	VP workshop
	VP for networks	- Scalable reach - Strong media partners - High demand: all verticals and platforms	New brochure		-	VP workshop
	All generic VPs	- Technology, BI - Owner of: platform, products, tech - Internal MB team - 5 years in business, top payouts	Print card for internal use		Train	VP workshop
Segmentation	Direct Advertisers	- Long term: 100% direct - Growth: 80–200 in 1 year			-	Yearly goals
	Networks	- Only highly profitable GP > 30%	Rule engine		-	Yearly goals
	Website owners	- Min size: increase entry level by 50%			-	Yearly goals

			Las Vegas		NYC	Yearly goals and budget
Events	Affiliate summit	- WW attendance of most industry - NY/Vegas - Important for: position, brand, networking, retention, new business - Table/booth - Define key messages				Yearly goals and budget
	Bluecon	- WW attendance of industry - FR/DE - Important for: bus new adv., apps - Internal social MB	-		Cologne	Yearly goals and budget
Positioning and messaging	Ad campaigns	- Important for brand: reach new partners - $2000 test budget - Campaigns between major events - Facebook, test search	-		-	VP workshop
	Website	- Updates for upcoming events - Push messaging	-		-	-
	Newsletter	- Pubs: monthly review top offers - Updates for system improvements - Success stories	-		-	-

(Continued)

Table 1 (*Continued*)

		Annual Marketing Planner				
Categories	Deliverables	Details, Purpose, Long-Term Goal	Jan Task	...	Aug Task	Dec Task
Marketing material	Exhibition booth	- Summits only: $1000 per event	-		-	Annual budget
	Giveaways	- Summits only: $1000 per event	-		-	Annual budget
Competitors	Competitive messaging for publishers	On-time payments	Update from summit		Update from summits	SWOT
	Competitive messaging for advertisers		Update from summit		Update from summits	SWOT
	Competitive industry trends	- Proliferation of media one-man-show - Increasing media cost on main platforms	-		-	SWOT
Playing field	Rules	- Acceptable publishers and advertisers - Minimum budgets - Prepayment policy - Payment terms - Cap on outstanding collection balance - Overruling result reports	Revise publisher rules		Revise publisher rules	-

Sales Organization Basics for B2B

Sales Function

33

Since the times of the Romans, it is known that an army is only as good as its logistics and supply lines. Indeed, the sales manager's job is to build and manage the support lines far more than to manage the front lines of sales representatives. Sales management involves planning, supply of information, approvals of deal structures, field and customer education, and channel development.

The following story shows how critical the planning can be. This was a global sales plan kept in the drawer in a state of *ready to pounce*. It brought about a change in the history of large computer systems and propelled its protagonist to the coveted leadership position of a huge segment that lasted for decades afterwards.

SALES IN THE DRIVER'S SEAT

In the early 1990s, EMC² was selling its large information storage systems, then already famous, into the mainframe computer market. Its amazing success was to create a separate segment for data storage within the mainframe market, which IBM had dominated for many

(Continued)

(Continued)

years. With innovative products, EMC^2 created a $2B company by *stealing* this lucrative part of business from IBM.

Realizing that the growth of mainframe is limited, however, EMC^2 expanded its product portfolio from the mid-1990s to address the growing open-systems market. The initial targets for the new products were the open-system environments of its existing mainframe customers; but they had a sales problem — these customers knew EMC^2 only for mainframe compatible storage and not as an open-systems supplier.

At the time, five major vendors covered the open-systems market by selling servers and their associated data storage units. HP and SUN, who were the most dominant of the five, competed fiercely for the leadership position. HP, who needed to rejuvenate their storage product line, found EMC^2 with its strong product line as the quick way for advancement. The HP–EMC^2 partnership gave EMC^2 the expected market reach and the partnership took off and soared with sales that doubled and tripled every expectation.

Two years later, EMC^2 achieved its goal to be accepted and well known as an open-systems vendor; the partnership generated 20% of its total revenue that was already counted in several billions. Then, in a well-prepared move, EMC^2 sales leadership negotiated with HP for better contract terms. When the overconfident HP refused, EMC^2 took a high, but calculated, risk and ended the partnership. The customers were content with the product line, therefore, they continued to buy it directly from EMC^2; sales grew and all the profit was now kept at home without having to share with the partner. Since that move, EMC^2 owned both mainframe and open-systems storage for many years to come.

(Continued)

(Continued)

The entire transition of EMC^2 from a player in the large mainframe niche, to addressing a much broader market, was watched as a spectacle in the industry and on *Wall Street*. The EMC^2 CEO led the company through growth that looked like jumping over steps on a moving escalator, from $2B to $8B in just 4 years. He continuously watched and balanced all functions in the company that operated around the innovative engineering and the aggressive sales — like a bipolar magnetic field pulling everybody inside.

There was no better story on *Wall Street* in the 1990s. EMC^2 won the honorable Stock of the Decade position, and developed strength that continued decades later, propelling it to more than $26B in 2016 when it merged with Dell. The partner, HP, that enabled this success in the critical stage, never received any credit for helping their inevitable competitor.

The entire plan was a sales-led coup d'état, conceived and executed completely in EMC^2 headquarters; field personnel joined the execution only when the plan came out in the open.

This story shows that a strong sales organization with a good plan has the power and capacity to lead strategic shifts. A coup of that magnitude is definitely rare, but even in normal periods with no plans for revolution, a strong and agile sales organization can and should keep the company on the right course.

*

Sales management is about creating an organization that can move fast. The key organizational features are as shown in Table 1:

Table 1 Sales Organization Features

Sales Organization Checklist
Access to information
Compensation models
Education of customers
Sales organization structures
Technical skills
Productivity, pipeline, prospecting
Sales cycles
Sales skills — consultative, closing

Access to Information

34

The most important supply line of the sales force is access to information. Yet, field sales personnel typically spend too much time on finding and customizing information. Content that comes from headquarters should be organized according to field needs for quick access to usable information; the authors' preferences are much less important. The time of sales representatives, sales engineers, and channel managers is measured in revenue and profit; therefore, optimizing their processes is crucial to the company.

A good content repository for sales follows standard and intuitive structures and each of the content items is designed for ease of browsing. The main user features of this repository are:

- *Administrative metadata* — electronic index card with information on the content item:
  - Type: presentation, whitepaper, brochure, marketing, technical
  - Title: product name, solution name, success story
  - Uses: handout, conversation, presentation
  - Author, date

- *Content metadata*
  - Executive summary
  - Main themes and messages
  - Target audience: technical, executive, and business
- *Search function*
- *Automatic alerts on new content*

Examples of *content metadata* that are both informative and easy to browse are:

- *Sales presentation* — The backbone of a presentation is the slide that lists the value propositions. With a few additional words on when to use it, it's a full summary of the presentation.

- *Whitepaper* — The abstract of a whitepaper is a short description of a solution and the successful results of the implementation.

- *Reference sheet* — Customer testimonial with demonstrated value propositions, relevant products, key selling points, and a few details about the customer's application.

*

The information that field sales personnel need comes from many sources. They should have convenient access to marketing and customer-base information of the following checklist (Table 1).

Table 1 Sales Information Checklist

Sales Personnel Information Checklist
Sales presentations
Value proposition statements and proofs
Recent service logs — the status of the account
Buying history from the CRM system
Pricing models and calculators
Latest product releases and their highlights
Reference sheets per product or solution
Whitepapers and Implementation Notes
Compatibility matrix
Information on solutions and their adoption

Compensation Models

35

Flow of information to the field is like fuel to a car, and the compensation model is the oil that lubricates the engine parts. Sales management should not be late with setting quotas and clear compensation formulas, and yet I've seen small companies where these aren't settled even weeks after the quota period started. Letting sales run without clear quotas and compensation rules creates attitudes of *them vs. us*, and that is not good for loyalty, commitment, and willingness to make extra efforts for the company to win.

Generating sales in modern B2B environments can be complex and involve efforts of multiple teams, and therefore, multiple commissions. Many companies also have commission-based incentives for management. Some scenarios of multiple commissions on the same revenue are described here. These could develop into a serious profitability issue for a company that's stressed with low gross-profits.

- Several teams work on winning a complex deal involving the company products, partner's products, and services. Do they all get credit for the deal and therefore commission? Are they competing amongst themselves, each one trying to make his part of the deal bigger?

- A product is sold to a customer site, but the customer's approval of the proposed technology is done from their remote corporate site in a different sales territory; two sales teams are working over a very long sales cycle to close the business. Who is entitled to the commission?

- Sales organizations with specialty overlays that assist general sales inherently have double commission structures.

- Deals of cloud-based enterprise software and internet-based services usually start on low customer budgets that grow with time as a result of the work of customer retention teams. How much revenue is credited (for commission calculations) to the sales team that sold it? And how much to the retention team?

- Management made a special commission arrangement with a sales superstar to attract him to the company. It is another added cost.

I have seen these scenarios in several small and large companies. They open a Pandora's Box of *who gets what and when* and generate multiple formulas that intend to split the commission fairly. However, the rules often work against teamwork, or become so complex that it's hard for the commissioned person to see the connection between the work effort, the results, and the commission payment.

A good set of commission formulas motivates the field and the support organizations to work as a team and sell; it is accepted as fair and balanced, and the links to results are very clear.

Fixed and Variable Compensation Components

Compensation packages for positions that are linked directly to revenue and gross-profit have both fixed and variable components:

- Fixed: base salary
- Variable: bonus, commission, stock options, profit sharing

The variable components are proportionally higher for front line positions — direct sales and channel sales — and for upper management.

Direct sales and channel sales create the new revenue for the company. *Upsell,* on the other hand, could come from the functions of telesales, inside sales, or retention teams. If it's not a required norm, it is better to compensate these teams with bonuses and leave the commission formulas simple and applicable only to direct and channel sales.

The variable compensation should not splinter into many small components; the connection between results and compensation needs to be as simple as possible.

THE COMMISSION FORMULA THAT DID NOTHING

In the following example, we can see how distorted the formulas can get. I recently examined the compensation structure of a company, where the formula for members of the retention team included five components for a commission that amounted to 20% of the total compensation. When their managers saw that the formulas created commissions they didn't like, they added yet another variable device called *manager's decision*. With this new device they adjusted the compensations of their employees to what they thought was fair. When I reviewed the history of payments, I could see that all employees consistently received 85%–90% of their variable every successive quarter. Obviously, the managers were straightening the line as they saw fit and the formulas were just a distraction. The employees learned to not pay attention to the formulas; instead, they trusted their managers to compensate them fairly. Instead of motivating desired behaviors and influencing results, the commission formulas did nothing, because they were overcomplicated. We changed the commission formulas to three components, and planned to reduce it further to two with the next product transition.

Commissions and Quotas

The language of sales compensation and commission formulas is complicated because there are many variations in the concepts of quota, revenue, and territory, and several optional rules that depend on the situation.

In relatively stable B2B environments we set the quotas quarterly. In internet services and e-commerce, they are monthly, because all payments between companies are done in monthly cycles. In these businesses, however, the monthly numbers are typically unstable and if the commission is paid on monthly results, the sales person sees payments that are going up and down frequently. It would be better to change the quotas to longer periods, from months to quarters, and stabilize the payment amounts. Stable numbers are better for motivation and consistent performance.

Each sales territory has its general quota that is sometimes divided into sub-quotas per product or service. With sub-quotas, overachievement in selling one product doesn't compensate for underachievement in the other. When the sales function is performed remotely, mostly without customer visits, the territories are usually virtual and not geographical. We define virtual territories by product, platform, or type of service.

To maintain fast cycles of reward-for-results, in situations where it takes a lot of time to calculate exact revenues and commissions, the company should pay *pro-forma commissions* followed by later corrections. Pro-forma commissions are also paid on *booked revenue*, in situations where customer payments are done in installments according to project delivery milestones. The corrections that follow are calculated on the *collected revenue*.

Companies pay premium commissions for *overachievement*, and it is usually done according to brackets that are capped by a maximum premium. For example, 10% commission premium for overachievement up to 130%, and 20% premium for anything above it. Underachievement is penalized, usually also in brackets. For example, achievement of 50%–80%

of quota receives only 70% of the calculated commission, and anything below 50% achievement pays nothing.

Some companies calculate the commission entirely or partially on *gross profit* and not on revenue. In internet services, for example, a commissioned employee's work is to buy media, add a service, and sell it; the gross profit is visible to the employee as an essential part of his work. With other products or services where there's no such visibility, the company sets *internal transfer prices* as the basis for gross profit calculations.

Effective commission formulas are simple, i.e., calculating revenue and gross profit results, and nothing else. I have seen attempts to add components to the formula to hold sales accountable for: collection rates, revenue growth rates, and deal dates — beginning-of-quarter or end-of-quarter. A complicated formula is difficult to understand; therefore, it doesn't work as a motivator.

Effective commission formulas are stable. For example, the formula pays 50% commission on gross profit and 50% on revenue. If the company changes its sales strategy to emphasize the gross profit more, it can change the internal transfer prices and leave the formula unchanged. Also when setting new sub-quotas, think long-term and stable. For short-term incentives there are other tools such as SPIF and Grace Period.

Growing companies should *raise sales quotas steadily,* but not too aggressively. As the company's position strengthens in the market, it's easier to sell their products; sales productivity increases, and quotas can, therefore, be higher. With increasing competition, however, selling becomes harder, and if the quotas are too aggressive, the best sales people will start to leave, going to companies where they could make more money; sometimes, they go directly to the competition.

The sales compensation policy should also recognize the company's market position; especially for startups, the rules cannot be the same as those for established and predictable companies. People who commit their time to a startup already take a huge risk; the sales compensation rules should be more forgiving, and realistic.

Performance Incentives

The company could use several types of variable components as non-commission incentives for temporary needs or for efforts that are linked to sales, but not directly on a deal-by-deal basis. These alternative compensation devices keep the commission formulas simple and stable, which is crucial for motivation and steady performance. There are two types of variable compensation components that are not commission. To drive performance, we use quarterly bonus, SPIF and grace period and to motivate employees to stay longer we use excellence awards and stock options.

Quarterly Bonuses motivate employees and teams who contribute to long-term goals and projects that benefit the organization. The quarterly bonus program gives weight and credence to the supportive supply lines. The *aim* should be to *pay bonuses in full* to all employees who are on the program as it's the company's interest that all employees accomplish their goals, and develop a habit of doing so. When the achievement is not 100%, as often is the case, the bonus payments should work like a carrot and a stick — full payment when they are close to the target and discounted payments when the gaps are large.

Examples of such support roles are technology experts who are fully dedicated to the sales organizations. If we pay them with bonuses they would focus more on teaching the sales organization and making it less dependent on their knowledge; the company's long-term interests would be served well. On the other hand, if we pay them with commission, they would be motivated to get directly involved with deals and become the expert closers. It might work for the short term, but they could quickly turn into bottlenecks. For the sake of the organization's health, it's better to prevent the development of such bottlenecks.

SPIF (sales promotion incentive fund) is a way to create temporary exceptions to the rules of the compensation policy. SPIF is additional commission for sales of a specific product that is supposed to generate incremental revenue. Usually, the program gives incentives for efforts to generate the first wave of sales of a new offering. The sales personnel should be aware of the limited time and budget, or they would develop an expectation to

receive the additional commission forever. When the program ends, the product rolls into regular quotas and commission calculations.

The *grace period* lets a new sales person ramp up to the expected performance without being subjected to penalties. During this period, he receives the commission for the full quota even if he didn't achieve it. Since the sales minds should be anchored on real targets and on seeking opportunities to achieve them, the grace period doesn't lower the target; instead, it eliminates the penalties for not achieving it. The grace period could be built in stages; for example, full quota commission initially and then gradually developing to the commission formula only for achievements above 70% of quota.

Excellence awards for top performers motivate key talent to stay longer with the company. These top performers are the people who have a *multiplier effect* on the productivity and work-quality of others. They carry the *big picture*, and when they're around, the organization functions a lot better. The awards are especially important for support roles; direct sales have the over achievement commission to compensate them for excellence; the support roles do not have it.

The excellence awards program should be sufficiently broad so that enough key employees are recognized and included. It shouldn't be limited to a few because that might encourage negative maverick behavior rather than positive teamwork. If awards are given frequently in the organization, the program creates an excellence buzz in the company. The size of the awards should carry a message of fairness — good awards for good results, exceptional awards for exceptional results.

Stock options became popular as a way to encourage key employees to stay with the company, though local tax codes in some countries affect their usefulness as a motivation tool. Smaller grants that occur frequently, as opposed to rare large grants, keep the key employees longer. The effect of the stock option plan on the organization will be significant if the program passes the critical mass of 20% of the employees. Long vesting periods encourage longer commitments to the company; but short and more aggressive vesting attracts key talent, especially in startups.

Responsibility to Customers

36

Relationships between customers and vendors in B2B environments exist over a long time. It starts with the first sales interaction, continues through the implementation process, and onto reaffirming value with the hope of securing more business, or to enlist the customer as reference for other prospective customers.

In a world where a lot of information is available online, a healthy relationship is about educating each other. From one interaction to another, the vendor helps the customer learn more in exchange for insights into his set of needs. *Free exchange of education* is the essence of ongoing account management.

The consultative salesperson educates without arrogance; he shares examples, helps in identifying problems, and leads the customer's learning without pressure. The depth of knowledge exchange should be just enough for understanding business and operational opportunities and bottlenecks.

This relationship starts even before the first interaction, when the customer visits the company's website, reads press releases, whitepapers, online demos, conferences, etc. All outbound marketing material should tell the same story, from different angles, with the same key messages.

Sales personnel are responsible for customer education during the sales campaign, and also throughout the implementation and post-implementation periods.

During the campaign, the intent is to raise the priority of our offering over the alternatives. The education is *customer focused* with only enough product information to make the proposal substantive and concrete. Once the customer visualizes the solution in his own reality, he will be interested to learn about the value and trade-offs. Knowledge and credibility are critical at this stage.

Selling a complex solution is rarely done in one shot; typically, there's too much to consider for one interaction. The vendor needs to know enough about the customer's purchasing priorities and comfort levels in order to progress the sales campaign from one step to the next.

Customers are generally reluctant to switch from existing vendors to new ones; but they would be open to the idea if they were disappointed by failures in service or relationship. Difference in features is less convincing, mainly because switching vendors is always associated with operational and business costs and risks. Therefore, during the campaign you have to educate the customer on the quality of your company as a vendor of service.

When the customer is ready to move toward purchase, they are interested in the implementation details. Be prepared with a chart that shows what they should expect during implementation, and save it for the right moment when they show the signs of interest.

When the agreement to purchase is made, the focus changes. In the anticlimax, immediately after a challenging sales campaign, the tension between the vendor and the customer converts to focus on fulfilling expectations. This is the time to strengthen the relationship and continue to educate with a focus on *the process and the vendor.*

From the customer's point of view, an implementation is a painful disruption. You approach the customer professionally with full transparency on delivery dates, timelines, preparations, and integration details. All customer-facing

employees need to be well trained in the principles of good service and the sales account manager is there to ensure it.

The vendor's *quality of service* is fully exposed during the implementation phase. It's about professional appearance of personnel, neatness of the work and the documentation, and empathy with the customer due to the disruptive nature of the implementation. The vendor's representatives on the customer's site need to be credible and dependable with information and actions, assure the customer that his concerns are addressed, and respect the customer who is waiting to realize the promised value.

The implementation phase is also the time to *close knowledge gaps* in the technical and operational aspects of the new system, and develop the new operational standards and guidelines. Any gap between the expected and confirmed value should be settled.

Post implementation, the value has been delivered and the customer approves all payments, but the relationship is certainly not over. Some sales presence continues to sow the seeds for future business or to ask for reference. Post implementation, the relationship is about collecting hard evidence on the product value for use elsewhere, or to further the relationship and reach higher connections with the customer's executives, now that the hard evidence of the value is already in house.

Value affirmation — reselling what is already sold — is not redundant; in a connected business world, there are no secrets and word gets out, for better and for worse. Sales' job is to get as much sales value as possible from the successful implementation.

In extreme cases, when the promised value is not delivered, the vendor should consider bearing the cost of replacement and keeping the customer whole. Admitting failure and delivering an alternative successfully leads to enduring relationships.

In the following stories from three different periods, I was on the vendors' side. In each of them we made difficult multimillion dollar decisions to do complete replacements, and in the aftermath of these events we came out as winners.

EFFECTIVE WAY TO ADMIT FAILURE

In the first story, the customer was a large multinational bank. With one of their computer systems not functioning properly they lost an entire day's stock trading. Originally, when they bought the system, they trusted its quality reputation, so much so that they had no redundant system to ensure the operation in the case of failure. When the event happened, we immediately created a task force of specialists who worked around the clock to minimize the damage for the customer. But we also installed a second system, free of charge, to ensure proper coverage of any vulnerability. Even though the customer had originally decided not to invest in this type of redundancy, our reaction in assuming full responsibility made them reconsider and invest in redundant systems throughout their operation. The customer's statement at the time said it all: ... *we've seen failures before, but we haven't seen a vendor that takes full responsibility for them...* The incremental business of the redundant systems paid for our decision, and more.

*

In the second story, the customer owned huge oil refineries and depots, and several oil pipeline installations crossing the Alborz mountain range near the Caspian Sea. They ordered the automation system for a new pipeline from an overseas vendor because we were experts in the field and we already had contracts with them on several projects. The system that we built according to the original specification proved to be very difficult to maintain, especially when considering the remote locations of the installations. As their system integration house contractor, we decided to redo the entire project with an improved design concept, even though the customer had approved the original design and had not requested the replacement. We knew it was a bad design, and we didn't want

(Continued)

(Continued)

the customer to find out later. There were delays in delivery, but the customer was happy to absorb the delays in exchange for receiving the improved systems. The relationship continued and the contracts continued to flow in.

*

In the third story, together with the customer, we, the main contractor, made the wrong choice of a core computer system for a chemical plant in the Dead Sea. The compute power and programming language of this special purpose real-time computer were inadequate; but the performance problems surfaced only during the full scale on-site testing. Fortunately, replacing the core system with a much more expensive one did not require the redesign of the whole system; the added cost was, therefore, limited. Yet, without admitting the failure and taking full responsibility, the project was sure to derail, and the long-term damages to both sides would have been huge.

The relationship between the vendor and the customer has real value. It is a *for-better–for-worse* partnership where the vendor has the larger burden of keeping the relationship working.

Structures and Functions

37

Legends of successful sales organizations are stories of audacity and triumphs on the front line, while the back-office usually stays out of the spotlight. A B2B sales organization may have many employees in back-office functions, and that depends on the nature of the business. The front lines are creative; they rely on exceptional success stories and organizational stamina. For the back-office functions, order and process are more important.

We will examine the front lines, and see the key features and structures of their organization, and then review the functions of the back-office and how to organize them to support their customer, the front lines, in the best possible way.

The Nature of Successful Sales Organizations

In a 2013 Harvard Business Review blog, Steve W. Martin summarizes his experience of successful sales organizations by working with two hundred B2B companies. He found seven shared characteristics of strength, stamina, leadership, and individual and teamwork excellence that shine a light on the front lines of sales.

1. **Strong Centralized Command-and-Control with Local Authority**
   Where there's money, and sales is certainly about money, there isn't much room for democracy. The fast pace of doing business demands quick decisions and full authority for the leaders. Strong sales leaders set goals and expectations, and they don't dwell on operational details. The limits of local authority are also determined from above.

2. **Darwinian Sales Culture**
   It is said that *a sales person is only as good as the results of his last quarter.* Young and successful sales people expect to be promoted regardless of seniority. They see themselves as hired guns; if they are held back, they tend to leave, as company loyalty for them is always secondary to income prospects.

   Darwinian *survival of the fittest* in sales organizations means higher employee turnover; three times as high as in the rest of the organization is healthy and acceptable.

3. **United Against a Common Enemy**
   Successful sales organizations, like the military, come together against a common enemy. Sales people are competitive in nature; an adversary gives them what they need — an enemy to fight. A well-defined adversary helps individuals and teams to develop focus and stamina to win; overtaking an adversary is a lot more rewarding for them than achieving the goals without one.

4. **Competitive but Cohesive Team**
   One of the best motivation tools in large sales organizations is the *overachievers club.* Upper management knows that the invitation to the club is more important than money to the salesperson; he gains the elite membership ticket with hard work, and in return he receives an elegant way to show-off his success. Peer competition for recognition creates winning attitudes that benefit the sales organization, much like sports superstars who improve the image and business of their sports.

5. **Do-It-Yourself Attitude**

Strong sales people are independent and they have *can-do* attitudes. They're highly creative in circumventing obstacles, internal or external, even when these are their own company's policies. Successful sales people quite often enjoy the preferred child status for whom the family rules are less enforced.

6. **Negative Beliefs Are Suspended**

Great sales people and organizations feed upon success; failures for them are *lessons learned.* Despite the many daily setbacks, sales people are undefeatable. The quota system is only a challenge for them. Unlike other jobs, every quarter starts with zero and last quarter's achievements no longer count. Sales people have the inner resources to overcome depressive symptoms, and the strengths of their leadership and teamwork help them to do that.

7. **Energy and Team Spirit**

Quoting Steve W. Martin in his HBR blog ...*great sales organizations are on a constant mission to prove to the world that they are the best...* Each win anywhere in the organization is for them a proof that it's possible; *success breeds success.* As much as they compete with each other internally for celebrity and elite status, the stronger drive in sales is that of a wolf pack — a larger group attacking bigger goals and always reaching higher.

Sales Representatives, Sales Engineers, Overlays

The organization of the front lines should be simple, with as few management layers as possible, to benefit the independent, can-do salesperson. The organizational processes create peer support groups and quick access to the central functions for knowledge and decisions. Some large organizations create a sales support desk to expedite field requests.

Typically, the organization of *sales representatives* is a simple hierarchy divided into segments by customer size, geography, vertical industry, and technology. For example, one group sells industrial class print-presses to print shops and another group sells slower and less expensive printers for home offices in the same territory. Their sales methods are completely different; one sells capital equipment directly to end users with values such as technology, industrial performance, cost per printed page, and financing options, while the other sells to commercial retailers with volume deals, mainly. Everything in their work is different; therefore, there's no point in combining these sales groups.

In the hierarchy, district managers *coach* the sales representatives and review every potential deal. A typical district manager for complex B2B products manages up to five sales representatives. The regional manager is a *consultant* to district managers; his job issues are staffing, strategy changes, and improvement programs, and he gets involved in high-profile deals. A region includes up to seven districts. Higher in the organization, sales executives manage geographies or segments. They are mostly concerned with strategy, budgets, and organizations, while the sales work is delegated to the regional managers. Sales executives have a central functional staff to support the organization — finance, legal, HR, and training.

In small organizations the managerial responsibilities are consolidated or shared in fewer hierarchical levels.

Channel sales representatives sell through or with a partner; therefore they need to understand the business of the channel partner and the businesses of the partner's customers. Channel sales is treated as a separate segment. Most of their work includes enabling the partner, providing training, and supporting deals, but also in resolving conflicts of interest when the partner represents competitors, or tries to push the cost of sales — staff and discounts — to the company.

Channel management needs patience, maturity, and authority. When multiple channel partners compete against each other for the same business, the company is in the line of fire, having to straddle more than one front line of conflicts of interest.

Pre-sales engineers know the technical aspects of the company's offerings and the customers' technology environments. They guide the sales representatives on the product fit and they guide the prospective customer

on the product and implementation. The number of SEs in the organization could be as high as sales representatives, if the product is complex or new and it requires pairs of technical and business professionals to win deals.

Even though they work hand in hand with the sales representatives, the SE organization is usually parallel, with its own management hierarchy. Having a separate SE organization ensures that their needs for developing knowledge are satisfied consistently, and they can continue to add value as technology experts.

In startups, SEs often do also the post-sale customer implementation. This could develop into a profitability problem as the startup transitions to its cost-conscious growth phase, and customers continue to expect the implementation to be a free service. Managers of startups need to position this free work correctly to prevent this problem in the future.

SEs advise the customers and are also close to the sales process. They see the product's true value firsthand and they know if it's easy to sell or not. Top SEs from all the segments of the company should be on the regular advisory board for product strategy, marketing, and engineering.

Technology and vertical overlay groups provide temporary support to the sales organization for a new technology or a new vertical market. This team of specialists identifies opportunities for the new strategy and helps the local sales teams and SEs win the business. With time, the sales organization learns how to do it independently, and the new business is rolled into the mainstream, or if the volumes justify it, the organization dedicates a team to work on it as a separate business segment. Overlays cost the company double commissions; therefore, they should be only a temporary organizational solution.

Sales Organization Structure

As soon as the sales group is large enough to include back-office functions, it's important to consider their processes with the field and to structure the entire organization correctly. We need to review and revise the organization regularly to get the best effectiveness and efficiencies with every change in sales strategy such as — phase transition, strategic moves, and coverage models.

Phase transitions of the company, from startup to growth and further to maturity, change the way sales personnel behave with customers. A startup sales person would move the entire company to close a deal; but in the growth phase such behavior is no longer realistic. Adjusting these behaviors in the field could only be done gradually; existing customers should not feel any bumps in the relationship, and field personnel needs time to learn how to work in the new mode of operation.

The cost of doing business during the startup phase is secondary and even the prices are flexible. The company wants to establish a meaningful install base, get product validation from a variety of real customers, and for that it is willing to bear almost any cost for securing customer satisfaction.

The way we talk to customers is also changing from phase to phase. The customers of startups are *early adopters*. Their expectations are different from the *second wave of customers* who expect professionalism and have little tolerance for experimentation. While an early adopter is excited to see the developer do on-site adjustments to a product, the second wave customer would consider such actions as indications that the product is unfit and not ready.

In the growth phase, the organization focuses on its processes — delivery and services, front-end and back-end functions. Yet, field personnel need to fill the gaps to satisfy both customer and company expectations as processes and policies are being built and adjusted during the transition. It's a fine balancing act of managing trade-offs until the company gradually reaches a more mature, well-established state.

With maturity, sales could reduce its expensive customer-facing activities or find other means to improve front-end and back-end efficiencies. Shifting resources between product lines, as well as consolidating support functions are common tactics during phase transitions. In the maturation process, the sales organization becomes more regimented, oriented to

process-and-procedure, with some methods phasing out while new ones phasing in.

Any one of the following *changes in strategic goals* drives adjustments in the front lines and back-office functions of the organization, and that is to ensure continued readiness.

- New product launch
- Focus program to grow or keep customers
- Open a new segment for an existing product
- Changing go-to-market cost structure
- Changing prices
- Responding to competitive pressures

For example, if the company wants more market share and revenue and it lowers its profit priority, it would need more prospects and more people to do prospecting. Reorganizing the sales teams in two levels of prospectors and closers could provide this additional coverage. Focus on footprint and top-line revenue also dictates processes with higher front-line independence and authority, while focus on profit and price-control points to organizations that are more centralized.

Any special field program, like a strategic goal to improve quality in the install-base, needs a dedicated, centralized group of professionals to manage problem cases and the corrective actions. You cannot expect the sales front lines to do this coordination work; they need to focus on creating new sales and managing existing accounts.

Another common scenario in sales reorganization occurs when the company moves to a totally new product set or a new target market, while the old strategy is still in place. The sales organization should split and dedicate a department for each strategy independently, as keeping them in one organization would hinder the growth of the new strategy, or cause the old strategy to deteriorate a lot faster than planned. For example, selling refurbished traded-in systems or older products in secondary markets is a good business that needs a dedicated sales organization. Managing cash cows should not intermix with creating new business. Having a sales team dedicated to the old strategy can also prevent the entry of a new competitor through the back door.

Organizational changes also follow every redefinition of market segments and their respective *Coverage Models*. For example, dedicated teams cover enterprise-level customers with high buying potential, while only a single shared team covers SMB customers. Or, a remote inside sales team covers long-tail customers, and support for vertical segments is done with a centralized team of experts.

Organizational adjustments due to coverage considerations are:

- Supporting value add resellers (VARs)
- Shifting small deals to online sales or inside sales
- Adding sales engineers to deepen coverage
- Pooling sales engineers to cover SMBs
- Redistricting of sales territories

Field dynamics are fast and the sales organizations should be equally fast. Restructuring and adjustment keep the organizations fresh and focused correctly on strategic goals. *Corrective plans do not work very well in the field*, and attitudes of wait-and-see are often damaging. These are the situations where management has to act fast and upfront.

Back-Office Sales Functions

The front lines are structured around the needs of coverage of market and customer segments, while the support functions follow the coverage needs of the front lines. Back-office functions should be centralized as much as possible for effectiveness and efficiency.

Ideally, front lines are invested entirely in hunting new business and the centralized support functions in the gathering of what the front lines hunt. Sales administration and sales operations share the work of delivery, field events, invoicing and collection, knowledge management, etc. Depending

on the size of the organization, back-office functions would have dedicated teams or just one administrator to handle all functions.

Sales Administration Functions

Sales administration handles the auxiliary tasks, and frees the front lines to spend their time on selling.

- *Customer logistics* — coordinating deliveries, registration of licenses and live accounts, updating customer status in the systems and quality assurance of delivery

- *Distribution* — coordinating product deliveries with field offices and distributors, inventory management, shipments of collateral material, process integration between the company systems and partner systems

- *Planning* — pre-planning and coordination with the manufacturing department and suppliers of auxiliary products

- *Execution of promotions* — managing discount periods, bundle programs, eligibility, inventories and supplies, data analysis

- *Reward and recognition programs* — managing sales motivational programs, quota overachievements and execution of SPIFs

- *Order administration, billing, and collection* — providing service to field personnel on legal and financial dealings with customers

Sales Operations Functions

Sales operations functions improve the quality and productivity of the sales activity. They collect and analyze data, and guide field decisions on cost of sales, productivity, knowledge, and forecasting. In small companies it's part of the job of the head of sales.

The *cost of sales* depends on the segment and how much the company invests in coverage and expenses. There are many shades of cost of sales ranging from minimal coverage to dedicated teams of experts with generous budgets for luxury invitations to golf tournaments. Sales operations manages the organization according to the coverage model and expense budget for each segment.

Sales operations builds financial models of each segment and summarizes them in the estimated P&L dashboards. The P&L dashboards are accurate enough for making management decisions and monitoring the business continuously. Without them, managers wouldn't know the state of their businesses. Accurate accounting P&Ls are usually too detailed and too late for making decisions; P&L dashboards from sales operations are an excellent alternative.

Sales operations also manages field transitions to lower cost of sales. A transition from direct coverage to resellers, for example, increases the cost of sales initially, as sales invest time and resources in enabling the reseller, and the cost reduction goal is achieved later. Sales operations, along with the partner management team will oversee this kind of transition.

Sales operations is also responsible for *Field Productivity*. They own the CRM (customer relationship management) system, analyze the data, and devise improvement programs.

The main productivity indicators that we want to monitor are wins and losses, distribution of deals based on revenue and profit, conversion rates, long-tail statistics and period-to-period comparisons. For larger sales teams, we also analyze the individual vs. group statistics, individual vs. benchmarks, and segment-to-segment comparisons.

The CRM is also the source of forecast data, however, most companies suffer from low quality of the forecasts. By running reports on historical forecasts, sales operations can develop insights and help reduce the wasteful fluctuations of decisions, especially in hiring. With more dependable forecasts, resource allocations and plans can be forward looking, effective and efficient.

Constant communication with field managers and continuous analysis of field productivity drive improvement initiatives such as training,

coaching of account managers, customer events, process improvements, and responding to field needs. Sales operations owns the field's calendar of events, and the execution of all the programs in it.

Training improves technical skills, sales skills, and team morale. An organization that invests in its field personnel will see better results and lower turnover of employees. Training, in addition to regular information feeds, deepens the field's knowledge and ability to apply it, and the best form of training involves teams engaging in live cross-pollination and exchange of experience.

It is Not a Mystery

38

Sales and its organization is not black magic. Rather, the function of sales in a B2B environment is more like a factory — inputs, process, and outputs. Measuring the quality of work is statistical, and the way to improve results is like in any other job — conscious and iterative cycles of assessment, testing assumptions, measurement and checklists, training, reinforcement, and no mystery.

And yet, the profession of sales is shrouded with urban legends and unfounded beliefs that *you either have it or you don't*. An old joke says that the difference between any sales person and a Swiss sales person is that *both will sell their mother in order to make a deal, but the Swiss will deliver*. The joke alludes to lack of integrity in the profession of sales. But, I have seen a lot of integrity in sales ranks; sales personnel that mostly go out of their way to keep customers happy and develop long-term relationships.

Believing that *the sky is the limit* is essential to the performance of sales organizations. Yes, a lot is possible, but the impossible is still impossible. Unrealistic goals will only train the organization not to take them seriously, and that everything is negotiable. *You cannot fool all the people all the time* is true with customers and with the sales personnel. The following story demonstrates this principle.

PRODUCT POSITIONING PROBLEM

Even the most exceptional sales team cannot fix the mistakes of product positioning. I examined a case some time ago with a client of mine. The company produced an attractive add-on hardware feature to a platform that was sold by another company. The price of the add-on, however, was two times higher than the average price of the platform. The sales team of the platform did not want to sell it, as it changed the position of the offering entirely and made it a lot harder to sell. My client did not want to listen. They believed that with more push and persuasion the sales team would change its mind. When I suggested producing a cheaper version, the CEO said it would not have protected intellectual property, so he didn't want it. As far as I know they're still trying. Unfortunately for them, customers didn't buy intellectual property, and sales people didn't hurt their own interests selling someone else's attractive add-on — it was a case of wrong positioning and no one, other than my client, could fix it.

The job of sales is hard. Like ballerinas they need to leave all their falls in the training studio, so that performance on stage is perfect. However, the preparation of sales people is never satisfactory; they rarely expose their mistakes in training, and in front of customers the conditions are always different.

The position of sales in the company should be the strongest of all positions. They are the face of the company and everything else follows. To earn this position, leaders of sales need to show that they are focused and in control; only from a confident baseline can they be demanding and influencing the strategy of the company.

Sales is a numbers game — the more nets you have out there, the more butterflies you catch. You always need more sales people; in rough times to increase coverage, and in good times to exploit the potential.

The language of sales organizations is in the statistics of productivity, market share, repeat sales, upsell statistics, recurring revenue, conversion rates, and in accountability — you are expected to deliver what you promised.

Sales leadership needs to constantly reinvent their organization; they should be intolerant of mediocrity and focus on improving the core of the organization. The workforce rule of thumb in large sales organizations is 20–60–20. The core 60% needs the organization's focus and support. All the improvement programs — training and processes — target this core group and aim to improve their performance. The top 20% already has the audacity and skills to do their job well, and marshal the company's resources appropriately. The bottom 20% is not cut out for this work; they are the watch-list of candidates for replacement. In small sales organizations, managers need to assess the performance of each sales person and decide to which category they belong.

The success of a salesperson depends on the offering and a supportive environment at least as much as on his skills. Having a Type A personality does not guarantee results. Experience from other places does not guarantee successful results either; the goose that laid golden eggs will need the same food and supportive flock around it to do it again.

Organizations: Culture, Structure, and People

PART VIII

Cultural Diversity

39

Cultural diversity occupies a prominent place in the global work environment. It is also a wild card for atmospheric internal jokes, fun-filled potluck lunches, and making the workplace a little more interesting. However, cultural diversity is also unjustifiably misused sometimes as an excuse for bad management practices, especially in multilocation organizations. For some managers, it's a convenient way to explain the problems of the organization; they blame the otherness of the remote group before checking their own house. We tend to forget that people in the workplace are pretty much the same everywhere, and to perform well, their needs are similar.

We should benefit from the power of diversity and enjoy it, else the world will continue and we will stay behind.

CULTURAL DIVERSITY STORY

This was going to be my first trip to India. It was squeezed into a very busy schedule, so my intent was for a quick one: arrive the day before, get a good night's sleep, teach my three-day course on management, and head back to home base. Somehow, despite all those years of traveling and globalization, India had not been on

(Continued)

(Continued)

my itinerary. My curiosity up to that point had been satisfied with the neighborhood of Little India in Singapore, where I had already bought the mandatory silk table-runners.

Thinking again, however, I changed my attitude entirely: Wow! My first visit to I N D I A!

A busy schedule not being the purpose of life, I rearranged a few things, and emailed my client a request to make the hotel reservation for a few more nights ahead of my course ... *because I wanted to do some sightseeing* ... Very uncharacteristically, he responded immediately and said ... *we will arrange that* ... but that's all he said, and nothing else. At that time, I wasn't sure what to make of his response — what arrangements exactly were included in *we will arrange that*? Later I found out that what he really meant was ... *we are so happy that you are interested in seeing our city, that we will arrange the hotel, the extra expense is on us, and we will have a few employees guide you on your visit; on the first day our office manager, who is into movies, will take you to Tollywood; on the second day, we'll have a young woman from the city center to guide you through the culture of the Muslim old city, and she will also take you to the Nizam's palace, and on the third day, one of our veteran employees will take you to Golkonda Fort and you will finish the day with dinner at a restaurant in the hilltop 7-Star Taj Hotel ....*

But, I had not known all that when a young fellow ran toward me in the airport arrival hall, asking if I were who I was.

What followed were 3 days of total immersion in the bustling city of Hyderabad, population of about one crore (ten million). I was being introduced to their glorious past as a princely state; to a place where it's hard to find the market because it is everywhere, with pedestrian and auto-rickshaw traffic that makes sense only to the

(Continued)

(*Continued*)

locals. I had luxurious breakfasts that tried to show me the entire Indian cuisine in one meal. The front pages of the daily newspapers and interactions with my guides gave me a glimpse into life below the surface; I found the Indian pride, deeply rooted in rich culture; I learned about the sources of popular entertainment — movies, weddings, food — and the atmosphere of a nation-on-the-move coexisting with massive frustrations from the state of politics and the endemic maladies of *the system.*

Monday morning when I arrived at the company building and was led to my cabin (office), I was greeted in a friendly manner which was absolutely beyond mere politeness. It occurred to me that they already knew me, as my guides had already shared their experiences of touring with me around the city. The fact that I showed interest in their surroundings, history, culture, society, and living conditions had transformed me, in their eyes, into a trusted friend. I was certainly not another B52 bomber coming to drop some American standards on them and leave swiftly.

The course I delivered in the following days was most enjoyable — the best I had had to date. We worked and laughed — a lot. When I wanted to demonstrate the importance of true quality, I referred to the food in India. The famous Shahrukh Khan and his film dances were an example of faked quality — we all knew that on film he looked like a perfect dancer, but also that he couldn't really do it without the help of camera trickery and film directors. For an image of perfection, I called upon that of Deepika (they knew which one). As you can see, those prior immersion days were worth their weight in gold.

The key to working in any multicultural environment is — as Aretha Franklin screams out of the top of her lungs — R.E.S.P.E.C.T. In my visit to India I realized how far respect goes when the women in

(*Continued*)

(Continued)

the office approached me for private consultations; these were all educated professionals in technology fields who wanted to achieve and advance themselves *…just like the women in the west…* they said. They thought I could advise them on how to break though society's constraining traditions. We had lovely heart-to-heart conversations, as I learned humbly, once again, that everything in life is relative.

Cultural diversity should be the cause for celebration and should never be used as an excuse for poor performance. Paying attention to the differences and showing interest in them will go a long way. There's no need to bow like the Japanese if you aren't one; nor should you be offended when they hold side conversations while you are presenting to them. People everywhere want to feel their value and make progress, and it doesn't matter in which currency their salary is paid. Wherever they are, and despite very different circumstances, people are not that different.

If you experience dysfunctional breakage between remote units, look for the tell-tale sign of one group that waits for orders from the other. Usually, it's the result of that group dominating them, thus killing all initiative and any good will to make improvements on their own. To fix this dysfunction, you have to turn the table and involve all sides in the solution — people whose input is respected will make the effort to improve results.

During my work with this company in India, I realized that hierarchy is highly central to the culture, so much so that they would respect it even when it's not there. In one situation, the responsibility for customer service was completely transferred and delegated to the team there, leaving only a program manager in the US headquarters of the company to represent the needs of this unit. The local manager and the team, who proved to be more than able during the long transition, found it difficult to assume total responsibility and ownership; they continued to refer to the program

manager as their manager, even though it was supposed to be the other way around. This difficulty could have been addressed as part of the transition plan and not as an aftermath, if we had paid more attention to the specifics of the culture differences and discussed them as part of the goals of the transition.

Whenever the idea of inclusion overrules the impulse to exclude, great things happen; the United States of America became great by following this simple rule — allowing immigrants to be included and succeed. Cultural diversity — embrace it or you will be late. The key to effective and efficient multicultural settings is to build organizations and relationships with *respect* as the guiding principle and to study the differences as part of this process.

Organizational Structures

40

Ideal organizational structure and reorganization are big concerns for CEOs. However, you cannot copy textbook structures in knowledge-based B2B companies, as so much depends on the situation, and on the skills and capacities of the extant leaders.

When considering *reorganization*, you should weigh the options and consider all the costs of the change, among them, mainly, is the loss of productivity during the transition. Especially, beware of managers who are trigger-happy with re-organizations. They might have been successful in the past, but that experience is actually a disadvantage, as they could be overconfident about the outcomes, and fail to consider all aspects of the new situation. Many reorg aftermaths take much longer than expected and cause unforeseen damage, such as key-employees leaving, and low employee morale.

The basic criterion of organizational structures is to form coherent groups that work effectively and efficiently, by themselves and with other groups. We will first approach the principles for forming independent work-groups, and then the processes and structures that connect them.

The Good Group

We often think of a group as several people fulfilling similar functions — customer service, development, accounting. A group could perform multiple functions if they have a shared and uniting interest, and still be a coherent group; for example, an account team with sales, pre-sales, services, and implementation, chartered together to cover one large customer, keep him happy, and ensure repeat business.

The first group type is organized by function, and the second by project, i.e., a customer in this case. We remember Chaplin's satire on industrial production lines in his "Modern Times" portrayal of Charlie, group of one, whose job is to turn one screw in a moving car-assembly line; a job he is doing all day long from his fixed location on the line. We also know that the car industry changed the assembly process from a moving line to a car fixed at one place with the team moving around it. Here, the transition from functional to project teams was about finding a more humane approach that is not less productive.

When forming a group, think of who they are, what they do, and how they do it. Here are some principles to consider.

Form follows function: The group's structure should suit the full flow of their function, i.e., how they receive inputs, their process and added value, and how they form and deliver the outputs. It should have the least possible friction, inside the group and with its giving and receiving constituencies. For example, the account team that covers a large and *mature* customer has people who are good at relationships, and only a simple structure to support the work which is mostly relationship building. But if technology transformation is happening in the account, the team needs technology experts and their key routine process is structured knowledge sharing — teaching and training. The form follows the function and the team organizes in two different ways — different *staff, process, budget*, and *operational plans*.

Learning: In the knowledge economy, with any new reality, new members, or a change in workload or process, learning is an important part of the

group's work. Learning is in the interest of the entire group, even if only one member learns one new skill. The structure of the group should make learning as easy and fast as possible. Pairing team members, two new employees or one new and one experienced, for example, will make the learning more effective and more efficient.

Since learning is fundamental to current work environments, consider the *learning curve* if you are not sure whether to organize the group according to function or around a project. If it's harder to learn the particulars of a project than to learn the skills to execute it, then the group should be a project group. The longer the learning curve, the more people should stick together as a team. System integration houses, for example, assign project teams to customers, because it's more difficult to learn the project and the customer than to learn the particular technical skills. Product development teams, on the other hand, are organized functionally — developers, QA, planners — because the skill is the bigger learning investment.

In startups people do multiple functions. As the company grows, they need to split into functional teams to allow learning and specialization, even though employees and managers usually resist this kind of change. Many people doing many things leads to context-switching, inefficiencies, and chaos. Good transition management into a functional organization could save a lot of agony in the life of a fast-growing organization.

The *learning workload* is so significant in Internet services, teaching hospitals, and law firms, that one of the organization's key themes is about learning — mentoring programs, internships, groups of one senior and multiple juniors, etc. The structure suits the effectiveness and efficiencies of learning as much as it suits the needs to perform the work itself.

Agility: So much of today's business environments is about strategic shifts, and immediate adjustments that reorganizing work and teams is a way of life in the workplace. Because of the natural resistance to change, managers should continuously talk to their teams about it, even when it happens elsewhere, and when it doesn't affect them right away. An agile team is always ready to make the necessary changes.

Group size: The right size depends on complexity of work, seniority of people, capacity of the group leader, expected amount of change, and the employees' stability. A small group is vulnerable because knowledge is very concentrated — one employee on leave could affect the group's productivity and contribution. A group too large, on the other hand, typically suffers from a manager who is stretched too thin. If employees wait for their manager to supervise, coach, or consult with them, then the group is too large for that manager to dedicate adequate time. An organization with many small groups also needs many managers, and that increases the general managerial overhead of the company.

Character: A good group has a character that its members are proud of. ... *We are the creative and audacious group — you need an idea, come to us... We are the execution machine — give us a project and we deliver...* A team with a character will develop excellence in everything they do to prove their claim to fame.

Organization Principles

The possible organizational structures of a collection of groups are hierarchical, matrix, independent pods, organic, and the *new-age* self-governing groups. Their key processes are either Agile or Waterfall. Organizing for business should not be confused with democracy and any form of social order. Contrary to their private lives, most employees appreciate more control, few and simple rules, and less choice, while they are at work.

An organization's hierarchy is *narrow* if there are many managers and the ratio of individual contributors to managers is low. The organization is *flat* where this ratio is high. The quickest way to examine the efficiency of an organization is to check the managerial span of control ratio. When we calculate this ratio, however, we have to be careful not to count as managers the individual contributors with the word *manager* in their title. For calculating the ratio, managers are the ones who have people reporting to them, and they are responsible for the work of other people.

Matrix structures, formal or informal, are common in modern organizations. More often than we recognize, employees find themselves directed by more than one person, and as often, they are confused by it. As a result of the dual reporting structure, a sales engineer, for example, is often caught between conflicting directions from his central management and the local sales team. From the center he is directed to learn new products, and if the local team doesn't see a fit for the new product in their target market, the sales engineer is caught in between the two positions. It is an example of a conflict of near-term goals vs. long-term strategy.

Specialty groups that aren't part of the organization's core, such as innovation group, advanced development, and business development, usually disrupt the organization, because they're understaffed to work independently. We create these groups to squeeze more value out of the organization; they usually have access and informal management authority. Creating these groups adds dimensions to the existing matrix of the core organization, albeit informally. Time and again, I see a new group whose job is to free the core organization from certain tasks, but the inevitable reality is additional managerial confusion. A specialty group should be staffed and budgeted appropriately, or it's better not to create it.

Solid lines and dotted lines of the matrix should suit the *learning workload*. Solid lines should trace the more difficult learning curve, or specialty, as the following example shows. The creative studio of a publishing company continuously learns new technologies, web libraries, and tools; for them the specialty learning workload is heavier than the learning of the specific projects that they serve. Therefore, the creative team should form a solid reporting line to their manager, and as a team they provide service to multiple projects. The resulting quality of service will be higher compared to assigning dedicated designers to each of the projects.

Centralized groups are more efficient than distributed teams as they enjoy visibility of the bigger picture and operate with better economies of scale.

Structural ambiguity should be minimal, i.e., if a function is central, it should be central across the organization without exceptions. Strong local leaders in large organizations often create their own mini headquarters to reduce the dependency on others, when the balance is incorrect or the process is inadequate between solid and dotted lines or central and local groups. This structure problem is hard to detect even though it's common, especially in large organizations where we find local teams performing central functions and central teams that create jobs to specialize in field local requirements.

To find such duplications and eliminate the waste in the organization, you have to investigate the different roles deeply, as job titles usually don't disclose the reality of how these employees spend their time.

A matrix is especially problematic if the organization has many managers who are not people managers. Project managers, program managers, product managers, coordinators, or expeditors are there to circumvent the organization. If you have many of them in the organization, it means that the formal matrix and its processes are failing.

Matrix organizations, formal and informal, are here to stay. Fewer organizations would need the matrix structure if employees and managers could give equal weight to the demand of service to other groups and the demands of their own function. However, like communism, it's a good idea, but impractical; we have to live with the trade-offs of matrix, and to learn how to balance and re-balance them correctly between the vertical solid lines and the horizontal dotted lines.

Independent pods, organic structures, and the new-age self-governing groups are still uncommon in businesses; therefore, they are outside the scope of this book.

Reorganization

If you are new to your team or organization, you should refrain from immediate reorganizations, unless you were appointed with a clearly communicated mission to reduce costs. The goal of significant reduction in cost unsettles the entire organization anyway. Unlike other reorganizations, it's better to do it all at once and resettle in a new structure as soon as possible. Long examinations prolong agony, and increase damage.

A normal reorganization starts with a shared feeling that *things could be better*. It continues with a group discussion of *what works* and *what doesn't*. The cost of the reorg should be justified in the eyes of most managers who would be affected by the change. If we proceed with reorganization after these discussions, we follow three steps: defining the *current problems*, building a *new structure*, and *testing* the new structure.

The problems that justify reorganization are *productivity challenges and specialization needs*. Here is a sample of such situations.

- Team Leads struggle to balance work and coaching responsibilities.
- Commitments are not delivered or delayed.
- Firefighting mode: no time to focus on important tasks.
- No time to vet tasks before execution; team is working on wrong priorities.
- Insufficient time to design tasks properly causes too much rework.
- No time to create a roadmap to allow groups to work independently.
- No opportunity to specialize; the competition is smarter than us.
- A lot of context switching in the workload.
- Not enough time to do everything we need to do.
- Unfulfilled potential of skills.
- Unexploited business opportunity.
- Cannot scale with current practices.
- New hire learning curve is too long.
- Other teams are not strong enough and we need to help them.
- Operational costs are too high.

Reorganization cannot make our problems disappear overnight. To find the best organizational structure, we should set a time in the future, for example in 3 months, and ask, *what should the structure be in this future?* By that time, many of the immediate problems will be resolved, and the new structure will focus on addressing the long-term problems. The planned-over-time approach is more likely to succeed than an overnight solution focused mostly on current needs. Time is certainly a healer of sorts as it lets us see a clearer picture.

The *new structure* that we chart for the future should be clear and detailed. The following is an example of a *restructuring plan*.

- The group splits into three, each with a team lead and area of responsibility.
- We have time from now until then, to complete all work in progress.
- We will assign all new tasks according to the new structure.
- We adopt the new process of roadmap and task management.
- The restructured teams have clear identity and function.
- We manage the transition with weekly coordination among the three future team leads.

We test the new structure by ensuring that the problems we identified initially are addressed. But even more importantly, we check the new structure relative to productivity criteria, and select the most important *goals for the new reorganization*. For example:

- Reduce context switching.
- Narrow the scope of each employee to allow specialization.
- Organize the groups around the longer learning curves.
- With time, all team members will need less supervision.

Once committed to the transformation into a new structure, we have to stick to the plan like religion. Along the way we will find new challenges and obstacles, but we cannot restart the process for every one of them. Organizational changes are not complete until they are fully tested over time; and if we keep changing them, we will never know what works and what doesn't.

From the simplest reorganization of office relocation, to the more complex changes that affect what people do and how they communicate, the reorganization process has to be inclusive; it's the shortest way to buy-in, collaboration, and reducing the harming effects of the aftermath. Even if you know exactly how you want to organize your team, you will have less damage to deal with if you take a step back and include as many people as you can in the process of change. Make the revolution feel like evolution — this is the secret sauce of reorganizations.

Organizational Processes

Management processes are a big concept that we often try to stay away from, so as not to overburden the organization, especially in small companies. However, we have to examine the managerial processes and fix them, when we see the symptoms such as many ad-hoc meetings, too many participants in meetings, long explanatory emails, repeated discussions, and lack of consistency and predictability in coordinating the work among groups.

Table 1   Company Calendar Checklist

Cycle	Internal Meetings and Cross-Functional Meetings
Annual	— Budgets — Kickoffs
Quarterly	— Strategy meetings — Company all-hands meetings — Marketing plan revisions — Product plan revisions — Technology roadmaps — Competitive reviews — Company policy committee — Individual employee-development plans
Monthly	— HR driven program reviews — Project roadmap reviews — Cost management — Operational and sales coordination — One-to-one meetings with two levels down in the organization — Knowledge sharing among teams
Bi-Weekly	— Agile cycle: sprint review, sprint demo, sprint reflection — Goal tracking — Progress reviews on new process — Cross-functional staff meetings (in stable environments) — Knowledge sharing inside teams — One-to-one meetings with subordinate managers
Weekly	— Cross-functional staff meetings (in fast pace environments) — One-to-one meetings with less experienced subordinate managers or new relationships
Daily	— SCRUM dailies — Daily briefings

At the top of the company the entire strategy and operational picture is concentrated within the heads of management; they don't realize, however, how much unaware their lower ranks are. It's often a symbiotic cycle of frustration; leaders at the top expect their lower managers to be innovative and break through glass ceilings, while the lower-level managers see only partial pictures that don't let them exploit their potential.

The optimal managerial process includes just the right amount of regular cross-functional meetings, roadmaps, and agile coordination processes.

Cross-Functional Managerial Processes

A *company calendar* is the right tool to rationalize the type and amount of cross-functional meetings to discuss and review strategy, plans, ongoing work, company events, etc. Your goal should be to replace as many ad-hoc meetings as possible with regularly scheduled meetings, so that managers cover all non-urgent subjects in them.

The preset calendar provides consistency and predictability, and keeps managers and employees at the highest performance levels. A stable calendar is the strong backbone that can carry a lot of weight and absorb changes, as the iterative process of correction is already in place (see Table 1).

Roadmaps

Everyone works better with more visibility to the next milestones, i.e., decisions that consider future steps save a lot of rework. Roadmaps are the main tool to set priorities and make multiple groups work in *balanced performance*. Roadmaps are good for every situation that involves progression, such as: infrastructure projects, new teams, new tools and processes, organizational changes, and the more common roadmaps of feature releases.

The following story of small internal project is an example to show the key principles of building a roadmap for saving project cycles and creating balanced performance among groups.

PROJECT ROADMAP

We wanted to develop financial *dashboards* for every business unit (BU) in the company, including key performance indicators (KPI) and estimated profit. Our BU managers already had a good grip on their responsibilities and basic KPIs. To complete the dashboard project, we needed to add the following:

- KPIs that interest other groups and upper management
- Direct cost allocation of systems and tools
- Indirect cost allocations of services from other groups
- Standard format of dashboard presentation
- Manual and automated data collection
- Data feeds from other groups

First, the project required managers' agreements on how to allocate costs, and then we needed the collaboration of multiple functions and groups, i.e., accounting, system administration, and sales operations. We didn't have a dedicated project manager; the COO of the company led it as a side project. We developed a monthly roadmap of 4 months and set the expectations from all groups in high-level detail, enough to tell the managers of the groups what was expected of them. The managers timed their tasks according to the roadmap, and all groups moved in parallel without having to wait for each other's actions. The biweekly reviews of the roadmap were the backbone of the project, and it was executed without pressure.

For a simple project like this one, there was no need to use agile methodologies. The steps were known and no assumptions needed validation. Each group worked on their tasks independently. The roadmap was good enough for driving all parties in a coordinated fashion toward the clear end result.

Roadmaps fail when they don't include everything related to the program; for example, product roadmaps that include all the new features, but do not include the changes in the license registration system that will manage the installations. Or, the common scenario of a feature roadmap that doesn't take into account the required software architectural changes. Partial roadmaps create delays because we assume that the project is managed, when in fact many important parts of it are not.

Agile and Lean Methods

The baseline for *Agile and Lean* methods is that most of our work is complex, made of many small tasks, and is based on insufficiently tested assumptions. As we progress with the work, our knowledge improves and the ability to test the assumptions also improves. If you work agile and lean, you start with a set of assumptions and then continually iterate cycles of testing, adjustments, and progress actions.

Agile and Lean use the intermediary ground between the flexibility you need to accommodate fluid requirements, and the stability you need for proper work. Since we cannot fix the requirements for long periods, we fix them for short periods; that's the essence of Agile and Lean. We covered the basic mechanics of Agile in chapter 9 as part of the principles for managing work. A more detailed discussion of Agile, Lean, and SCRUM is outside the scope of this book.

Conversion to Agile is not easy when other processes like Waterfall and Lifecycle Management are entrenched in the organization. For modern dynamic projects, converting to Agile makes a lot of sense. But you need a broad and deep consensus, and the commitment of the higher company ranks before you start.

Even though Agile has the mechanism of *Spike* to let product owners or project leads break the rules and cycle of the sprint for emergency requirements, the spikes should only be used rarely. If they're used often, it's a sure sign that the organization is not committed to Agile, and that pressure or direction from above takes over control. You justify a spike

only if the entire team needs to work on a bug that handicaps the operation of the business. Any other interrupt of the sprints' cadence could ruin the system and its benefits.

Agile methods increase the level of sharing and teamwork and reduce the amount of waste and rework. Once they get used to the method, teams are usually excited with the change to Agile. If converting to Agile fails, however, the feeling is of defeat and lower morale; therefore, it's better to consider all aspects and then commit to it for a long term.

I'm a People Person!

41

The organization should support managers with their people management responsibilities. We are *not* born managers; therefore, we need systems, policies, training, coaching, and role models.

New managers are often unprepared when they discover for the first time that … *they (the employees) are not like me* …. I was appointed to my first management role because I managed projects better than my peers. My teams were more professional, my customers happier, and the profits much better. I was, therefore, promoted to be the manager of project managers, but I was totally unprepared for the responsibility. Whenever I faced a problem — a paused project, mishandled customer, or any other failed execution — I would ask myself in frustration … *how did they end up in this situation?* Obviously, this was a wrong question; I was selected for the managerial job *because* I was not falling into those traps! My new job was, mainly, to teach others how to avoid such mistakes as well.

Good managers come in all shades of character, from the highly reserved to the extrovert, and anything in-between. Contrary to common belief, overconfident people are not better managers, as they tend to rely too much on natural leadership and skip the lessons of good practice and procedures; in contrast, the less confident manager would do more analysis and act according to best practices. Good management is more about experience than about pure talent.

Most of what you do as manager is to follow rules that you learn and practice as you gain experience. There's very little art in becoming a *people person* in the work environment.

Every new assignment of a manager to a team or organization starts with the work, but the challenges that hide and wait to be discovered are not necessarily there: rather, they are on the people side of the job. Training and coaching should prepare managers for these challenges. Even though it's hard to give them recipes, at least they should be aware of the symptoms, and of concepts and approaches to address them. The following are the most common challenges that new managers face.

People Management Challenges

Friend and colleague boundaries are not clear. In knowledge-based companies, work is much more than a place to earn a living; the boundaries of work and life are blurred. *If I was your peer and now I am your manager, how do I treat our past relationship? How much of a friend should I be to my new team?*

Every person is a full world unto himself. The philosopher Martin Buber said ... *every person born into the world represents something new, something that never existed before, something original and unique ...* People are unique, and the manager needs to learn how to work with all of them. New managers typically struggle with the question of how much to exert authority and direct. It takes them time to get comfortable with authority, especially when they deal with strong personalities.

More is hidden than revealed. When you ask for the full details of a task or a project, your wish is a command, and you typically get more than what you wished for. If, however, you asked your team members openly how they preferred to be managed, the best of the answers would be confusing and certainly not what you discover later.

Maslow's pyramid of needs. On the job people's needs start with the *basics* such as compensation, knowledge, and tools to do the job. Then *safety* needs to work in a team and be unthreatened by it. Further up the pyramid are the *social and esteem* needs to be accepted as a valuable team member, and

lastly, to have the opportunity for *self-actualization* — to feel accomplished and recognized.

The team members expect their manager to satisfy all of these needs. However, as a new manager you are not ready with the specifics of each person, and in real life the needs are mashed-up and not well organized in layers as in the model; the needs emerge as problems without prior warning, especially when the employees see an opportunity to raise latent issues that were not resolved by the previous manager. The hierarchy of needs, as explained by the model, helps the manager understand problems deeper than what they appear on the surface. And understanding the root causes is the first step toward resolution.

Work–life balance is personal. What is acceptable to one person may not necessarily be acceptable to others. The manager needs to be friendly and open with the team members and manage the differences without affecting the quality of the teamwork.

Inside competition in the team. Team members always compete for attention, recognition, and the opportunity to advance. Tacit as it might be, this undercurrent is a source of tension that influences what the members say and do.

Money is powerful but it doesn't solve everything. Managers who make a special effort to improve the compensation of their team members with bonuses or raises are often disappointed when they aren't satisfied with the outcome. As with anything else you buy with money, once the employees are accustomed to their new pay, their focus is on the next improvement.

Managing in good times and in bad times. Motivating and influencing the team in good times is easier, as the common focus is on achieving more with what we already know. However, it's a lot more difficult if you are a new manager whose job is to solve the issues of a bad period. You're expected to know better, even though you know nothing at first. Your job is to focus the team on opportunities beyond the low point and build their confidence to go through the corrective programs. This requires leadership and a lot of shoulder-to-shoulder teamwork.

Learning curves. Some people learn fast, but we cannot conclude that slow learners aren't good enough, as they could be more thorough, meticulous, and cautious. A known fact is that the best learning happens by experience and in pairs, but somehow we often expect employees to develop skills without any investment from our side, just by reading or following free online resources.

Feedback. The manager is responsible for feedback to, from, and within the team. A new manager should create more feedback flows than usual, until both the team and the manager get to know each other well.

*

Learning to manage people is about fine balancing of give-and-take, and the best approach is to play with open cards and get involved with the people and the work. Over 30 years in various leadership positions, I was almost always parachuted into the position from outside the team or organization; I had to establish myself as the manager and leader without the benefits of knowing the place and its people, and without being known to them. I learned the hard way — and later found out that was the best way — that working with people on shared tasks makes everything about management much simpler. Team members enjoy exhibiting and sharing their knowledge, and in so doing help the new manager become their leader.

Active coaching of team members benefit the manager directly, and sometimes more than it benefits the team. Your information on projects and tasks becomes direct and unfiltered, and once you know the work and the team, you will delegate it with confidence as the workload grows.

If you are a manager of managers, most of your tasks will be delegated at some point. Use any possible opportunity to work with someone on these tasks and prepare them for that time.

Manager's Self Awareness

One of the main issues in being a leader is that people in your environment refrain from giving you true feedback. The only hard feedback that's

continuously flowing is the actual results of the organization; for the rest you have to look for clues.

Managers and leaders usually have strong opinions on their strengths and their needs to improve; but the people around them may have different opinions, especially about how the leader influences them. What you think are strong points might actually be harmful to the organization. For example, a manager who is a good organizer might be the only organizer of the team and the ultimate crutch without which the team cannot move. Or, a leader with many ideas that might, in fact, train his organization to rely solely on him for any sort of innovation.

Managers and leaders have blind spots, i.e., behaviors that they fail to see or to recognize their influence on other employees. Righteousness and arrogance are always in the blind spot zone. Only once they see and understand the effect on others, can leaders expand their scope of positive behaviors and improve.

All methods of leadership evaluation use some form of panoramic view, i.e., how people in the work environment see the manager, leader, or the leadership team. The more diverse the collection of feedback, the more helpful it is — like the combined reflections from mirrors in different angles that give the complete view.

One common panoramic tool used in large organizations is the annual *Employee Satisfaction and Motivation Survey* (ESMS), or the newer versions of it, with better marketing spins, known as *Employee Engagement Survey* or *Best Place to Work Questionnaire*. The anonymous survey covers the workplace conditions, company policies, and the general quality of leadership. ESMS highlights broad issues of the entire organization but it's only marginally effective in identifying specific manager's issues, and then only when these are extreme. Typically, the ESMS findings affirm known issues, rather than revealing new ones.

More helpful to managers who are interested in real self-improvement is the *360° leadership assessment tool*. The voluntary survey collects detailed inputs from 8 to 20 people surrounding the leader, from all sides — internal and external to the organization. The assessed behaviors typically align with these categories:

- Result driven, responsibility
- Accountability
- Managing people
- Communication
- Leadership and management
- Solving problems and adaptability
- Influence on both people and organization

The *360° leadership survey* often surprises the evaluated leaders with findings that are both positive and negative. It's a very powerful tool. One of my clients decided to do it as a mandatory survey on all managers and team leads. The competitive undercurrent among managers actually helped the process; we gave managers the choice to keep the findings private, but once one of them decided to open the discussion about his corrective actions, all of them followed, and the process was very effective.

It Is All About Teamwork

Teamwork has become the credo for all organizations, irrespective of the size. Even in the smallest of companies, one superhuman soldier cannot win the war.

One of the simplest approaches to assess the quality of teamwork in the organization is to follow *Patrick Lencioni's* checklist from his book *The Five Dysfunctions of a Team*. His assessment criteria look for gaps in teamwork traits. If the statements are highly true, the team needs more corrective action or intervention.

- To what extent does the team suffer from *lack of trust*?
  Nothing can be built without the foundation of trust among team members. We need to trust each other that we *can* deliver and that we *will* deliver.

- Are the team members *afraid of conflict*?
  People in the team have different opinions, naturally; if we refrain from discussion because we fear conflict, the team is not functional; frequently, the team is dominated by certain members, and achieves the appearance of consensus, but not a real one.

- Is there *lack of commitment* from team members?

  Decisions are made, but there's no full commitment to follow these decisions. We meet and discuss, but later, it is to each his own.

- Does the team allow its members to *avoid accountability*?

  Team members do not follow the team's commitments, and there are no consequences. We pretend we are a team, but we don't progress.

- Do we pay enough *attention to results*?
  The team is just passing time and not taking their charter seriously to achieve measurable goals. We decide to meet again, or appoint someone for the task without specifying the expectations. The actions are interpreted freely.

The response to teamwork issues is usually to tighten a process or add feedback steps; unless these measures are iterative, checked, and rechecked over time they will not be effective in resolving the teamwork issues.

Serious dysfunction in teams needs intervention from a facilitator to avoid dysfunction in the process of assessment itself. Minor dysfunction can usually be discussed and resolved internally.

It's good to learn from extreme situations of team dysfunction. In a couple of them, I got involved when the lingering frustrations and fear of conflict caused the team members to stop talking to each other, and all their relationships were severed. Just like rebellious teenage kids, they would not sit together in a meeting, and I had to interview each of them separately to get their versions of the full story. Only then could I force them to share these stories with each other; and I did it by telling them that if they didn't, I would.

The team members' views were so different that they would not agree on the current state of things; I could only make them agree on a future desired point, but not on how to get there. Once they agreed, however, they had to commit to get there by themselves, since they couldn't help each other. These were very bad situations where the only way to get a resolution was to step in and out of the facilitator role and involve myself in follow-ups. To unlock the stalemate, I acted as a *facilitator*, forcing the sides to talk to each other with a threat that I would disclose to the team what they had told me in private. To ensure progress of the resolution, I acted as their *manager* following up in a collaborative fashion on the action items that resulted from the agreement.

Team Motivation and Morale

High morale and motivation in the team is contagious, but the reverse is also true, i.e., one bad apple can spoil the entire cart. The emotional strength of the team is the responsibility of the manager, and the way to achieve it is to create and narrate its story from several angles. Creating the team's stories is sometimes the only task that engages the entire team, all at once. What better way is there to develop teamwork than to have them develop their own identity as a team?

Team elevator pitch makes every employee an ambassador for his team. Your team members would not steal the show from you; on the contrary, you should encourage them to narrate the story. The more they do it, the stronger you are perceived as their manager. Develop the story as a team exercise, and you would be amazed at how much pride people take in their work.

Team BoD presentation is another cut of the team's story. Imagine a hypothetical board of directors that oversees your team's performance as a business. It could be the employees of the rest of the company, their managers or your peers. You impress them with the team's performance with a presentation that covers all the important aspects of the work; if they were impressed, they would keep you on the job.

This BoD actually exists, albeit tacitly, and its most important members are the employees of the team itself, whom you engage in creating this

presentation and updating it regularly. In addition, it's an exercise that unites and strengthens the team as they understand the full scope of their contribution to the company and its value.

Finally, *Monthly Reports* are not simply an old concept. Involving the team in generating its monthly report is yet another way to develop the shared responsibility and accountability in the team, and with it the motivation and morale. Employees feel a lot better about their work when they see how it adds to the true value of their team.

Make the Most of the Experience!

In almost every aspect of the management role, there's no replacement for experience. How, then, do you approach each of your management roles to gain the most experience from it?

Correlate your experience with an onion. The work of your team is the core of your knowledge and experience. The more you learn about the work of the other teams, layer by layer from the inside out, the bigger and juicier the onion gets. And that is how your experience grows. Unlike research, where experience is about digging deeper and zooming in, with management it's about zooming out and seeing more of the same in other situations.

Encourage your team members to expand their interest in other teams, and involve them in as much cross-functional activity as possible. You will see them grow faster and in turn you will grow with them. In one of my prior positions, the company offered a rotational program to exceptional university graduates. They had the opportunity to work in three different jobs and departments during their first two years, and then select the area that suited them the most. As an executive mentor to the program, I worked with my trainees on building and accumulating the most experience from these 2 years. The results were amazing. One quote in particular summed it perfectly; my colleague who hired one of my trainees for his permanent position after the program, said that … *he worked and acted like a talented person with at least five years of experience*… You could say that I received an ROI of 2.5 on each year of mentoring him.

Another way to broaden the experience is to follow the example of a company where I coached the leadership team. They assigned each of their key employees a personal project that went outside their direct responsibility. Beyond benefitting their respective teams, these continuous improvement tasks enriched the experience of these key employees which amounted to a net gain for the company.

Friend of Numbers

PART IX

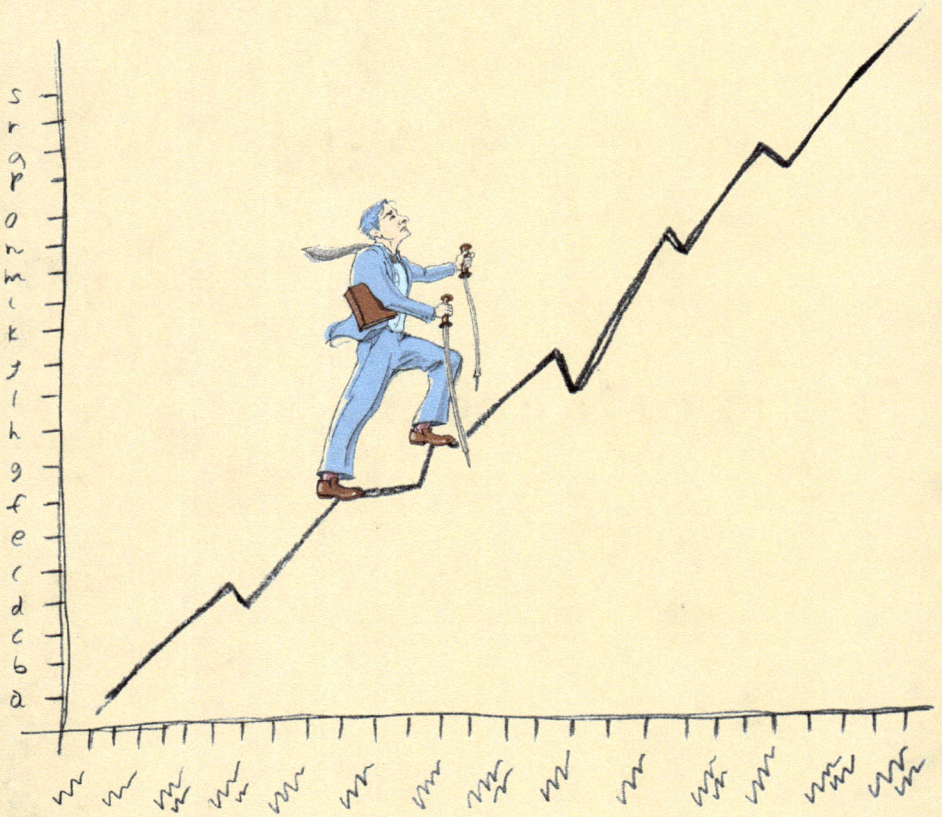

Process Metrics and Feedback

42

It always makes me smile when I am talking to someone and they reach for their phone to calculate five times forty-nine, while I have already figured that two hundred and fifty minus five is two hundred and forty five. But no more than a reserved smile, honestly. I am not worried about the loss of calculating skills — there's plenty of computing power around; I do worry about managers neither understanding numbers nor interested enough in getting them, when there are no machines to fill in the gaps. Even the most automated stock-trading machinery that makes micro decisions in microseconds is continuously watched and overruled by people who understand numbers.

Watch Hans Gosling's 2003 Ted Talk and you too could smile in the company of numbers. There's no one better to show us the importance of tools to understand data, the development of health metrics, and the ridiculous overuse of averages when there are such huge differences inside the groups of numbers. In our context we would call these concepts *dashboards, business unit health metrics,* and *segmentation and statistical distribution.*

We need numbers. The corrective mechanisms that are the essence of the knowledge economy do not work without them. MIT's *Beer Game* (well, not that one) developed back in 1960s by Jay Forrester shows how bad things could get without corrective mechanisms.

The game simulates a complete supply chain, starting from a beer factory through distributors and wholesalers and retailers — four main stages in the chain. Players are stations along the chain that receive orders for beer, and based on them they decide how much to order from the next station upstream. While playing, they are not allowed to communicate and collaborate; they see the incoming order from the player downstream, and decide solely on that input how much to order upstream.

Without spoiling the surprise of the game, I will say that after the game is played the statistical analysis shows that there was neither rhyme nor reason to the players' decisions. They were not allowed to cooperate — they had no way to correct their actions. Without a corrective mechanism the chain of input–process–output creates chaotic behaviors and much waste in the operation of the business.

Accurate data is essential for business transactions and automation, for which we have accounting departments and powerful machinery. However, as managers, we don't need accurate numbers for most of our decisions and to keep the corrective mechanisms working. The goals that we set for the business are not scientific either; we usually pick a number after applying a few rules, top-down or bottom-up. Our interest is the gap from the current status to the goal, with some allowance for an acceptable tolerance in either direction. We know that we work correctly when our actions reduce the gap.

Numbers can be very deceiving. There's a famous story (not sure if it's true) about the Raytheon missile that in its first test hit the target like Newton's apple (not sure if this is true either). So accurate was the hit that the test was declared a success. To the dismay of the test team, it was sheer luck that granted them the perfect result; the missile guidance was found later to be not so great after all. *Repeatability of measurements* within an acceptable range is a key concept in understanding numbers.

To be sure that the numbers are valid it's better to measure in two different ways and compare the results. For example, before proceeding with Lasik

surgery, eye surgeons take two sets of measurements from two separate sets of equipment. The equipment is identical, and yet, the measurements are not; and since absolute accuracy isn't possible, they take the average of the two.

Surprising numbers are always suspicious. Save your emotions until after the numbers are validated in different ways, because the way we measure affects the results, sometimes profoundly.

Averages are meaningful for making decisions when the spread of the numbers is low. A *narrow bell curve* means that most of the numbers are similar to the number in the middle; we can therefore use the average. However, *a flat bell curve* means that the numbers are all over the place; their average is meaningless to most decisions.

When the numbers are spread, statisticians say that the standard deviation is large. To make good decisions, we need to divide such a set of numbers into groups and treat each of them separately. The most common example is from sales — segmenting customers by volume of business, to: enterprise, SMB and long tail, and treating each segment with different methods and budgets. We have several names that are roughly synonymous for the graphical presentation of the subdivided groups: *distribution, bar graph, histogram, Pareto charts, percentile,* and *80/20.*

Day-to-day managerial decisions are mostly related to process, organization and productivity; types of measurements relevant to each of them are discussed below.

Process Metrics and Feedback

We generally consider a process as a sequence of actions. But, we have seen that without a corrective mechanism the results will not be what we expect. The process is, therefore, the sequential actions *with* the corrective mechanism. In science and mechanics, these corrective mechanisms are mathematical models programmed into computers. In human work, we adapt similar principles into rules of behavior called *corrective actions.*

The corrective mechanism narrows the gap between what we have and what we want. If the action is good, the gap narrows and we reinforce the action; conversely, if it's bad, the gap grows. Therefore, we take a different action in reverse. We continue to measure the gap relative to the goal as it goes up or down depending on the circumstances, and we continue with the appropriate corrective actions. These are the workings of a process.

The familiar Broken Telephone game we played as kids in kindergarten shows that if we don't correct *quickly,* the accumulated gap grows as the players add bits of incorrect information. This is the principle of *dead-time.* When there's no corrective reaction to the gap, time passes and steps are taken, and we get bigger gaps.

Unstable work environments have managers that change their minds or priorities frequently. They create new gaps, do not measure the right gaps, do not understand them, and therefore, they create long dead-times by not correcting them. It is physics. It's impossible to stabilize a process with *long dead-times.*

For corrective mechanisms to work, we set several measurement points and goals along the process, and feed the gaps (back) upstream to make intermediary corrections. If it sounds complex, it should not. We know these checkpoints as *Key Performance Indicators (KPIs).* The first rule for a good process is: *more checkpoints with smaller delays between them reduce the dead-time and the accumulated effect of gaps and overreactions.*

The second rule is about *how we react.* If we react only in proportion to the current gap, we might be overreacting or underreacting. For example, our goal is 500 and our current measurement is 400, but we also see that the trend is upward. Therefore, even if we changed nothing, the gap would become smaller. Our corrective action should react to the gap of 100 with a discount, because of the *trend.* If the trend were down, our corrective action would be to react to the gap of 100 and a little more. Another possibility is that the measurement of 400 is only a blip on the chart, when we expected it to be at 300; we know that because we have been watching the *history* of the measurement. Our corrective action reacts to the history of these numbers more than to the current measurement because we see that it's a

blip. The *best corrective actions respond to a combination of the history of the gap, the current gap, and the future, as seen by the trend.*

These rules are easier to apply when we have numbers. For most decisions, however, we just apply the principles. *The process that works well has a lot of checkpoints and corrective actions that don't overreact or underreact, as we understand the historical behavior and the trends.*

The following are samples of KPI lists in numbers. We also have samples of feedback for when numbers are inapplicable — human inputs, assessments, formal, and informal (Tables 1 to 5).

Table 1   Business Metrics Sample

Business Metrics
Dollar amounts: revenue, gross profit, net profit
KPIs: lead funnel conversion rates, inventory metrics, sales cycle
Ratios: growth rates, cost of sales to revenue, ROI
Quality: LTV, retention rates, market share

Table 2   Operational Metrics Sample

Operational Metrics
KPIs: order fulfillment cycle, downtime
Ratios: inventory to revenue, inventory turns
Quality: time to market, yield, failure statistics
Service: problem resolution stats, customer satisfaction (C-SAT)

Table 3   Organization and Performance Metrics Sample

Organization and Performance Metrics
Revenue per employee
Employee satisfaction
Employee turnover
Cost per employee

Table 4   Informal Feedback Sample

Informal Feedback
Acknowledge and paraphrase during conversation to confirm that the message was received and accepted.
A manager who is present and available sends a message to the employees that they are important and that he is there to help.
Any information that passes through a conversation.
Emotional reactions.

Table 5   Formal Feedback Sample

Formal Feedback
Information passed in meetings: one to one, group, spot checks
Meeting summaries, action items
Reviews of work and performance of employees
Agile process checkpoints

Because we have a mix of KPI numbers and human feedback to feed the engines of the corrective mechanisms, managers need to be the drivers of these fire engines and get involved in all the corners of their organization continuously because *a system that doesn't correct itself will go out of control!*

But what if the drivers are in place, the corrective engines are running, but there are still failures, because these processes are not perfect. We would be looking for the *failure mechanism*; is it a *bottleneck* in one area that causes delays in other areas? Do we rework tasks because people dabble in too many activities and do not have enough *focus* to do a good job? A simple *fishbone analysis* (a foundational quality control tool) can start the investigation and narrow the search for clues; it will also help to set priorities and fix the root cause problems according to their real importance.

The corrective mechanism and process metrics need to *move continuously in the right direction* of improvement; it is less important to reach the goals, as long as we are improving. In any case, if we reached the goal, we should raise it and keep improving.

Organizational Metrics

43

A startup or a very young company doesn't need to care much about organizational health until it grows. With growth, however, and division into functional groups, we do need to worry about health. Already in an organization with 30–50 employees, the organization's head needs to manage the following basic metrics:

- An organization with too many layers of management, or with a low ratio of employees to managers is *narrow* or *tall*.

- When most managers struggle with time management, it could be a symptom of too much responsibility — a *wide or flat* organization.

- The people who create, maintain, and sell products and services are in *direct roles*. Coordinators of work are *indirect* — product, program, project, escalation, and backlog managers. Administrative functions, such as accounting, HR, and office management, are *overhead*. An organization is *fat* when the ratios of indirect-to-direct and overhead-to-direct are excessive.

- *Fitness* of the organization is measured by execution metrics, such as time to market (TTM), release cycles, competitive features, transaction cycles, and productivity. An organization that is slow, or consistently behind the competition in these metrics, has low fitness level i.e., it isn't *nimble*.

- An organization that continuously revamps structures or processes lacks *mental stability* and will not develop the necessary stamina for achieving success.

The *acceptable ranges* for organizational health metrics are wide, and there's no science that dictates the absolute truths. An organization might have excessive layers of management because it's investing and preparing for a big surge in business. Each situation is unique, but relevant benchmarks are easy to find.

The company cost structure, gross profit, and cost of sales depend on its type; a services company in enterprise cloud software has very different costs compared to medical care services; a capital equipment company has different costs and risks compared to a software company. The cost structure, gross profit, and cost of sales also depend on the company's stage in its life: during growth the company invests in its future; maturity is when it controls its costs; and during decline the company focuses on saving. Cost structures and expectations for gross profits in each market segment help set the ranges for the health metrics.

Once we set a *baseline for the health metrics* we can monitor and control them. Usually, the difficulty is in counting correctly because we tend to confuse *critical* with *direct*; for example, a critical coordinator job is indirect, but we would likely count it as direct. As in human health, some fat is good, and indirect jobs are not necessarily bad for organizational health. More important, however, is to keep the counting method stable so that the periodic checks serve as meaningful KPIs.

We address organizational health problems with changes to process, structure, and budget allocations. All improvement programs should *increase focus* and be *above the point of critical mass*. A little investment in training would not fix a serious skill shortage, as much as a crash diet cannot solve an obesity problem. Any time we address a health problem with short relief, we might hurt the organization instead of helping it. For example, a group is so overtaxed that it needs five more people to cover the workload. The solution is adding five people or automating the work. Due to budget constraints, the manager is giving them one more person as relief, but in fact, he just added training workload to the overstressed team

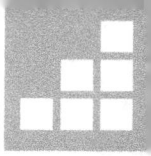

that should be focused on preparing their work methods for automation. The solution in this simplified example is both below critical mass and defocusing; it's like pretending to solve a problem and delaying resolution, instead of implementing a real fix.

An organization is only as healthy as its managers. Read articles about Finland's educational system and there's no doubt that you would support investment in teachers to get better students, and investment in managers to get better employees. On-the-job coaching and workshops are effective in seeing real improvements in managers and leaders. External courses are better at explaining the world of work, and the theories. Both approaches are valid and the best is a mix that provides external references as well as internal enrichment of experience.

You should invest in the skills of mangers the moment you reach 30–50 employees and it's an organization, rather than a group. The leader of the organization and his experience should focus entirely on strategy and execution and not in management training. I have noticed CEOs of small companies giving speeches to their managers about principles in management and considering it as a part of their education. Learning has different dynamics, though. While learning, the manager takes time to analyze, digest, and draw personal conclusions; when he is listening to his boss, however, his brain works differently.

The method to gauge the strengths of the management team and their skills is done in periodic leadership assessments.

Tables 1 through 5 are samples of organizational health metrics. Some of them are relevant even to small organizations.

Table 1 Recruitment Metrics Sample

Recruitment Metrics
Quality — first year turnover
Stability — constant flow of candidates
Statistics — time to fill, cost of hiring
Number of open positions relative to candidate sources
Candidate funnel statistics

Table 2 Organization and Workforce Metrics Sample

Organization and Workforce Metrics
Turnover of employees
Industry and local market benchmarks
Compensation relative to standards
Reorganizations: frequency and analysis
Investment in key employees
Diversity goals and compliance

Table 3 Employee Development Metrics Sample

Employee Development Metrics
Investment in education
Skill maps
Key Employee and Talent Development programs
Upward mobility

Table 4 Work–Life Balance Metrics Sample

Work-Life Balance Metrics
Employee satisfaction
Company policies
Investment in social events
Levels of stress in the organization

Table 5 Managerial Strength Metrics Sample

Managerial Strength Metrics
Managing situations of questionable employee performance
Bench strength: succession plan
360-degree surveys
Employee satisfaction surveys

Productivity and Performance Metrics

44

The simplest definition of *productivity* is how much money each person produces on average. Calculated for the whole company, it's the net profit divided by headcount. If we expand the definition to results that are not measured directly by money, we overlap with the definition of *performance*. With productivity and performance (P&P) we measure how well the entire system works, i.e., people, equipment, capital, and process. To explore P&P concepts and metrics, we examine them by how managers see and use them.

- Managing pipelines
- Managing quality
- Principles and metrics for making decisions
- Business performance and cost allocation
- Management dashboards

Managing Pipelines

Pipelines are work items that are queued to be processed, e.g., sales leads, bug lists, and service calls. Unlike supermarket queues where all customers have equal stature, the work items in the pipeline could differ in importance, urgency, and weight. Therefore, we assign them categories and priorities; the items can jump the queue, and managers can assign the work appropriately.

We review common pipeline examples first, and then the basic queue metrics and their respective managerial decisions.

- *Sales pipelines* and funnels start with leads that convert to prospects that further convert to customers. The categories in this pipeline are: size of potential deal, expected time to close, offered products, probability, existing customer Y/N, reference Y/N, etc.

- *Accounting collection pipeline* is the list of invoices that have not been paid yet. The important attributes would be: billed amount, age of invoice, customer's history of payment, stop-service until paid Y/N, etc.

- *Service call* pipelines queue requests for service. The most important attributes are: level of urgency, customer expectation for response time, level of service entitlement, severity, complexity, call-initiation (voice, email, automatic alert), etc.

- *Bug lists* help software development set priorities to their work. The most important attributes are: subsystem, severity, exposure, effect on customers, effect on marketing, age, etc.

- *Feature lists* help engineering plan their work. They also guide sales and marketing campaigns and strategy decisions. The important attributes include: competitive need, expected incremental revenue, feature of a bundle, customer expectations, level of effort, subsystem, etc.

*

The basic statistical metrics apply to all pipelines because they are (mathematical) queues; the names might change for the different pipelines but the principles and meanings are the same.

- *Segmentation, histogram, or distribution*: The first analysis of any pipeline is to divide it into groups according to one or more

categories. For example, in an enterprise sales pipeline, we are interested in the *main deals*, i.e., large opportunities with high probability, and in their volume of potential business. We are also interested in the *long tail* — many small opportunities that consume our resources but do not generate much business. We might decide to move the long-tail business to an inside sales team where costs of sales are lower.

In a service pipeline, for example, the histogram divides calls into subgroups of committed level of service. We could shift service agents from Tier-2 to Tier-1, if we have a surge in Tier-1 calls and we're about to miss the committed response time. In bug lists and service pipelines, we also give priority to groups with high urgency, severity, or exposure.

■ *Time-related KPIs*: Anyone who has ever waited in a queue knows that time is a key factor in the quality of service. While responding to voice initiated calls (VICs) we measure the *abandonment rate* and if it's higher than our goal, we change the assignments of personnel to shifts. In a bug list, abandonment is all those *non-critical bugs* that accumulate in the pipeline and are never fixed. For customers who raised these non-critical issues, the sheer volume of them may be annoying enough to reflect badly on the product. You would not call an exterminator to kill an ant, but you will do it for a swarm of them; engineering teams typically announce a campaign to sweep an accumulation of non-critical bugs when the volume becomes annoying enough. In a sales pipeline, abandonment is leads that were not processed.

For each subgroup in the pipeline we also measure several other time statistics: time for first response, time to resolve, and *aging reports*. We borrow the concept of aging from accounting practices, where it's used for the collection pipeline, as follows: we divide the customers into good payers and questionable payers, and then subdivide the outstanding invoices according to their age. Our pipeline rule could be: call good payers if the invoice is outstanding for more than 60 days, and questionable payers after 30 days. Aging reports are used for bug lists, service calls, and sales pipelines in a similar manner.

From accounting practices, we can also borrow the concept of DSO (days sales outstanding). It's an *overall metric* for the *entire* collection pipeline. If our calculated DSO is 35 days, it means that on average it takes 35 days to collect the money that we invoiced. We aim for lower DSOs i.e., to collect the money for what we sold. If our DSO is getting worse, we examine the quality of the customers that we serve, or do a campaign to resolve collection issues. DSO calculations are very useful to manage any pipeline. For example, if our average time to release new features is worsening, we know that product marketing is running ahead of engineering, or that the engineering organization needs attention.

- *Efficiency in the pipeline*: In accounting we measure collection rates. Not all invoices are paid; some customers cancel orders and ask for a *refund*, others request a *chargeback* from their bank, or just refuse to pay. The Collection Rate is the ratio between real business and assumed business, i.e., money collected vs. money invoiced. Visa and MasterCard, for example, refuse to work with companies whose chargeback rates are more than 1–2%. Collection rate measures the overall efficiency of the invoices in the pipeline. In a feature list, we could similarly measure how many features engineering developed that had no use later, and then know the efficiency of feature requests. In a pipeline of service calls, we could look at reopened calls as cancelled resolutions and measure the efficiency of our service staff against the percentage of reopened calls.

- *Conversion rates*: In sales pipelines, they mean the ratios between prospects to leads or customers to prospects. If the conversion rate for a company is 2.5 to 1, we know that for a good chance to reach the quota we need 2.5 times greater prospective business in the pipeline. That is how sales organizations work.

In the context of online marketing and e-commerce, conversion rates are much more complex. The prevalent combinations are: views or exposures of advertisements or content, one-click events, two or more clicks, viewers who enter data in a form, viewers who subscribe, returning viewers, clicks to buy, etc.

- The *queue length* in each conversion state is the basis for all optimization work. In the context of online marketing, it means to change something in the way the advertisement appears and see if the conversion rates improve.

  Another interesting application of queue length is in engineering problem lists. It would be time to re-architect the software if we see many different problems that are associated with a particular area. The queue for that area will be unusually long, which will signal the need to revise the architecture. If we counted the problems only by type and not by area of software, we would have missed the root cause of these problems, i.e., the outdated architecture.

- *Level of effort*: Managers should understand the amount and type of work for each subgroup in the pipeline before doing budgeting and resource allocation. They segment the pipeline according to the providers as opposed to customers in order to see the respective workload or level of effort. Typically, you would find assignments of pipeline segments to: inside sales group, new team members, experts, level-1 teams, advanced support teams, customer relationship tiers, etc.

Managing Quality

Some of the pipeline metrics measure the quality of how well we process the work in the pipeline. Usually, however, when we discuss quality we talk about failures — their occurrences, frequency, severity, root cause, etc. But we should also take a more humane approach to quality and measure the level of annoyance; a smartphone that sends us software updates frequently may not have serious failures, but it sure is annoying.

We manage and analyze *quality* by understanding the following *concepts* and *metrics*.

- *Amount of failures* and the associated *level of effort*, per period and per system, help us plan the work of resolving failures and improving quality.

- *Repeat failures* and *mean (average) time between failures* (MTBF). Worsening MTBF or failures that occur again are symptoms of deeper root causes that need to be addressed.

- *Average time to resolution* is both a service pipeline metric and a product quality metric.

- *Severity* indicates the failure's damaging effect on users or other systems. For example, as users of banking systems, we have learned to expect data to be always online and available, on the ATM machines and other access systems. However, we know that behind the scenes systems occasionally fail. The bank's IT decisions on costly redundant systems depend on the severity and exposure. Complete data-loss (DL) incidents are rare in banking, because the systems can recover the important data if necessary. The time that the data was unavailable (DU), however, is almost as bad from the quality of service point of view. DU/DL occurrences are a metric of the highest severity.

- *Annoyance metrics*: Uptime, downtime, planned downtime, and number of version updates — all of these affect the quality of service and translate to customer satisfaction metrics.

- *Bubble charts* and *heat maps* are meant for identifying areas that are prone to problems. *Troubles come in Bundles* should be taught in engineering schools, since poorly designed systems are buggy and problematic in more than one way. For example, if a popular website has areas that are rarely visited or with high rates of abandonment, it's probably a combination of poor design, lower quality of content, issues of graphics, user clicking flows, annoying colors, font, etc. Website visit analysis or advanced web analytic tools could discover the various problems occurring in the area. A relatively large bubble of problems calls for a complete overhaul.

- *Usability failures* and *infancy failures* occur with the introduction of a new product or system. The time from introduction to normal and expected failure rates indicates the quality of the product's user features and the system's overall quality. The *bathtub curve* shows

the high occurrences of *infant mortality* failures that decrease with time to *constant random* failures, and as the system gets old, the *wear-out* increases the number of failures again. This analysis is mostly used for hardware systems. A good bathtub that has a sharp drop on the left, a long flat stretch, and then a slow incline at the right indicates that the system is easy to learn and durable.

■ *Relative vs. absolute*: It is often difficult to find out the correct quality benchmark and then make comparisons to it. The more common approach is *continuous improvement (CI)*. You take a measurement as a baseline and improve continuously from this starting point. This is the iterative nature of lean and agile; you know where it starts, but not where it goes, so you keep iterating as long as you are improving.

Principles and Metrics for Making Decisions

Return on Investment (ROI) is the most well-known criterion for making decisions. We use *estimated* ROIs, because we cannot predict the future. And because ROI estimates are often optimistic — we know it from past performance — we need to use other tools to assess the investments, results, and risks. Gut feelings and hunches are good, but not enough; they need to be supplemented with data and tools. First check the facts and see what they mean, and then decide on the most sensible options.

■ *Sunk cost and loss aversion* were already discussed earlier in the book. The principle is simple, though. ROI terminology is about the *future* return on current investment decisions. Anything from the past, investments or results, has no bearing on the decision at hand.

■ *Data*: The best practice for making business decisions is to review data routinely and not only when we need to make a decision. Quality of data takes time to perfect. Only with routine use of data over time can we examine the data, and make it reliable and complete. That is why the first stage of building a BI function in the company starts with collecting data and ensuring its coverage and integrity.

■ *Checklists* were already discussed in previous chapters. They are another way to create relevant data to review routinely.

Routine use of *checklists* and *data* helps us find and address problems methodically, and not by intuition or crisis. That's the only way to ensure that we don't miss important issues and that priorities are correct.

■ *Potential vs. incremental*: We like our successes, so whether intentionally or not, we tend to set goals that would make success likely. *Better than last time* is usually how we set the goals. But, especially in sales, we should approach it differently. *Inch it up* by 10% over last year, for example, is not necessarily great success. In an enterprise account, if we sold them 2% of their budget last year, it would mean that this year we would sell them 2.2% of their budget, if it remained the same. We were, however, insignificant to them last year and we would remain so this year. It's very likely that another vendor with more influence in the account will expand his reach and take us out of the account. In such cases, we should aim higher to increase our wallet share in the account based on potential.

■ The method of *clean sheet design* applies beyond sales. As the name suggests, it starts from a position of no history and no baggage, and checks the potential. It's about *asking the right questions,* such as:

— What if we used a new technology for the product design, could we get a better product fast and move ahead of competition?

— What if we sold a partner's product instead of our own, could we achieve better market share? Could our total profit be higher even though the profitability is lower?

■ *Critical mass* as a decision criterion could be confusing, because it's hard to know whether our decision is *too little-too late* until we test it. But we *could* test it as an assumption in most cases. If the solution proves to be under critical mass for a sample, it's almost sure that it would not be better on large scale. Any action that is below critical mass results in waste and damage. When

you suspect a critical mass issue, think in simple phrases: *is it a drop in the ocean? Are we spread too thin? Is it just a Band-Aid? A cosmetic fix?*

Business Performance and Cost Allocation

Business performance is measured by top line and bottom line, i.e., revenue and net profits. But these overall company numbers would not help heads of business units (BU) understand the performance of their unit if costs are shared and mixed with other BUs. Overhead costs (HR function, finance, administration), and indirect costs of internal services (systems, service, marketing, engineering, BI, etc.) — are typically shared in small and medium companies. Some BUs consume more of these services than others, so the costs per BU are unclear.

But if we want to manage the BU properly, we need to develop a P&L dashboard for it and allocate the shared costs correctly. We can estimate the cost allocations, and it would be good enough for accountability and decisions. The P&L dashboard is a simple spreadsheet updated every month or quarter. Table 1 is the high level structure of the P&L Dashboard.

Monthly P&L for Business Units in Small or Medium Companies

Revenue and *direct costs* (COGS) can be traced easily; heads of BUs know how much they sold and how much they paid for the ingredients that

Table 1   P&L Dashboard for BU

BU Revenue	Gross Profit
	(Company cost employees)
(Direct costs/COGS)	(Direct services)
	(Allocated services)
	(Allocated Overhead)
= **Gross profit (GP)**	= **Net profit (EBITDA)**

enabled the sales, i.e., they have access to the data; for example, hardware components and software licenses inside the product, or media costs to run an online sales campaign. The gross profit calculation is relatively straightforward.

To calculate the estimated net profit we need estimated data of the four types of expenses: direct and indirect costs of employees, services, and overhead.

Company cost employees: For each BU, we have to include the cost of employees who work in the BU and the cost of employees who share their time among several BUs, but not the overhead employees. We create a table of all employees and allocate them to the BUs. For example, Alex in the sys-admin team shares his time equally between BUs A and B. His cost would be allocated 50% to each of these BUs. We have thus established the *BU cost size* — employee costs for each BU.

For *allocation of employees in overhead*, we create a table for the employees in overhead functions — HR, finance, administration — and spread their cost in proportion to the BU cost sizes. We now have the total *company cost of employees* for each BU, which is the first cost in the P&L dashboard model (Table 1).

Direct services is the second cost category. These are the services that the BU buys for its own use; for example, customer credit checks or any type of subcontractors that work in the BU.

Allocated services is the third cost category. Assume, for example, that we use Amazon's web services (AWS) as the infrastructure for the BUs. We could tag the AWS subsystems and know exactly how to allocate the shared costs to each BU. Similarly, if we have significant costs in one BU, legal services for example, we should separate it and allocate it correctly.

Allocated overhead: Everything else — the structural overhead — is allocated to different BUs according to their relative cost size. Allocated overhead includes office rent, communication, utilities, admin systems, etc.

Net profit (EBITDA) for the BU is the bottom line of the P&L model, and it serves as an adequate estimate to make ongoing decisions related to business performance.

The P&L dashboard models assume that *all expenses walk on two feet*, which means that all overhead allocations are in proportion to employee costs of each BU. This broad assumption works very well in knowledge-based companies and services companies. If the business is more complex, more rules could be used to develop the P&L Dashboard.

The P&L dashboards have a lot of value; heads of BUs that know their top and bottom lines behave like business owners, and that is exactly what we want of them.

One question remains open and that is how to allocate executive management costs. If the executives consider the exposure too risky, you exclude these costs entirely or bundle them with the overhead. Another approach is to treat the executives as an internal service and ask them at the end of each month how they spent their time per BU.

Management Dashboards

Unlike Chanukkah candles or Christmas lights, management dashboards are not for pleasure or symbolic value only; we are supposed to use them for a productive purpose. What KPIs should we include in them? Think of a car dashboard: while we drive the car, we want to see the main health metrics such as speed and fuel level, and to have an alert system for unusual events such as overheating and system failures. It would be nice if it also showed us when the front or back light bulbs need replacements. We only need the metrics and signs that we are *programmed* to react to. Anything else is a distraction. Some hybrid cars, for example, have included in their dashboard an energy monitor that shows a live diagram with real-time updates on how the car switches from engine to battery to electric motor. It's cool to watch, but does it serve a purpose? Would the driver do anything with this information, or rather train himself to avoid looking at it?

Management dashboards are essential for running any type of operations. We need to develop them with the concept of checklists in mind — just the right amount of information, and no distractions. Good dashboards include three categories of functionality:

- *Health metrics.* Main KPIs of the business, including trends
- *Alert system.* With adjustable thresholds that would keep the alerts relevant and prevent distractive false alarms
- *Drill down.* A dashboard on a computer screen or mobile device with clickable links to provide drill down analyses

Dashboards are both real-time, online instruments, and offline tools for managers. Either way, they follow the same principles of just the right amount of information to react or make decisions. Any periodic metrics review of a business, department, or operations is a dashboard. For example, the *startup canvas* of Steve Blank's course on lean startups is such an offline dashboard. In it, the information from all main aspects of building a startup is updated before every review cycle; each metric leads to further action.

Friendly to Facts and Numbers

Management depends on facts, and the best facts are numbers. The internet is about people, businesses, and now also things (Internet of Things); but it's all about what the facts and numbers say. See how the concept of business intelligence (BI) is already somewhat outdated; trends in *machine learning* are all the rage. The systems are getting more intelligent day by day. In a business world of this nature, we cannot remain ignorant of understanding the basics of numbers. These trends will not go away; they will eventually be replaced by other trends with even higher demands on understanding numbers.

Good metrics systems grow in their influence with time, because there's nothing more convincing than facts and numbers. From any starting point, if we already have metrics or are starting anew, we should keep developing

them, refining the meaning, and always expanding to more areas of the operations or business. The natural journey of a BI department starts with collecting and cleaning the data, and then building data models and language, on to automation based on the data. Only from here the more advanced stages begin: analysis, optimization, prediction, and prevention.

Turning the Curve with Sprezzatura

The SYR Story — Ahead of Its Time

Knowledge, power, and wealth are like blood, they need to flow freely and spread evenly or they form clots and clog the system. We are here to spread the knowledge about management, and expose the secrets that are not so secretive — it's all about teamwork. It would seem that there are a lot of recipes to keep in mind, perhaps too many to memorize, but, as with any type of craftsmanship, you learn to do it the right way, start practicing, and all of a sudden people notice — it looks as elegant as if you were born into it.

I learned about sprezzatura ("zz" as in pizza) from Professor Robert Greenberg's lectures on "The Life and Operas of Verdi". *Opera* in Italian, he reminds us, means *work* — all things working together, when *the whole is greater than the sum of its parts*. Opera in Italy was a big business in the centuries just prior to recording technology; there were 50 new operas a year in Venice alone. For so much work to be successful it needed to suit the tastes of the masses, to accomplish lyrical beauty in the service of dramatic expression. Composers and librettists worked very hard, often to exhaustion, to create volumes of musical beauty while conforming to structural rules that make the results light, elegant, and digestible for the audience. Their trick, though, was to hide the sweat and only show the elegant results. They worked with *...style and panache that made it look* *easy...* as Professor Greenberg describes it; they kept refining the work and resolving all difficulties with an *appearance of effortless mastery,* — the definition of *sprezzatura.*

...all things must be done with sprezzatura... said Baldassare Castiglione in the 16th century as he advised courtiers, and that is what we want to do in management with our teams — marry the form to function, perfectly, and achieve great heights with simple and elegant mastery — the realization of *team sprezzatura.*

THE SYR STORY — AHEAD OF ITS TIME

Think of a time in the future when we are so health conscious that we forget about privacy and equip ourselves with personal health metric chips, voluntarily, of course. As a community we advocate it because it's good for society; about 85% of the population agrees. We are so advanced with our systems that the chips collect our vital signs and transmit the information to a central database every time there's an exception to normal health ranges. Technicians at the center of operations monitor the incoming alarms and contact the person to validate the concerns before transferring to a doctor for first response. The general system also tracks us when we travel, and sends us information on high UV index, smog, questionable water quality, and any other health related hazard on our way.

The first operational problem that we encounter is that most calls are validated as a nonissue ... *yes, my heart rate went up, but it's because I was running* ... or ... *I just ate a cake, should I really worry about my sugar level* ...? We could then build a Rule Engine that adjusts the settings according to circumstances and filters out those false alarms. I'm sure you are already seeing how this rule engine isn't satisfactory. A few more steps of thinking through these

(Continued)

(Continued)

hypothetical systems and we arrive at a complete health system with rules, regulations, training, institutions, laws, governing bodies, etc. — just what we have today, which is slow and cumbersome, albeit more automated.

The technologies to realize this vision are already here; however, when we mix ethics and societal needs into a technology problem, the complexity becomes prohibitive to the solutions that otherwise would have been very nice to have.

Back in the mid-1990s, we had a similar health vision for the install base of the most popular information storage systems — about 10,000 units spread around the world's largest computer centers of global 2000 companies. The service motto for our company at the time was *guilty until proven innocent*, which meant that we would assume the responsibility for any alarm call detected in the units in the field, whether it originated in the unit itself or from any other connected equipment. However, we set the acceptable ranges so tight that we received too many health false alarms.

The technicians at the service operations center weren't happy. They felt that most of their work was to validate problems that did not exist. Customers weren't happy; even though remote dialing did the validation and checking of the unit; still, they were aware that this operation was going on, and they didn't like it when it happened often. The operations manager wasn't happy because of the service costs. Something was not right in a big way, and yet, the head of engineering was reluctant to change the range settings; he wanted to ensure that no real problem was missed.

The install base continued to grow rapidly; the units were calling with spurts of alarms whenever there was a wave of upgrades or

(Continued)

(Continued)

installations of many new units. Moreover, systems that did not call for a while for some reason were assumed healthy; because there was no automated mechanism to validate it — we missed real problems despite the over caution of our policies.

With this starting situation, the decades-long history of SYR started. (The project's first programmer gave it a temporary name and it stuck.) We felt that there must be a better way and it should start with getting closer to the data; we needed a central database to collect data, and a system to analyze it.

We knew that the software of the storage units already collected data, locally on the units themselves, to help remote diagnosis. The first goal was to upload this data from the field units to a central system and store it in a database. In modern technology this step would seem very basic, but back then, prior to internet connectivity, we had to develop batteries of modem dialers to access the field units once a day, and trigger the software to call the center and transmit this data. We also developed a parser that deciphered the incoming data and presented it in the database in readable formats. We still hadn't solved any false alarm problem, but the first heavy lifting was done. In addition to the incoming stream of alarm calls we had a searchable database with all the configuration data from the field, i.e., the foundation for a rule engine. We also started to collect and save the alarm data so that we could correlate it with the configuration data and analyze it.

At that point we exhausted the budget; the head of engineering no longer wanted to fund the project alone, and securing it from the services department was not realistic — the current situation already made them vulnerable. From previous experience of presenting to the president of the company I knew that he understood numbers.

(Continued)

(Continued)

We showed him a sample of what we could see in the data that we had not known before, and invited him to think with us about how this information could be used in the future; he was the head of a large information management company after all. The budget was approved and never surfaced again as a problem.

The software developers, on the other hand, gave us a cold shoulder when we told them what we had. Responding to calls was someone else's problem. They focused on making the product more attractive to customers: faster, more compatible, and with broader applications, i.e., in a sense, they were creating more conditions for generating alarms. So new was the concept of automated install base management that we had to show them value rather than vision, which at that point was not very clear, even to us.

To build the case we analyzed the data from all possible angles, dividing it into segments, cross-cutting from many directions, by date, configuration, version, geography, or anything else on which we could pivot the data. We tried to find patterns in what was a cryptic text to us. We didn't know what it all meant or what we were looking for, we just hoped it would mean something to the developers, who did understand the language of bits and bites inside the systems. The entire analysis was done with the original goal in mind — to find the root causes for false alarms so that we could reduce them. We generated a very thick book of graphs and called it The Red Book — red for the color of alarm.

In hindsight, it should not have been a surprise that in the heap of junk information that we generated, we hit upon some shiny pearls, as any research into material is bound to reveal valuable information, on purpose or by accident. The software developers at the time were setting priorities and other criteria for their work

(Continued)

(Continued)

based on field assumptions; and here, for the first time, they could stop arguing because real data of 85% of the install base was right there. Now, they too started dreaming about immediate feedback to anything they released to the field, instead of the unclear results that they were normally receiving from the practice of *release and then wait-and-see.*

The monthly edition of the Red Book was now much anticipated— it had the right followers, and we were ready to address the false alarm problem. The developers then revealed to us that the software in all the units in the field included a mechanism to change the range settings for alarms; as good developers they had not hard-coded anything that could be changed later. The next SYR goal, therefore, was to build the rule engine in the center, and use the connectivity to and from the install base units to create the feedback mechanism.

The first rules that we implemented had a dramatic effect on the rate of false alarms. In a rollout of a new software upgrade, for example, we could set a simple rule that a certain error *dials home* only after 10 repeated occurrences of the same error. We could manage, and indeed prevent, the call-home spurts; and we implemented broad based rules after every investigation that discovered a correlation of events. Flex Filter, as the rule engine was called, was so popular that it became a mission-critical system — software developers and service personnel used it daily in their work. As the word spread, however, SYR started to attract more creative ideas about how to use it for the benefit of customers and the company, beyond the automation of install-base management.

Appetite comes with eating. With new and broader interest we started collecting and analyzing more data, and then integrated SYR

(Continued)

(Continued)

with the call management system (CRM) to do even bigger things. We divided the customers into two groups, for example, those who gave us advance authorization for preventive maintenance actions and those who wanted to approve actions one by one. We could now automate the installation of fixes and upgrades as all the pieces were in place and working together. Most of the fixes and upgrades that the software developers created were now with nondisruptive characteristics to suit the automated processes — SYR had benefits that reached much farther than originally envisioned.

Even the legal department of the company benefited; they were able to settle a patent infringement court case at 1% of what was claimed for damages, as the hard evidence from the SYR system on the real exposure left the claimants in a very weak position. The risk of hundreds of millions of dollars and a long drawn out case was averted.

When marketing started to inquire about install base information from us, we enhanced SYR to be more marketing-friendly. For example, to create sellable packaged solutions, they wanted to know the statistics of how customers used the storage systems, and what applications were connected to them. At that point, we only had information in SYR that was related to solving problems, because that is what we could access from the storage units. However, everything that was connected to the storage — servers and network equipment — could, if customers agreed, leave footprint data files on the storage units, and from there we already had SYR to collect and analyze it. This next step — Server Software Tracker — gave us access to an unprecedented large sample of real-time data without the need to do cumbersome and totally inaccurate surveys. SYR became a standard marketing advisory tool as well.

(Continued)

(Continued)

Over the years, SYR grew to manage the install base that doubled with multiple generations of the storage units. The demands on it had also grown; hardware versions could now be collected to help manage field logistics. Connectivity and security features had to adapt to increasing customer demands and new technologies, and paper red books transformed to real-time dashboards. We went deeper and deeper with stronger functionality. With SYR, the entire support and management system for this product was a world apart from the other, much bigger, install bases that the company managed. It was time to go wide and absorb them into the system. Product by product, SYR grew to manage 200,000 units in the field — a long way from its humble beginnings of 10,000 units of a single product.

One of those products offered a new pay-as-you-grow model. The only way to manage it on a large scale was to have SYR track usage and report it to the local sales representatives. They became even more interested in what we could do to help identify sales opportunities and manage their customer relations. We also discovered that it was cheaper for us and for the customers to install full units upfront, and enable the step-by-step growth by software licenses, rather than doing onsite hardware upgrades every time the customer wants to buy more of the same. We came close to what is so obvious today for certain applications — use data storage as a utility.

Another product had a large proportion of its sales done through channel partners. Connecting SYR to their systems was both unrealistic and involved too much risk. We couldn't reach the 85% SYR penetration rate that was the benchmark from the original install base. However, any effort that increased the connectivity rate from 30% to 40%, for example, meant thousands of averted calls and

(Continued)

(Continued)

much higher customer satisfaction. We could not set a perfect goal, but each improvement was worth the effort and the investment.

The story of SYR is an example of what we call today the Lean Methodology — never ending cycles of test-implement-correct — that took place on a big scale over a long period; it's a story of bottlenecks and pressure points. Like turning a huge aircraft carrier in the ocean, it involved many systems and different organizational hierarchies at every step of the way. It survived two major overhauls of the company's ERP/CRM replacement projects, and as far as I know it's still there, deemed irreplaceable for its unique functionality. From the beginning the SYR team always maintained a lean and flexible architectural design with a good balance between independence and connectivity to other systems.

The SYR team, through all its generations, was a small group that understood the idea of developing excellence step by step. They worked with a mission, starting from the thick red book that was the voice of *talking facts creating ideology*, and not like Mao's little red book that did the opposite. They had to convince groups and sometimes even whole departments to change process and focus, and give attention to the next potential improvement.

Going against the grain, again and again, is not easy. The team worked always from behind the scenes, making their collaborators comfortable with each of the steps before moving to the next one — never seeking the aura of a prime-time project. The team secured the support of executives; they knew how to talk to them with real results and small incremental budgets. It also secured the attention of the best in many departments — people who could see big opportunities from using a system approach to solving problems.

(Continued)

(Continued)

> In the end, this small team stitched it all together; they created a mission-critical system with the collaboration of several business units; in each of them they worked with software development, hardware development, customer support, IT, legal, marketing, sales, and logistics — field and corporate departments. Every piece required hard work and constant reinvention. To convince the collaborators they had to show that these pieces are achievable, and not too hard. Overall, with many small steps, they turned a huge curve with *the appearance of effortless mastery — sprezzatura!*

The SYR story has elements from every chapter of this book. The managers who were involved understood their role as the combination of their responsibility, as well as influencing the big picture. This was the spirit of the company's culture — driving execution by setting goals of incremental steps, even when the long-term goal was just an unclear dream. Many other Continuous Improvement projects were running during that time. SYR was operating in an environment that understood the principles and lived them.

When I spoke to one of the team leads years later she said ... *this was the project where we could make mistakes and come out as winners; that is how well management supported us. We were Agile before we knew Agile existed ...*

The company's customer strategy was the umbrella under which projects like SYR could be funded and successful. The company was very close to its customers in understanding their needs and strategies. SYR increased this intimacy by adding knowledge and operational security to the customers' systems. For a long time, SYR remained the main tool in guarding customer

satisfaction and excellence in execution — it was fully compatible with the company's strategy.

The team continuously used the principles of how to sell ideas of internal and external value to increase the support from all the departments. Everywhere in the company, people liked to contribute to something big that touched so many aspects of the strategy and gain benefits for their own jobs. Working the system included a lot of education, finding personalized value statements, understanding each type of audience, and how to influence them — and above all, presenting facts professionally and with a lot of enthusiasm.

Facts and numbers were the engine that drove this project for such a long time from one conquest to another. It was about organizational and process change, and yet, it was received with open arms as the facts did most of the talking, showing how to free bottlenecks, and find pressure points that affect the entire nervous system and create a lot of benefit. Sprezzatura, indeed!

Peek Through a Small Window

46

The management principles in this book work for big scale projects like SYR, as well as for a very small scale, as the following story shows.

As an exception in my consulting practice, I agreed to coach an individual, as opposed to management teams in a company setting, as I normally do. A close friend asked for a favor, and I agreed.

QUICK TURNAROUND

The person I was coaching presented his role as customer success manager, which includes responsibilities for direct customer relationships as well as continuous management of the customers' online assets and actions — websites and promotions. This combination of front-end and back-end functions bundled into one role is typical of the online marketing tools industry. Some companies in this field charge proportional success fees for their products and services. This company, however, sold licenses and service packages. In both business models, the company depends

(Continued)

(Continued)

highly on generating successful incremental results for its customers; no results means no pay, or discontinued service.

My client was struggling in three areas which are very common in knowledge economy companies: time management, customer relationships, and position in the company. He described his problems as follows.

- Time management: Despite working long hours every day, he couldn't keep pace with his workload. He was assigned more customers, but was unable to give them appropriate attention.

- Customer relationships: Though my client prepared for meetings with customers, he always felt that he had not presented all the main points; according to his own assessment, he skipped important arguments, and wasn't as sharp as he wanted to be.

- Position in the company: Indirectly he was recognized for delivering good results by receiving assignments to more customers. In every other respect, however, his direct manager rejected him or overtly showed disrespect. The manager delayed all of my client's suggestions for improvements; gave credit to other people for his work; and plainly wasted his time by giving him *go fetch* assignments. My client was frustrated and didn't know how to manage this situation.

Addressing problems of this nature requires time and effort; I suggested we start with the first problem, so we could free some time from his very busy work habits. We analyzed how he was spending his time and realized the following time-management issues.

(Continued)

(Continued)

- He delayed important tasks because there were always urgent issues that took over his time. I suggested blocking timeslots on his calendar as quality time that cannot be interrupted.

- His support portfolio included many customers. He organized his tasks one customer at a time, instead of grouping similar tasks and executing them in sequence to reduce context switching.

- His calendar's structure changed from week to week depending on the workload. He needed to fix times for certain types of tasks and preschedule regular meetings with internal groups instead of relying on ad hoc meetings.

- He spent 40% of his time on writing emails to customers, internal support groups, and engineering.

We discovered the fourth issue of his email time-sink while working on reorganizing his calendar. We examined a sample of emails and saw clearly that he did not use any structure or style; he wrote them according to how he discovered the information that he wanted to convey. Therefore, his education started with realizing that the purpose of these emails and the needs of his customers and internal audience followed highly repeated patterns. We discussed his email readers and how *they* would want to receive information, and learned how to structure an email with the three golden rules for effective communication — *delivering a message, writing for retention,* and *stating the actions clearly*. We reviewed and revised a broad selection of emails, practiced... and... amazing result! 2.5 hours a day saved, consistently.

We could now approach his second challenge and learn how to present status and proposals to customers. He learned how to tailor

(Continued)

(*Continued*)

messages to customers and present the story in the most convincing way, using the best practices and methods for effective presentations. We practiced with preparing for real presentations that became so successful that my client forgot that he once saw himself as deficient in presentation skills. The customers moved in the direction that he wanted and made the decisions that he proposed.

His third problem of position in the company and the political nature of the relationship with his direct manager was more challenging to address. First, from my vantage point as a complete outsider hearing only one side of the story, I couldn't validate any of the observations; it was only a peek into the company through a very small window. Was the manager really so blatant in his actions and still thought he could get away with it forever? I advised my client not to take any proactive action at first, and to follow tactics of prepare-and-wait.

- Observe quietly if others in the company experience these same behaviors and attitudes from his manager. Apparently, I was late with this suggestion, as people were already discussing the subject freely, behind that manager's back.

- Do not approach the manager directly unless provoked. Address the issue of giving credit for your work to someone else with a specific message and a short email of the main facts, and request to discuss it in a meeting. The manager reacted to this email with a written apology. In essence, he was admitting his action and behavior — in writing — without noticing that he was doing it.

- Wait for the CEO to start asking around, and prepare short factual answers, in advance of any question he might ask. We examined a few possible scenarios and prepared answers. The idea was to make sure my client did not trip in the

(*Continued*)

(Continued)

political atmosphere, as situations of that nature tend to hurt more than just the instigators. The proper tactic was to stay reserved, professional and ready with answers, show you are focused on work and on the success of the company, while keeping out of politics.

It so happened that opportunities presented themselves and events unfolded in this company a lot faster than I anticipated. The problems that this manager created were simmering for quite some time, so much so that the CEO had to take corrective action and remove the manager from the company. My client, who stayed professional throughout this ordeal, was promoted to his first team-lead responsibility.

The techniques that we used to manage my client in this situation were not the immediate reactions one would think of, especially when you're in the trenches and hurt continually by the situation. Active listening and discussing sensitive matters with facts only, worked perfectly in this case. While the manager was hurting himself with his behavior, my client had the opportunity to stay aloof, focus on self-improvement, and show strength by delivering professional results consistently, despite the bad atmosphere. Six months of hard work, calculated restraint, and a bit of luck helped this turnaround with sprezzatura.

Afterword

I hope I have put a rainbow in your clouds, and I hope you find beauty in management and leadership.

The stories in the book show how the principles and methods work in real managerial situations. I covered a broad range, i.e., large and small situations, new technology businesses, and more traditional ones. In all likelihood, you found many similarities to your situations that could guide you on how to construct your personal approach.

It's all about change and working with your team to achieve and perfect it. You could transform an entire company or just one corner that's in your control. You could address many aspects at the same time or take them one by one. Every bit counts; every improvement makes life at work easier and more enjoyable. You might be comfortable in your managerial state of affairs, and feel that everything is fine and doesn't need change; in which case I would advise you to find out from your team if they feel the same way. Change in business is like exercising for fitness; it's healthy even in small bits; it reinforces excellence in everything and everybody, and it helps shed stale habits.

Understanding the problem is the first step toward a solution. Every topic in this book leads to a checklist that could serve you both ways — defining the problem with its known and less-known aspects, or as a guiding structure for the solution. Obviously, each checklist depends on the situation and they are all different. The guidelines are only half of the homework, the rest is for you to choose what is relevant, adapt to your situation, and add the missing parts.

If nothing else, once you understand the principles, it will help you learn from others. You're continuously observing other people's behaviors; now you have the tools to judge what is good and what is not so good, what contributes to progress and what impedes it.

As final words, I repeat my apology from the Foreword. I confess, every time I typed *he* or *his,* it hurt my fingers. Converting it to a she-book would not have helped me either. May we all be gender-free when we think about management!

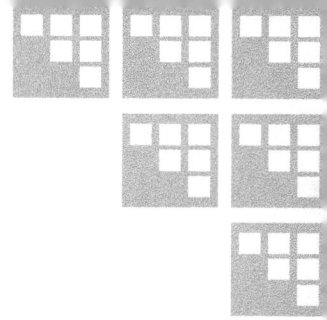

Index

www.ingramcontent.com/pod-product-compliance
Lightning Source LLC
Chambersburg PA
CBHW050537190326
41458CB00007B/1810